W9-AZB-776

Who Knew?

Who Knew?

Hundreds & Hundreds of Questions & Answers for Curious Minds

Bob Strauss

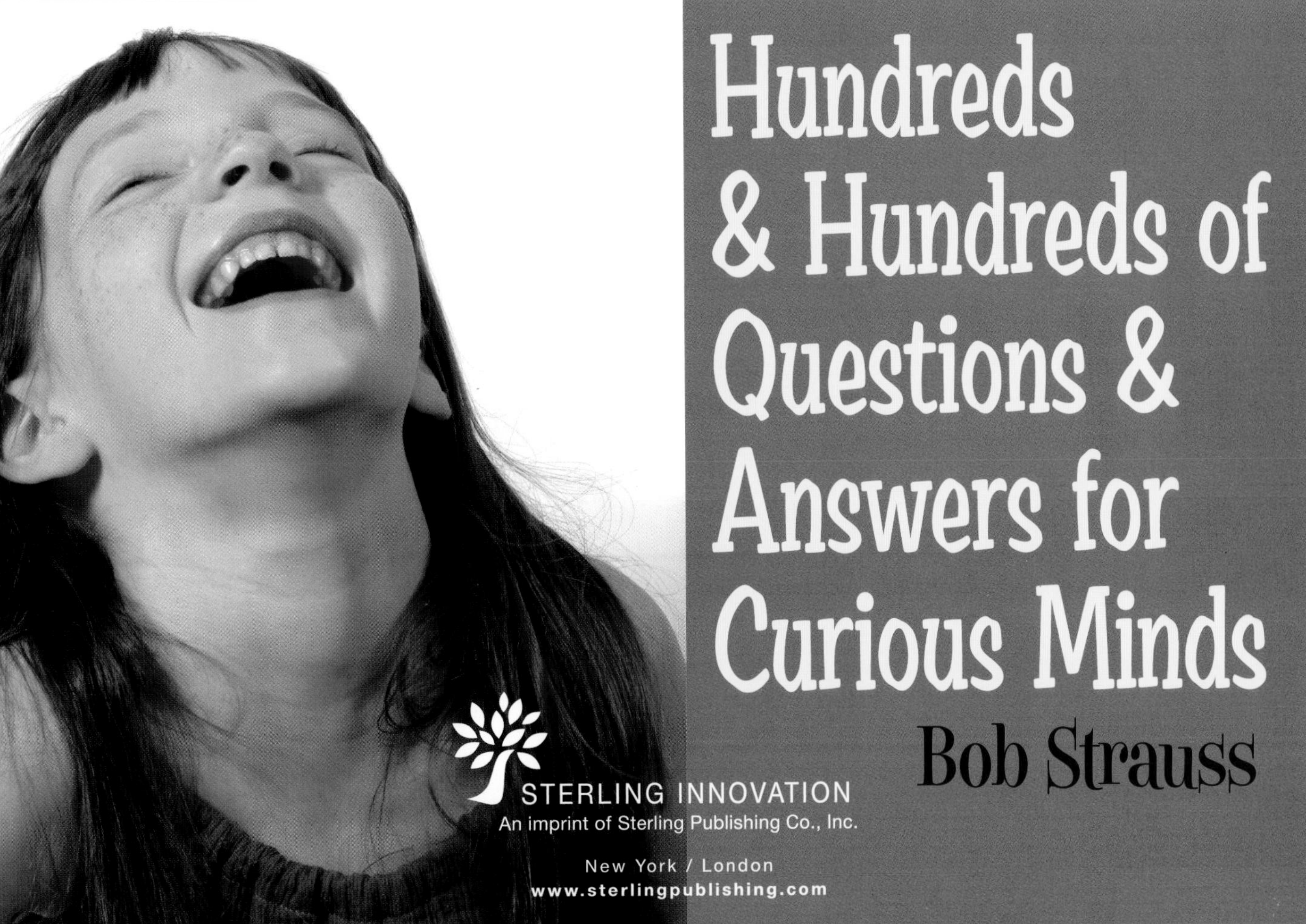

STERLING INNOVATION
An imprint of Sterling Publishing Co., Inc.
New York / London
www.sterlingpublishing.com

Library of Congress Cataloging-in-Publication Data

Strauss, Bob, 1961-
Who Knew? : hundreds & hundreds of questions & answers for curious minds / Bob Strauss.
p. cm.
Sequel to: The big book of what, how, and why / Bob Strauss. 2005.
Includes index.
ISBN-13: 978-1-4027-4456-3
ISBN-10: 1-4027-4456-0
1. Children's questions and answers. I. Strauss, Bob, 1961- Big book of what, how, and why.
II. Title. III. Title: Who Knew?.

AG195.S77 2007
031.02--dc22 2007001585

10 9 8 7 6 5 4 3 2 1

Published by Sterling Publishing Co., Inc.
387 Park Avenue South, New York, NY 10016

Distributed in Canada by Sterling Publishing
c/o Canadian Manda Group, 165 Dufferin Street
Toronto, Ontario, Canada M6K 3H6
Distributed in the United Kingdom by GMC Distribution Services
Castle Place, 166 High Street, Lewes, East Sussex, England BN7 1XU
Distributed in Australia by Capricorn Link (Australia) Pty. Ltd.
P.O. Box 704, Windsor, NSW 2756, Australia

Printed in China

Sterling ISBN-13: 978-1-4027-4456-3
ISBN-10: 1-4027-4456-0

For information about custom editions, special sales, premium and
corporate purchases, please contact Sterling Special Sales
Department at 800-805-5489 or specialsales@sterlingpub.com.

Table of Contents

Section 1
Nature & Health

Section 2

Culture & Government

Customs & Traditions

Leadership

Society

Law & Order

Section 3
Science & Industry

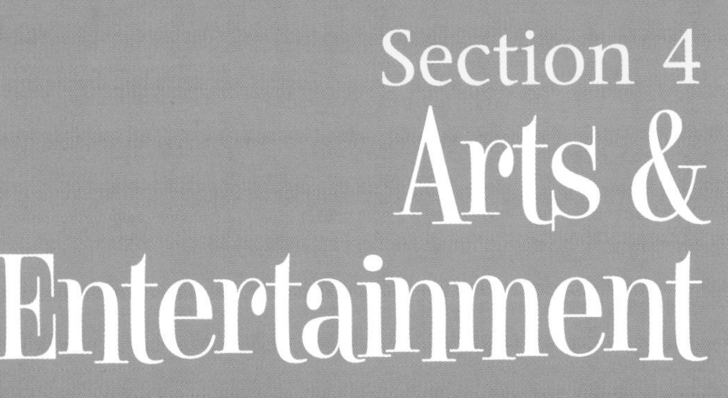

Section 4 Arts & Entertainment

Creative Arts

Myths & Beliefs

Places

Fun & Recreation

Introduction

Have you ever pestered your parents or teacher with questions like "Why are there so many cartoons on Saturday morning?" "What's the difference between a lizard and reptile?" or "How was brunch invented?" They probably encouraged you to go get a book and look it up. The trouble is, until now, there hasn't really been a kid-friendly one-stop shop that answered these types of questions. But now there is, and it's the book you're holding in your hands: *Who Knew? Hundreds & Hundreds of Questions & Answers for Curious Minds*.

In this book, I go way, way beyond obvious questions like "Why is the sky blue?" or "How does popcorn pop?" (You probably know the answers to these, anyway.) The questions in *Who Knew?* are for *really* curious minds and range from entertainment ("What was the first science-fiction movie?" "How was jazz invented?") to science ("How do atoms stick together?" "What is the difference between an android and a robot?") to everyday life ("Why do we pay taxes?" "How does health insurance work?"). I've also thrown in a few questions about topics your parents may have a hard time answering, like "What is a nursing home?" and "Why do some kids stutter?"

While this book is easy to read, you may find some of the topics hard to understand. This is entirely on purpose: I was a kid once, and I know kids like to be challenged. Hopefully you're curiosity will grow and you'll want to investigate these topics further. But if you still can't quite figure out what quantum physics is, don't worry—the fact is, most adults don't understand quantum physics either!

—Bob Strauss

Nature & Health

WHAT is diabetes? HOW was anesthesia invented? WHY do sharks need to keep swimming? In this section, you'll find questions and answers about the human body, as well as some of the plants and animals with which we share the planet.

How did bullfighting begin?

Bullfighting in Spain dates back almost 1,000 years—to the 11th century A.D.—but historians aren't quite sure where the sport originated. According to one theory, the ancient Romans introduced this practice when gladiator combat was outlawed (only for a very short time, though, since Roman crowds loved watching warriors fight). It's also possible that bullfighting was brought to Spain by the Moors, a North African people that conquered Spain in the 8th century A.D., or that it was somehow picked up from a similar ritual in Minoan Crete (an island south of present-day Greece).

During the first 700 years of Spanish bullfighting, it was customary for matadors to be mounted on horseback with javelins—making a bullfight more like a chase than a duel. It wasn't until the early 18th century that a matador named Juan Belmonte insisted on challenging the bull on foot, which made for a fairer (and, for the crowd, more exciting) fight. Because modern bullfighters can't run away fast enough, they're in constant danger of being gored by the bull's horns—though there are plenty of people nearby who can rescue a matador if he gets himself in serious trouble.

What is the Running of the Bulls?

Every year, in the Spanish town of Pamplona, a herd of bulls is let loose in the streets to chase anyone brave enough (or foolish enough) to try and outrun them. The Running of the Bulls attracts thousands of townspeople and tourists, and a few of them usually wind up gored or trampled (though fatalities are rare). The bulls don't fare so well, either, since their hooves aren't suited to Pamplona's cobbled streets!

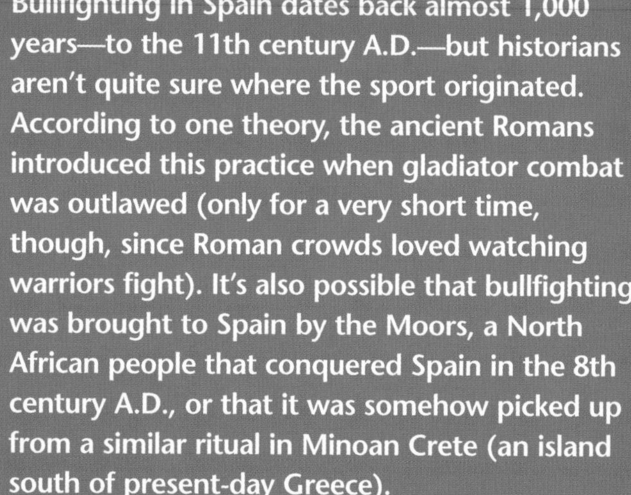

Why don't we use bulls for food?

Because male bulls are more muscular than female cows, their meat tends to be tougher and less appetizing. Also, because of their aggressive nature, it's a lot harder to tend a herd of bulls than a herd of docile cows. For these reasons, the main function of bulls on dairy farms is to impregnate the cows and (hopefully) create more cows, not to be slaughtered and used for food themselves.

What was "bull-baiting"?

Bullfighting isn't usually associated with medieval England, but that's exactly where the closely related sport (if you can call it that) of bull-baiting was practiced. This spectacle involved tying a bull securely to a post, enraging it by (for instance) blowing pepper up its nose and letting loose a pack of dogs to attack it. It sounds like the kind of thing that could be enjoyed only by illiterate peasants, but sadly, this sport was a favorite of English royalty. Even Queen Elizabeth I was known to enjoy a good bull-baiting every now and then!

As you might have guessed, bull-baiting involved the breeding and training of what is today a beloved pooch—the bulldog. Most bulldogs today couldn't tackle and destroy a roasted chicken, let alone a full-grown bull, but in their time these dogs were known for their ferocity and single-mindedness. Once a bulldog had bitten into a bull, it would hold on for dear life, and many of these dogs were killed as the bull flung them off or trampled them.

You'll be glad to know that bull-baiting (at least in England) was outlawed by Parliament in 1835, along with other sports that involve cruelty to animals, such as cockfighting.

Why do matadors wave a red cape?

Despite what you've seen in cartoons, bulls aren't enraged by the color red. What does get their interest are things that move, so waving a cape in front of an angry bull is an invitation to be charged. The reason the matador's cape is red is because that signals to the cheering crowd that the final part of the bullfight is about to begin, when either the matador (or, much more likely, the bull) is about to be killed.

What happens to a bull that wins a bullfight?

Although bullfighting is a controversial sport, the least that can be said about it is that it treats the bull with a certain amount of dignity. Every now and then, a bull that gets the best of a matador will be spared to fight another day (usually, bulls are killed by the matador at the end of the fight). Some especially fearsome bulls are allowed to retire and go to stud—meaning they're bred with cows to (hopefully) produce a new generation of ring-worthy beasts.

Chickens

Why do some people keep chickens as pets?

You may not want to know this, especially if you're a big fan of chicken nuggets, but chickens are actually friendly, gentle creatures—and like dogs and cats, they can be bred to have specific characteristics, such as long, hairy feathers or bright red wattles (those weird, fleshy things that hang off the chicken's neck). And there's another advantage: unlike the family pooch, a pet chicken can help earn its keep by laying eggs!

What do chickens eat?

Like people, chickens are omnivorous—that is, they'll eat anything from bugs to vegetables to other chickens (well, most people don't eat bugs, but they could if they had to). In crowded chicken farms, this tendency toward cannibalism is prevented by a procedure known as "debeaking," which involves clipping off the sharp part of the chicken's beak.

Why do we only eat chicken eggs?

For the same reason we only drink cows' milk: chickens, like cows, are domesticated, meaning they can be raised on farms and handled by people without too much fuss. If our distant ancestors had figured out a way to domesticate pigeons or penguins, we'd probably be making omelets out of pigeons' or penguins' eggs!

Why don't chicken eggs have baby chicks inside?

An adult hen will produce eggs on a regular basis, whether or not she's been visited recently by a rooster (a male chicken). If a hen has been fertilized by a rooster, the eggs she lays will contain baby chicks, which will shortly hatch their way out. If not (and the hens in egg farms are kept well away from eager roosters!), her eggs will contain all the nutritious stuff a growing chick needs, but not the chick itself.

By the way, despite what you see in grocery stores, not all chicken eggs are white. Hens lay eggs of all sorts of colors, ranging from pale green and blue to various shades of brown. While there's no nutritional difference between different-colored eggs, most folks in the U.S. prefer their eggs pearly white, so that's the color the billions of hens on chicken farms have been selectively bred to lay. (Some shoppers prefer brown eggs, but white eggs and brown eggs have exactly the same ingredients inside!)

What are free-range chickens?

Every year, the billions of chickens raised on U.S. chicken farms wind up as someone's dinner. Because the demand for these "broilers" (as they're known in the industry) is so great, many chicken farmers try to raise the fattest possible chickens they can in the shortest possible amount of time, which, as you can imagine, creates overcrowded conditions in the pens. In the worst of these "factory farms," broilers never live to see the light of day, going directly from egg to pen to slaughterhouse.

Although farm conditions have been improving lately (thanks to negative publicity among consumers and intervention by government authorities), some people still prefer to eat chickens that have been raised in a "free-range" environment. As they're reared, these chickens are given enough room to occasionally strut around outside, which results in a happier, more contented chicken (presumably resulting in a tastier specimen). Because they're much less common, though, free-range chickens usually cost more to raise than everyday, factory-bred chickens.

What is the difference between a chicken and a turkey?

Although turkey and chicken meat look similar when they're inside your sandwich, turkeys and chickens belong to entirely different species (although, of course, they're both part of the larger family of birds). The chicken originated in Europe and Asia, while the larger, more quarrelsome turkey is strictly a New World creature that evolved in North and Central America. Because they're harder to breed on farms, turkeys are usually eaten only on special occasions, like Thanksgiving.

Why did the chicken cross the road?

No, we can't answer this age-old riddle, but we can at least try to figure out where it came from. The most likely explanation is that, not being the brightest creatures in the world, chickens escaping from their coops would obliviously cross a nearby road and get run over by chariots (or cars, depending on the historical era). One can imagine a person watching this tragedy and asking, quite seriously, "Why did that chicken cross the road?" at which point someone else made a funny wisecrack!

Desert Life

Why do some camels have two humps?

Camels come in two different varieties: "dromedary" camels, which have one hump, and "bactrian" camels, which have two. One-humped camels live in the desert, while their two-humped cousins are found in the slightly cooler climates of central Asia. If this sounds topsy-turvy, keep in mind that camels' humps don't contain water; rather, they're used to store deposits of fat that the animals can draw on between feedings.

How tall can a saguaro grow?

It had a near brush with death after a wildfire in 2005, but the saguaro called "The Grand One" remains the biggest specimen in the world: it's a whopping 46 feet tall and 8 feet in circumference at its base. Botanists (experts who study plants) believe this saguaro, located near Scottsdale, Arizona, is almost 200 years old—comparable to the age of the next-biggest saguaro, which resides in the vicinity of Tucson, Arizona.

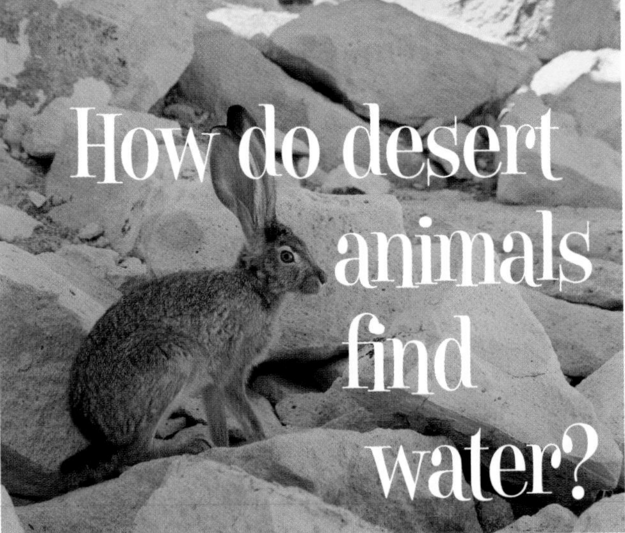

How do desert animals find water?

As you can guess, the most reliable source of water in a hot, rainless desert is plants—whose roots extend deep into the soil to extract H_2O from underground aquifers. Unfortunately for the average rattler or kangaroo rat, desert plants (such as cacti) have developed spiny defense mechanisms to keep from being eaten—so it's up to a desert's less glamorous inhabitants, its bugs, to extract the plant's valuable water. This way, the larger creatures obtain their water indirectly, by eating the bugs that eat the plants!

When you're a desert critter, however, finding enough water to stay alive is only half the story: it's equally important to conserve the water that's already in your body. For this reason, desert animals sleep underground or behind rocks during the hottest parts of the day, and have evolved ingenious ways to rid themselves of excess heat (for example, a jackrabbit's big ears radiate heat back into the environment) or to conserve water (a kangaroo rat's kidneys, like those of many other desert creatures, are specially adapted to filter most of the water out of its urine).

Why will vultures circle a dying animal?

Although desert vultures aren't quite smart enough to follow a bus full of lost tourists (in the hopes of scoring a tasty meal within a few days), these big birds are able to sense when an animal is on its last legs—probably because the dying beast is moving very slowly, or doesn't immediately react when the bird ventures near. As gross as it is, vultures have even been known to start feeding on their prey before it's officially dead—though the victim is hopefully far enough gone that it doesn't realize it's being made into a meal!

Because they feed exclusively on dead (or almost dead) animals, vultures have developed a sophisticated immune system, which protects them from the bacteria that decompose the flesh of these unfortunate beasts. (If a stranded tourist attempted to eat a three-days-dead antelope, for example, he'd probably exchange a slow death from starvation for a quick death from blood poisoning). Turkey vultures, which live in the American Southwest, are even resistant to botulism toxin—a tiny amount of which can kill a full-grown human.

How deep are a desert plant's roots?

When you're a plant, you have to get your water where you can find it—and in the desert, that's often dozens, or even hundreds, of feet beneath the surface. Most desert plants have long, thin "tap roots" that extend deep into the soil toward sources of underground water. Some trees in the Kalahari Desert in Africa have taproots more than 200 feet long—or almost the height of a 20-story building!

Why are they called Bedouins?

Although they're known in the west by the generic name of "Bedouins," the nomads who roam through the Arabian, Saharan, and Sinai deserts actually belong to a variety of different tribes (the word "Bedouin" is derived from the Arabic "badawi," meaning "desert-dweller"). Today, there are fewer Bedouins than there used to be, as many of these tribes have settled in the populated areas of the Near and Middle East.

What is the most dangerous cactus?

In cartoons, characters always seem to be falling into cactus patches, then ruefully plucking spines out of their rears afterward. In real life, though, if you fall into a cholla (pronounced "hoya") cactus, you'd better hope there's a hospital nearby. The barbs of this extremely spiny Southwestern cactus are shaped in a way that they remain embedded in human skin, and can cause severe damage (or even death) if they're not carefully removed.

Why is it called a "litter" of puppies or kittens?

Well, for one thing, there's nothing like seven or eight newborn pups to mess up an entire house! Seriously, though, a person can spend her entire life trying to figure out why groups of animals are named one thing or another. Not only are there "litters" of newborn puppies and kittens, but "gangs" of elks, "bloats" of hippopotami, "wakes" of buzzards and "murders" of magpies. Wherever "litter" ultimately derives from, it's almost certainly not related to the "litter" people throw onto streets or the "litter" used in cat boxes (which your typical dog would certainly be offended by!).

Speaking of litters, you may have wondered why puppies and kittens are born with their eyes closed. It's not clear exactly why this is, but the fact is that many animals are born before they're completely "done" (human babies, for instance, are born before their brains are fully developed, because a full-sized head would be impossible to push through the mother's birth canal!). It's probable that, in the course of evolution, a tradeoff was made between keeping a litter of kittens in their mom's womb for another two weeks (which might have adverse consequences for both the kittens and their mom), and allowing them to be born in a slightly vulnerable condition, with their eyes closed.

What is a puppy mill?

When you buy a purebred dog or puppy, it's important to deal with a reputable breeder or pet store, which can be counted on to mate appropriate male and female dogs together and raise the resulting puppies in humane conditions. "Puppy mills" are fly-by-night outfits that breed puppies indiscriminately, and are notorious for churning out badly socialized, aggressive dogs with health problems (which you may not even notice until you've taken your new pet home!).

How can you tell a dog is rabid?

Thanks to regular inoculations, there are far fewer rabid dogs (that is, dogs suffering from the disease rabies) in the U.S. than there used to be—in fact, you're far more likely to encounter a rabid squirrel or raccoon. That said, you can usually tell a rabid dog by its extreme aggressiveness and its foamy saliva (which is why angry people are often said to "foam at the mouth"). Unfortunately, since there's no way to cure a rabid dog, it has to be put down to keep it from infecting other animals (or people).

Why do cats use a litter box?

One of the biggest differences between dogs and cats is the way they go to the bathroom. While a dog has to be walked two or three times a day to go number 1 or number 2, a cat can be trusted to do its business in an indoor litter box, which can be filled with anything from plain sand to scientifically formulated granules that absorb moisture and mask odors. Even better, most cats (and even kittens) don't have to be trained to use a litter box; they just instinctively know what it's there for!

As with most pet behavior, the reason cats use litter boxes is rooted in millions of years of evolution. In the wild, the ancestors of domesticated cats were accustomed to burying their pee and poop in loose soil, most likely to keep its smell from attracting larger predators. Dogs, on the other hand, are descended from wolves, who were much higher up on the food chain. A prehistoric wolf had no incentive to bury its poop; in fact, if a big pile of wolf doo happened to attract a hungry critter, that was a good thing—from the wolf's perspective!

Why do dogs have dewclaws?

You may have noticed that pooches have a fifth claw raised an inch or so above the back of their front paws. These "dewclaws," as they're called, don't serve any useful function; rather, they're all that remains of a primitive "fifth toe" comparable to a human pinky. Because prominent dewclaws can catch on clothes or furniture, many pet owners choose to have them removed surgically.

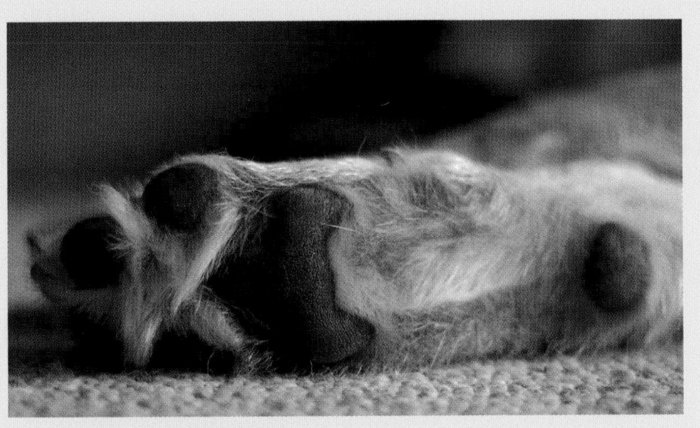

Why are dog shows more popular than cat shows?

If you're a true cat lover, there's nothing better than a cat show, in which purebred cats are judged on their appearance and demeanor. But if you're just an animal lover in general, dog shows are much more interesting, because dogs can be trained to obey simple commands—while your typical cat will just sit there, looking smug. For this reason, dog shows have more individual events than cat shows, and usually get higher ratings when they're shown on TV.

Fungi

What are fungi?

In the grand scheme of things, fungi—organisms that include yeasts, molds, mushrooms, and yucky creatures called "slime molds"—may seem like an insignificant afterthought. But in fact, fungi comprise one of the four major "kingdoms" of nature, the others being plants, animals, and one-celled bacteria.

Although fungi are similar to plants and primitive animals, they're set apart by two major differences. First, unlike plants, fungi don't convert sunlight into starches and sugars by way of photosynthesis, so they need to obtain their nutrients elsewhere. And second, unlike animals, fungi don't directly ingest other organisms; rather, they secrete chemicals that dissolve food externally, and then they soak up the resulting nutrients.

Fungi come in all shapes and sizes, from microscopic organisms that cause disease (in much the same way that bacteria and viruses do) to enormous underground growths that extend for miles in all directions. They can also be found pretty much everywhere on earth, including the oceans, the soil, and even the air you breathe!

What is ergotism?

No, it's not related to "egotism," which means having a high opinion of yourself. Ergotism is a disease caused by a fungus called "ergot," which can infest grain. The symptoms of ergotism include hallucinations and seizures, which has led many historians to speculate that outbreaks of so-called "hysteria" in the Middle Ages were actually caused by peasants eating ergot-infected bread. Some people even think the Salem Witch Trials may have been provoked by young girls suffering from ergotism!

How was penicillin discovered?

It's one of nature's ironies that one of the most important medicines ever discovered came from a lowly bit of fungus. In 1928, the Scottish scientist Alexander Fleming discovered a species of mold that inhibited the growth of bacteria, and called the chemical he isolated from it "penicillin." Since penicillin could cure diseases (such as pneumonia) that were otherwise fatal, its discovery was a huge advance in medical science.

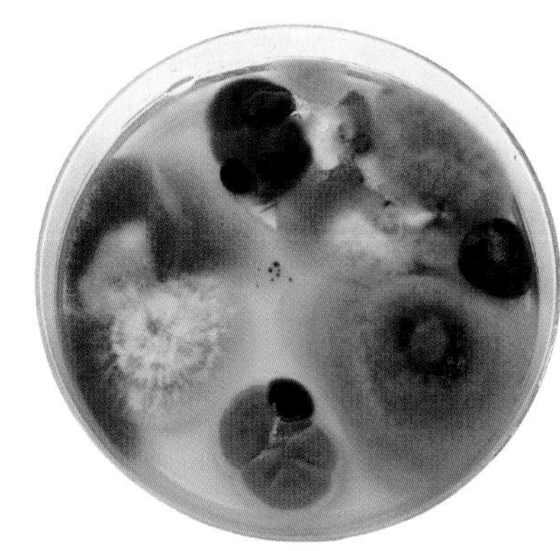

Why are fungi important for the ecosystem?

Like bacteria, microscopic fungi feast on the stuff other plants and animals won't touch—such as dung, rotten wood, and the carcasses of dead animals. By digesting these substances, and then being eaten in turn by other animals, plants, and bacteria, fungi help to recycle the essential nutrients that sustain life.

How do slime molds reproduce?

One of the most fascinating organisms on earth, the slime mold (a kind of one-celled fungus found mostly in forests and soil) shows how ingenious nature can be when it comes to, well, making more slime molds.

In its life cycle, this creature goes through various incarnations. To begin with, slime molds are microscopic, one-celled creatures, much like amoebas (which are technically animals). But when they undergo stress—say, because there's not enough food in the immediate vicinity or the temperature has suddenly dropped—the individual slime molds join together to form one big organism called a "pseudoplasmodium," or slug (because of its resemblance to an actual slug).

But wait, we're not finished yet. Once it has formed, the pseudoplasmodium crawls off slowly to a new location, where it sprouts a long stalk with spores at the end. When the wind blows, these spores fly off, seeding the surrounding territory with more of the single-celled slime molds that kicked off this process in the first place!

Why does mold grow in bathrooms?

A microscopic fungus that can be found virtually everywhere, mold thrives in moist environments, so it's especially attracted to toilet bowls, shower curtains, and the tiles in your bathtub. Although most kinds of mold are harmless in small quantities (if not especially pleasant to look at), the best way to prevent dangerous mold infestations is to clean your bathroom regularly, and to leave the door open after you use the bathroom so the shower and tub can dry more quickly.

What makes toadstools dangerous?

There are various species of toadstool, but the most dangerous by far is the deathcap mushroom, technically known as "Amanita Phalloides." This killer 'shroom contains a slow-acting poison that causes vomiting, diarrhea, liver damage, and death (these symptoms appear about 12 hours after the mushroom is eaten, and become progressively worse over the course of a few days). Unfortunately, the deathcap looks just like a plain, ordinary mushroom, which is why you should never pick and eat mushrooms in the wild!

What is the difference between lizards and reptiles?

Let's put it this way: all lizards are reptiles, but not all reptiles are lizards. According to the classification system used by biologists, the class known as "reptilia" (the name is derived from the Latin verb "repere," which means "to creep") consists of four orders: "crocodilia" (crocodiles, alligators, and caimans), "testudines" (turtles and tortoises), "rhynchocephalia" (two species of tuataras, a strange reptile native to New Zealand), and the biggest order, "squamata," comprised of the thousands of lizards and snakes found all over the world.

Although there are a few odd exceptions, most reptiles share the same basic features. First, they're covered by scales (and not skin, fur, or feathers); second, they're cold-blooded (meaning a lizard or snake takes on the temperature of its environment); and third, they give birth by laying eggs. Another thing that sets reptiles apart from other, similar-sized animals is that they need to eat very little to stay alive, one of the benefits of their cold-blooded metabolism.

What is the smallest lizard?

Not only is Sphaerodactylus the smallest lizard in the world, but—as far as scientists can tell—it's the smallest animal yet discovered among the thousands of species of reptiles, birds, and mammals. First found on the British Virgin Islands in 1965 (a second variety was discovered in 2001), Sphaerodactylus can fit easily on a dime, measuring only three-quarters of an inch from its snout to the tip of its tail.

How often do tuataras give birth?

It's no wonder that tuataras are among the world's rarest reptiles: female tuataras take a full 10 years to reach sexual maturity (by comparison, most small animals begin to breed when they're only one or two years old), and then they lay eggs only once every four years! The weirdness doesn't end there: unlike most other animals, which reach their full height and weight within a few years of birth, tuataras grow continually for the first 35 years of their century-long lives.

What is a gecko?

Perhaps because they have such a funny name, geckos have always been a particular favorite of reptile enthusiasts. These small lizards are extremely mobile, with sticky pads on their feet that allow them to climb up walls, and some species are talkative as well, chirping to each other constantly. Dozens of species of gecko can be found all over the world, ranging from the gargoyle gecko to the stump-toed gecko.

How closely are lizards related to dinosaurs?

It's easy to look at a big, hulking Komodo dragon and picture it as a direct descendant of long-extinct dinosaurs. However, in evolutionary terms, it's a tricky matter to say that any creature is closely related to a beast that lived tens of millions of years ago. The fact is, some modern-day lizards are as different from dinosaurs as cats are different from monkeys—and in the absence of direct DNA evidence (it's not like we can ask a dinosaur for a blood sample!), their true heritage may remain a matter of speculation.

In fact, it may surprise you to learn that scientists have identified a class of creatures that appears to be directly descended from dinosaurs—and it's not reptiles! Careful analyses of the bone structure of birds have shown that our feathered friends have a good claim to be the dinos' real descendants. If this is true, then the first birds likely evolved from smaller dinosaurs that escaped extinction tens of millions of years ago, while lizards (which are still related to dinosaurs, though not as closely as birds are) "split off" from the dinosaur lineage somewhat earlier.

Why do reptiles have scales?

The scales of reptiles have a slightly different function from the scales of fish (aside, that is, from protecting these creatures' internal organs!). Reptile scales are waterproof, and prevent moisture from evaporating out of a snake or crocodile's body (unlike mammals, reptiles don't have sweat glands). This is one of the adaptations that allow reptiles to thrive in hot environments, in which they can survive with scarce food and even scarcer water.

What is a Komodo dragon?

The largest lizard in the world, the Komodo dragon of Indonesia can grow to a length of 10 feet and a weight of more than 150 pounds—which is a good thing, since this creature likes to feast on hefty prey like pigs, goats, and even water buffalo. However, the Komodo doesn't qualify as the largest reptile: two of its reptilian cousins, the Australian saltwater crocodile and the leatherback sea turtle, have been known to grow even bigger.

Lobsters & Crabs

What is a lobster's shell made of?

The outer shell of lobsters (not to mention crabs, beetles, and other assorted creatures) is made out of a tough protein called chitin (pronounced "kie-tin"). What makes chitin especially interesting is that it's a naturally occurring polymer—that is, a strong, protective substance made out of long chains of identical molecules. Since most polymers used today are man-made, scientists study chitin to get some clues from nature about how to make tougher, more durable materials. (By the way, chitin is the second most abundant natural polymer on earth, next to cellulose, the stringy material found in plants.)

Because of its unique properties—it's natural, non-toxic, biodegradable, and doesn't provoke any allergies—chitin has many medical uses as well. When applied to human skin, chitin has been shown to accelerate the healing process (don't worry, patients don't wind up growing their own lobster shells!), and some doctors use chitin-coated sutures to sew up the patient after surgery. Chitin can also be found in antibacterial sponges, artificial blood vessels, and even contact lenses.

What is that green stuff inside of lobsters?

If a first-time lobster eater isn't put off by the way these creatures are cooked (alive, in a pot of boiling water), their numerous legs, or their small, beady eyes, she may well wonder what that oozing green stuff is in the lobster's insides, around the white meat. That's the lobster's liver, technically known as "tomale," and wouldn't you know it, some people consider it a delicacy!

What insects are lobsters related to?

You may not want to tell your parents this the next time they sit down to a lobster dinner, but in evolutionary terms, the closest relative of the lobster is the common cockroach. In fact, some people call lobsters "the cockroaches of the sea," because both roaches and lobsters are omnivorous feeders, and will gobble up anything they find lying on your kitchen counter (or on the ocean floor). Now, wouldn't you prefer to have a hamburger?

How big can a lobster grow?

The majority of lobsters weigh only a few pounds each, but every now and then, fishermen dredge up monster specimens weighing as much as 35 or 40 pounds. You might think such plump, juicy monsters would earn a one-way ticket to the dinner table, but most triple-extra-large lobsters wind up in aquariums instead, as tourist attractions. (By the way, the biggest lobsters are also the oldest—these creatures can live for 20 to 30 years.)

What is a horseshoe crab?

One of the most fascinating creatures on earth, the horseshoe crab isn't technically a crab at all, but an ancient, alien-looking arthropod closely related to the spider. The horseshoe crab's most noticeable feature is its long, sharp, solid tail (called a "telson"), which it uses not to attack other creatures, but to flip itself over if it happens to wash up on a beach upside-down!

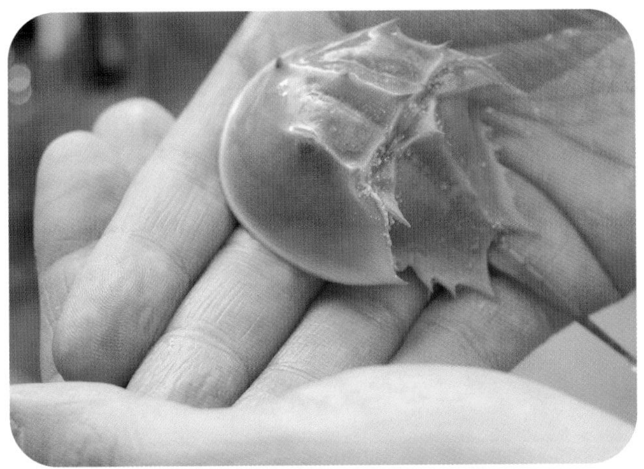

Why are they called "fiddler crabs"?

Because one of its claws is much bigger than the other—and because it eats by scooping up food with its small claw and bringing it up near its big claw—a male fiddler crab appears to be playing the violin, which is how this species got its name. (The reason for the unequal size of a male fiddler crab's claws is that big claws are helpful for attracting more symmetrical female crabs.)

How did people learn to eat lobsters?

You have to admit, lobsters aren't the most appetizing-looking creatures on earth, and their close kinship to cockroaches (see the facing page) doesn't make them any more appealing. Still, archeologists have found the remains of lobster shells in ancient human settlements, indicating that these creatures have long been part of the human diet. (Then again, prehistoric humans were always on the brink of starvation, and ate pretty much anything that hopped, jumped, or crawled their way.)

Even people who have gotten over their squeamishness about lobsters' looks are often put off by the way these creatures are cooked: by plunging them, still alive, into a pot of boiling water. If it makes you feel any better, researchers who study such things have determined that lobsters don't feel pain, because their nervous systems are way too primitive. Even still, some cooks prefer to freeze their lobsters before boiling them—although, from the lobster's point of view, it's hard to see how this is much of an improvement!

Why are rats taught to run mazes?

Scientists who study learning and memory often find it convenient to experiment with rats, for two reasons: first, these pesky rodents are in plentiful supply, and second, they share enough traits with human beings that the results of these experiments can often be extrapolated to people. (Rats and humans are both mammals, for instance, and despite what you may think, rats have relatively advanced brains, at least compared to fruit flies!)

Experimenters usually teach rats to run mazes by offering incentives (like a tasty nugget of cheese at the other end) and punishments (such as nasty electric shocks when the rodent makes a wrong turn). By studying how these stimuli affect the rat's choices and repeat performances, scientists can learn a lot about how the brain retains short- and long-term memories, as well as how animals (and humans) learn specific tasks. Unfortunately, unlike human subjects, rats are often killed humanely and dissected after maze-running experiments, so scientists can explore the physical effects of learning on their brains.

How do rats know when to leave a sinking ship?

It's considered an insult to compare someone to a "rat leaving a sinking ship," but this should really be taken as a compliment. The reason rats can be seen leaving a ship just before it sinks is because many of these critters live deep down in the hold, and can see water accumulating long before the humans on board do. A rat leaving a sinking ship is just (very sensibly) trying to get out while the getting is good!

What is the difference between a mouse and a rat?

Well, for one thing, mice make for adorable cartoon characters, but you're unlikely to see a TV show starring a rat! Technically, mice and rats belong to two different (but closely related) families: the genus "rattus" for rats, and the genus "mus" for mice, which both belong to the much larger category "rodentia" ("rodents" to you and me). Generally, though, rats tend to be bigger, more aggressive, and much less cute than their smaller, meeker cousins.

How big are the biggest rats?

Legend has it that some rats in New York City are as big as well-fed cats, but this is a bit of an exaggeration: most city rats weigh a pound or less, though that's probably not much of a consolation if one happens to be staring at you on a subway platform. Many rodent species (like the colorfully named Gambian pouch rat) are significantly bigger, but although they're close relations, technically they aren't rats at all but members of an African group called muroid rodents.

Why do mice only eat cheese?

This is one of those incorrect facts that's been hammered into the heads of grade-school kids by years and years of TV cartoons. Although mice certainly enjoy the occasional bit of gorgonzola (if any is available), these adaptable creatures will eat anything from grains to seeds to small insects, as well as any crumbs you happen to have lying around on your bed or floor.

Why are rats called "vermin"?

"Vermin" is one of those catchall words that means everything and nothing at the same time. Technically, vermin are any animals that human beings consider to be pests, whether this means mice, rats, crickets, or rabbits. (It's also the source of the colorful word "varmint," which settlers in the American west used to describe larger creatures like foxes and coyotes.) Today, since you're unlikely to find a coyote living in your basement, "vermin" is most often used to refer to rodents.

While we're on the subject, although the word "rat" has negative connotations in the U.S. (it's used to refer to Mob turncoats, for instance, and people often say "rats!" when they're disappointed), this isn't necessarily the case in other parts of the world. The rat signifies one of the 12 years of the Chinese calendar, and a person born in the "Year of the Rat" is supposed to be creative, honest, generous, and ambitious. There's also a temple in India where people worship rats (which they believe will be reincarnated after their deaths as Hindu holy men).

How long can a mouse live?

It all depends on where it calls home. A mouse kept as a pet by a responsible child (in a nice, warm cage) can live for as long as three years, but out in the wild, the life span of rodents is usually measured in months rather than years. This is because mice are pretty far down in the food chain, and usually wind up eaten by owls, cats, and other assorted critters.

Pet Fish

Why do fish float upside-down when they die?

This is kind of disgusting, so stop reading if you have a weak stomach. Immediately after it dies, a fish will sink to the bottom of its bowl or aquarium. Shortly after that, though, bacteria inside the fish start eating away at its insides, producing gas in the process. Some of this gas becomes trapped in the fish's body, causing it to float to the surface like an inflated balloon—usually upside-down, because the fish's belly is lighter than its back.

Why is it dangerous to overfeed fish?

Despite what you may have heard, you can't kill a fish by overfeeding it (though you may wind up with a very fat and unhealthy fish). The reason you shouldn't put more food in an aquarium than your fish can eat is because the uneaten food will sink to the bottom and decompose, fouling the tank's water. So if you like to give your fish extra portions, be sure to clean out its tank on a regular basis!

How many kinds of goldfish are there?

This question may seem kind of obvious, if you're only familiar with the plain, yellow goldfish that millions of kids keep in fishbowls. But goldfish aficionados know that there are dozens of breeds of this famous fish, some of which look as different from the "common" goldfish as a bulldog does from a Chihuahua. You can get a sense of how strange some of these goldfish are by their names, including "bubble eye," "telescope eye," and "lionhead."

Many of these odd varieties of goldfish are most popular in China, where goldfish originated over a thousand years ago as a sudden, harmless mutation among populations of carp kept in ponds. When their Chinese tenders saw these "golden" fish, they started a program of selective breeding, deliberately mating the mutants with one another to produce a line of increasingly ornate fish. Essentially, the most exotic goldfish are bred according to the same principles as the most exotic dogs and cats!

How do fish go to the bathroom?

Unlike cats, which instinctively use a litter box, and dogs, which wait until they're taken outside, fish pretty much pee and poop wherever they happen to be swimming—and their excretions contain the chemical ammonia, which is deadly when it's allowed to accumulate. That's why it's important to treat your fish well, and to clean its tank every now and then!

Why is it called a Neon Tetra?

Probably second only to goldfish in its popularity in America's fish tanks, the neon tetra earned its name because of the two bright stripes on its body: blue-green along its back and red along its tail. As is the case with goldfish, there are many varieties of tetra, including the cardinal tetra, the glo-light tetra, and the rummy-nose tetra (that's "rummy," not "runny," and refers to this fish's bright red snout).

Why can't some fish be kept as pets?

Like some brightly colored parrots—which are illegal to remove from their native habitats in South and Central America—certain colorful varieties of fish aren't supposed to be sold as pets, usually because they're on the verge of extinction. If you insist on seeing these fish, though, you can often find them at your local aquarium, which may be allowed to keep a few varieties (just as a zoo keeps endangered animals like pandas).

How does a home aquarium work?

If you keep fish at home, you know they require more advanced care than your average cat or dog. Because it lives in a liquid environment, maintaining a fish "out of water," so to speak, can be as complicated as keeping an astronaut alive in the farthest reaches of outer space.

Basically, the idea of a home aquarium is to duplicate the conditions a fish would have in its native habitat. It's not enough to simply pour water into a tank and plop in the fish; you also have to invest in a filter (which constantly removes waste and impurities from the water) and a heater (which keeps the water at the optimum temperature). It also helps if you keep the tank away from sunny windows, vibrating appliances, and your hungry cat!

One of the most challenging things about owning an aquarium is its sheer weight—because water is surprisingly heavy, your average 30-gallon tank (when you factor in all the equipment) can weigh more than 200 pounds! That's why you need to place the tank in a secure location, and away from where people might accidentally bump into it.

Pigs

What does a pig say?

Well, if you're American, the answer is obvious: a pig says "oink!" Other languages, though, use different words to imitate the sounds animals make. In South Africa, pigs go "snork," while they "buu" in Japan and "grok" in Serbia. Oddly enough, the language that uses the word closest to the English "oink" is Spanish, in which pigs go "oing" or "oinq."

How did pigs become domesticated?

Just as dogs are descended from wolves, pigs are descended from a relatively untamed relative: the European Wild Boar. Despite its name, the European Wild Boar had characteristics that made it a perfect candidate for domestication (the process by which animals are raised to coexist peacefully with humans): it's a social beast that craves body contact, whether with other wild boars or with people.

About 10,000 years ago, experts believe, wild boars wandered into a human settlement in present-day Turkey, and were slowly molded into the tame, friendly animal we know today. (In fact, scientists now think the European Wild Boar was domesticated a half-dozen separate times, in areas as widely separated as China and Italy.)

In a way, though, pigs have been big losers in the domestication lottery. While dogs and cats are bred as pets and horses as transportation, pigs have been domesticated for one reason: as a source of meat. (Yes, farms also have domesticated chickens and cows, but at least some of these animals are spared so they can lay eggs or produce milk!)

How many pigs are in a litter?

Part of what makes pigs such a dependable source of food is that they multiply very quickly: a female pig can give birth up to twice a year, to anywhere from 8 to 12 piglets at a time (and sometimes more than that). You can recognize a brand-new mother by the squealing piglets desperately trying to secure access to one of her teats, which supply the milk the piglets need until they're old enough to eat the usual pig slop.

What is a Vietnamese pot-bellied pig?

If you're in the market for an exotic pet, you might want to ask your parents to look into a genuine Vietnamese pot-bellied pig. As its name implies, this pig has a prominent pot belly, but it's considerably smaller than a farm pig—"only" about 200 pounds full grown. Pot-bellied pigs are fashionable pets among people who a) have enough room to keep one and b) enjoy being stopped on the street by curious strangers!

What is the difference between a pig and a hog?

Like cattle farmers and chicken farmers, pig farmers have their own, highly specialized terminology. Big, fat pigs raised to be pork chops are called "hogs," while a female pig is called a "gilt" (unless she's had a litter of baby pigs, in which case she becomes the more familiar "sow"). An adult male is referred to as a "boar," but if he's been neutered (that is, rendered unable to procreate), he becomes a "barrow." As for "pig," that's pretty much the generic term used to describe the entire species!

What do pigs eat?

Like humans, pigs are omnivores, meaning they'll eat pretty much anything they can lay their hooves on, ranging from grains to birds to the remains of other pigs. However, it's unfair to say that pigs, well, eat like pigs—like any animal, a pig will eat enough to satiate itself, but it won't keep eating and eating until it explodes!

What part of the pig does bacon come from?

There's a funny line from the TV show *The Simpsons* in which Homer is told by his daughter that bacon, ham, and pork chops all come from the same animal, and he replies sarcastically, "Yeah, right, Lisa. A wonderful, magical animal."

Well, the fact is that bacon, ham, and pork chops all do come from the same animal (and if you haven't guessed what that animal is by now, you and Homer Simpson may have something in common). High-quality pork chops come from the pig's loin (that is, the top side of the pig under its back), while lower-quality chops are derived from the muscles of the pig's shoulders and the area near its front legs.

But wait, we're not finished yet. As you can guess, the fattest (and tastiest) part of a pig is its enormous belly, which is the source of spare ribs and most cuts of bacon. As for ham, that comes from the pig's back legs (you can understand why "smoked ham" is a more appetizing name than "smoked pig butt"). Because the rear end of the pig is leaner (that is, less fatty) than its front and bottom, this is considered the healthiest part of the animal to eat.

Why are they called nurse sharks?

It's hard to imagine a creature that sounds less harmless than a nurse shark—but although these medium-sized sharks usually stay away from people, they have been known to attack when threatened. The reason they're called "nurse sharks" has nothing to do with their temperament; rather, this word is derived from the old English "nusse," a name that was once applied generically to the "catsharks" of which the nurse is a particular species.

While we're on the subject, you may be curious about where the word "shark" itself comes from. This word first appeared in the English language in the late 16th century, when a specimen of "sharke" was brought to London by a captain named John Hawkins. Etymologists (scholars who study language) don't know for sure, but one possibility is that "shark" was derived from the German word "schurke," which means "scoundrel" or "villain." In fact, it may well be the case that real sharks were named after "loan sharks" (unsavory characters who lend money at high interest), rather than vice-versa!

How many people are killed by sharks every year?

You can do the math: in 2005, there were only 58 instances of sharks attacking people without provocation, resulting in five fatalities (the organization that tracks shark attacks is careful to distinguish unprovoked from provoked attacks, which result from tourists or fishermen unwisely teasing nervous sharks). By comparison, humans kill tens of millions of sharks every year, either directly for food or as an indirect result of trawling for fish!

Why can't sharks stop swimming?

Because they're so fast and muscular, sharks consume more oxygen than most other sea-dwelling creatures. While the average fish can keep still occasionally and allow a slow ocean current to drive water through its gills, a shark needs to keep swimming in order to filter more water (and extract more oxygen). Even so, some species of shark have been known to take occasional naps, provided they can find a strong current that meets their oxygen needs.

How do sharks detect their prey?

As befits creatures that spend most of their time looking for food, sharks are equipped with the sharpest underwater senses nature can provide. The details vary slightly by species, but most sharks are extremely sensitive to the scent of blood, as well as to various chemicals in the waste products of fish (which usually indicate that the fish itself is somewhere nearby). Sharks also have extremely acute hearing (they can pick up the nearly inaudible sounds of swimming prey thousands of feet away), as well as sharper-than-usual eyesight.

But wait, we're not finished yet. A shark's head contains a network of organs called the "ampullae of Lorenzini," which can sense the tiny (as low as a few billionths of a volt) electrical signals emitted by the nerve cells of living creatures, as well as slight changes in temperature and pressure. Some sharks will use their senses of smell, hearing, and sight to navigate within the general vicinity of their lunch—then will switch to "electric" mode to detect their prey cowering under a nearby rock!

Why did Hawaiians once worship sharks?

Well, think about it for a second—if you lived on an island surrounded by thousands of miles of water on all sides, you might worship a shark or two yourself. Shark gods featured prominently in ancient Hawaiian mythology; the most important of them all was Kamohoali'i, who could take on the form of any fish or person. Another shark god, Kane-i-kokala, was said to save shipwrecked sailors by dragging them onto the shore.

Why do hammerhead sharks have such weird heads?

The hammerhead shark has one of the most distinctive heads of any creature: two thick stalks jutting out at right angles from the neck, each with a big eye at the end. Scientists have only recently discovered the reason for this weird configuration: like other sharks, the hammerhead has an "electric" sense, and the wide, antenna-like separation of its head allows it to detect the incredibly small electric currents generated by its prey.

Why don't more people eat shark?

It's not (as you may think) because sharks are more difficult to catch than "food fish" like cod or salmon. The fact is, shark meat contains a chemical compound that, if it's not immediately removed, turns into ammonia—and even a properly prepared shark fillet will often have a strong ammonia taste. Since most people prefer less aromatic fare, they're content to stick with a nice fillet of flounder!

Snails & Slugs

What is the difference between snails and slugs?

In a sense, a slug is nothing more (or less) than a naked snail. Both slugs and snails belong to the class of animals known as "gastropods," which translates roughly as "stomach foot." (Gastropods themselves belong to the mollusk family, which includes other shelled creatures like clams and mussels.) Essentially, a snail is a gastropod that has a coiled shell (which is secreted from the snail's body and grows into the hard shell you see), while a slug is a gastropod without a shell (or, occasionally, with a very small internal shell); there are also creatures called "semi-slugs," which have rudimentary shells that don't serve much of a purpose.

Aside from their shells (or lack of them), snails and slugs lead fairly similar lives. Most land-dwelling varieties are gentle vegetarians that thrive in moist soil and feed on decomposing vegetable matter, but there are also carnivorous species, which aren't quite as dangerous as they sound because they feed mostly on other snails and slugs (or the occasional earthworm). Because of their protective shells, snails can venture away from the soil for brief periods of time, but slugs need constant moisture to stay alive—so they're not likely to try to cross a paved sidewalk!

What is the biggest slug?

In the U.S., the bright yellow banana slug can grow to a whopping length of one foot (it's pretty speedy, too, as slugs go, capable of a top speed of about 30 feet per hour). Technically, a European slug called "limax cinereoriger" is even bigger, but its dull color and relative obscurity have pretty much relegated it to the slug sidelines. Besides, you have to admit, "banana slug" is a much more attention-grabbing name!

Why does salt kill slugs?

Because a slug doesn't have a protective shell—or even what we would ordinarily consider "skin"—pouring salt on one will suck all the fluids out of its body, causing it to dehydrate and die. If this sounds like a disgusting (and cruel) way to get rid of slugs, gardeners have hit on a more humane solution: they fill a bowl with stale beer, which attracts (and drowns) any curious slugs in the vicinity.

HOW do snail shells get their shape?

Because of the way they're gradually secreted from the snail's body, the striped "whirls" of a snail shell have a precise mathematical structure, known as a logarithmic spiral. Many snail shells also utilize something called the "golden ratio," another quantity that derives from pure mathematics. By the way, snail shells are composed mostly of calcium carbonate, the same chemical secreted by other mollusks (such as clams and oysters) to create their shells.

HOW long can a snail live?

There seems to be something about moving very, very slowly and having a protective shell that extends a creature's life span. Just as a giant turtle can live to be more than 100 years old, some species of snails have been known to live as long as 30 years—which is close to an eternity for a creature that size!

What is the biggest snail?

Well, it probably isn't a match for a charging rhino, but the giant African snail measures almost a foot from end to end, and has an enormous, striped shell that can attain a height of a few inches. Unfortunately, this monstrous gastropod has found its way out of Africa, and is rapidly multiplying in many of the countries bordering the Pacific Ocean (including Brazil, the Philippines, and even parts of the U.S.). The reason this is unfortunate is that, as you might expect, a snail this size needs to eat a lot of food—in New Zealand alone, the giant African has been known to feast on lettuce, potatoes, onions, sunflowers, and Eucalyptus leaves!

While we're on the subject, another enormous gastropod is the freshwater apple snail, which is fairly close in size to a genuine apple—up to half a foot in diameter, with a surprisingly hefty weight. What makes the apple snail even more fascinating is that it has gills on one side of its body (which breathe water), and a lung on the other side (which breathes air). This makes the snail amazingly well adapted to living on sea or land, and as a result, it has proliferated to the point that some people consider it a pest.

What is the difference between a swamp and a marsh?

The English language is rich in words describing wet, soggy patches of land, including "swamp," "bog," and "marsh." But although they're often used interchangeably, these words actually describe slightly different things.

Technically, both swamps and marshes are low-lying wetlands (that is, large areas of land submerged beneath still, murky waters only a few feet deep) located near rivers or oceans. The main difference between them is that swamps are dotted with trees, while the plant life in marshes consists mainly of grasses, making a marsh a much less interesting place to visit!

As damp and buggy as they are, the average swamp or marsh is paradise compared to a bog. Bogs are wetlands that have accumulated acres and acres of "peat," or dead plant matter (which, in a few million years, will most likely turn into coal). Unlike swamps and marshes, bogs aren't wet because they serve as drains for nearby rivers or bays; all their moisture comes from rain or other precipitation. This makes their water especially acidic and unfit for consumption by humans (or, for that matter, by most plants or animals).

Why is it called the Great Dismal Swamp?

You mean, besides the fact that it's great and dismal? This huge, 100,000-acre swamp straddles the border between southeastern Virginia and northeastern North Carolina, and it's famous for two reasons: first, future president George Washington founded a company in 1763 to drain part of the swamp, and second, before and during the Civil War, the Great Dismal Swamp was populated by hundreds of runaway slaves!

What is a quagmire?

It sounds more interesting, but "quagmire" is basically another word for "swamp" (it's derived from the words "quake" and "mire," which roughly translates as "wet and shaky"). The word "quagmire" is most often used not to describe specific wetlands, but a bad situation that just keeps getting worse: for example, in the 1960s, some people referred to the "quagmire" of America's involvement in Vietnam.

How can people live in swamps?

If you don't object to lots of bugs—not to mention a lack of utilities and paved roads—it's possible (if not especially comfortable) to live in the middle of a swamp. The trick is to build your house on stilts, which raises you above the standing water and keeps your living room from flooding every day. These stilts need to be made out of a strong material, since standing water tends to eat away at soft wood!

How big is Okefenokee Swamp?

The largest freshwater swamp in North America, Okefenokee (the name is Native American for "trembling earth") occupies 400,000 acres of land between Georgia and Florida, with a National Wildlife Refuge taking up most of the Georgia side. Today, Okefenokee is a popular tourist destination, and an especially good place to catch a glimpse of some really big alligators.

What is the world's biggest swamp?

You might not expect a swamp to be found so close to a desert, but the biggest swamp in the world is located in Sudan, south of Egypt, where the upper Nile River gets bogged down in a vast network of wetlands covering an area larger than the state of Pennsylvania. There have long been plans to drain parts of the As-Sudd Swamp, as it's known, and reclaim the land for crops, but a continuing civil war in Sudan has put this project on hold indefinitely.

Why are swamps drained?

Historically, people drain swamps (that is, siphon away their standing water by building a network of canals, ditches, and levees) for two reasons. First, swamps are notorious breeding grounds for pesky insects, such as the mosquitoes that spread malaria or the West Nile virus. And second, the land covered by marshes is unusually rich in nutrients, making the reclaimed soil perfect for planting crops. (On the down side, many environmentalists object to draining swamps, because this destroys the ecosystem of the plants and animals that live there.)

One of the biggest (and longest) marsh-drainage projects in history took place in southeastern Missouri, starting in 1905 and ending in 1928. During that span, engineers built almost 1,000 miles of ditches and 300 miles of levees to create the Little River Drainage District, reclaiming a huge expanse of land that had previously been swamped by floodwaters from the Mississippi River. By the time they finished, workers had removed more soil from the Little River area than had been dug up during the building of the Panama Canal!

Coffee & Tea

How much coffee is drunk every day?

Next to water, coffee is the true global beverage: every day, more than one billion people have at least one cup, from the Western to the Eastern hemispheres (not to mention the small, frozen research outposts of Antarctica). Coffee is so popular, in fact, that the price charged for beans by coffee-growing countries like Brazil and Guatemala has almost as much of an impact on the world economy as the price of oil!

What is the difference between espresso and cappuccino?

Regular coffee is made by percolating ground coffee beans in water, but espresso—a darker, thicker, more bitter concoction that's meant to be drunk in small quantities—is brewed in a special machine that forces blasts of steam through finely ground, dark-roasted beans. Basically, cappuccino is espresso that has been "watered down" with steamed milk and various flavorings.

How did people learn to drink coffee?

You have to admit, it's a big leap from stumbling across a squat, unremarkable coffee plant and figuring out that its beans can be used to brew an addictive beverage. Legend has it that a traveler in Ethiopia (where coffee beans grow naturally in the wild) noticed that the local goats had a lot of energy, and made the logical connection to the coffee beans on which they nibbled. This may or may not be true, but it does seem likely that this "Kaffa" region of Ethiopia is where coffee got its name.

Whatever the case, throughout history, once people learn how to start drinking coffee, they find it very difficult to stop. Coffee was so popular in Arabia that it was briefly banned in various cities in the 16th century, but this ban was later rescinded (probably thanks to some very groggy, very grumpy coffee drinkers). This was around the time that coffee made its way to Europe: by 1675, there were thousands of coffeehouses throughout England alone, and settlers sipped coffee at similar shops in the American colonies.

Why can drinking tea be good for you?

While scientists have yet to show any health benefits from drinking a cup or two of coffee a day—other than keeping people from falling asleep at work!—it has long been known that drinking tea can be a very healthy habit. The reason is that tea contains substances called "antioxidants," which help keep the walls of your cells from breaking down (a contributing factor to aging and disease).

Although the "black" tea that's popular in America has some antioxidant properties, the true champ in this regard is green tea, which is traditionally consumed in the countries of East Asia. Green tea has been shown to help prevent cancer, heart disease, and diabetes, and it lowers your blood pressure as well!

However, this doesn't mean that you can eat cheeseburgers and fries all day and make up for it with a nice, steaming mug of green tea. It's possible that part of the reason green tea has such a beneficial effect on Chinese and Japanese people is that they have a more balanced, low-fat diet. Drinking green tea certainly can't hurt, but it's important to pursue other healthy habits too.

Why do some people grind their own coffee beans?

For the true coffee enthusiast, freshness is everything. The most demanding coffee drinkers buy their own beans at specialty shops, grind them at home, and brew up and drink a pot of coffee without allowing it to sit for an extended period of time (which can spoil the flavor).

What are herbal teas?

Practically any kind of plant (or tree bark, for that matter) can be soaked in hot water to create "herbal" tea. There are hundreds of different herbal teas, ranging from raspberry to sassafras to ginger root, and some are associated with medicinal effects (for instance, it has long been believed that echinacea tea can help cure colds). Since these effects are unproven, it's better to drink herbal tea because you like the taste, not because you want to cure your athlete's foot!

How is coffee decaffeinated?

The most popular way to remove caffeine (the chemical in coffee that keeps you awake) from coffee beans is to soak them in hot water, which causes the caffeine to leach out. Unfortunately, this soaking process also removes most of the coffee beans' flavor, so there's a second step: the caffeine is removed from the water by means of a carbon filter, and then the beans re-soak-up the caffeineless water to recapture their flavor.

Condiments

Why is it called ketchup?

When it first began to be used in the American colonies in the 16th and 17th centuries, "ketchup" referred to a tomatoless flavoring sauce made with vinegar—which makes sense, since its name was probably derived from a tomatoless fish sauce from Malaysia called "kechap." It's also possible that "ketchup" descends from the Chinese word "ke-tsiap," which refers to a kind of eggplant sauce. In any case, tomatoes didn't come into the picture until the early 19th century, when U.S. citizens overcame their irrational fear of this harmless vegetable.

While we're on the subject, you may want to know why ketchup is so hard to pour out of the bottle. This condiment is what's known as a "high-viscosity" liquid, which means that it flows very slowly (water, on the other hand, has very low viscosity, and flows quickly). For this reason, the best way to pour a bottle of ketchup is to hold it at a slight downward tilt, so the ketchup can slowly ooze out. If you hold the bottle upside down (or slap its bottom), the ketchup will usually wind up stuck uselessly on top. (Today, most kids get their ketchup from squeeze bottles, so this isn't as much of an issue!)

How do you pronounce "Worcestershire" sauce?

Names from England are notorious for looking a lot longer than they actually are. "Worcestershire" looks like it should be enunciated with four syllables, but "wooster-shear" is the proper pronunciation. Now that we've gotten that out of the way, this popular steak sauce is made from a long list of ingredients—usually a base of vinegar, corn syrup, and molasses mixed with a variety of spices (such as shallots, cloves, peppers, and garlic).

What are the ingredients of mayonnaise?

Unlike other popular condiments—such as mustard—mayonnaise isn't made from a particular kind of plant. Rather, it's a mixture of vegetable oil, egg yolks, lemon juice (or vinegar), and assorted seasonings. Because mayonnaise is so rich (almost two-thirds oil), it's usually avoided by people on low-fat diets. By the way, mayonnaise made without egg yolks is usually sold as salad dressing.

What is vinegar?

French for "sour wine," vinegar is pretty much what its name implies: wine, beer, cider, or fruit juice that has been fermented by bacteria into a pungent liquid loaded with acetic acid. Historically, vinegar has been used as a folk medicine or even as an ingredient in shampoos, but today you're most likely to find it in salad dressings or preparations of pickled vegetables.

Why are frankfurters served with sauerkraut?

As you can guess from the name—"Frankfurt" is a city in Germany—frankfurters were introduced to this country by German immigrants, who sold them from street carts in the late 19th century. Because sauerkraut (sliced, fermented cabbage) is also a German favorite, it only makes sense that the earliest frankfurters were served with optional sauerkraut toppings—a tradition that has persisted to the present day.

Why is it called horseradish?

The origins of the word "horseradish" (a bitter root related to mustard and cabbage) have been lost to history. Some historians think this name is a mistranslation of the German word for the plant, "meerrettich," meaning "big radish"—"meer" may have became "mare" (a female horse) in the English language. On the other hand, it's possible that "horse" was a deliberate choice, meant to signify this condiment's strong, untamable taste.

How is mustard made?

As is the case with many condiments, mustard comes in two basic varieties: a milder "American" style prepared from white mustard seeds (which are obtained from plants called mustard greens), and a spicier style made from brown mustard seeds, which are harvested from a species of mustard green native to Asia. Whatever the style, the basic recipe is the same: the seeds are dried, ground up, and mixed with water, vinegar, and various other ingredients, depending on the desired result.

American mustard is usually mixed with a spice called "turmeric," which gives it its characteristic bright-yellow color. Brown or golden mustard, though, looks pretty much the way it's supposed to, since it's derived from darker mustard seeds.

By the way, many people mistakenly believe that mustard gas (a toxic gas used on the Western Front in World War I, and by some countries in modern times) is made from mustard seeds. In fact, this deadly gas received its name because it smells uncannily like mustard (or, depending on the formulation, garlic or horseradish); it's actually made from a chemical containing sulfur.

Meals

Why is it called breakfast?

As you might have guessed, "breakfast" means, literally, to break a fast—"break" meaning "end" and "fast" meaning a long period of not eating—usually the eight or nine hours you just spent sleeping. By the way, American kids are pretty much alone in starting the day with a big bowl of cereal and milk—in other countries, breakfast consists of beans, cheese, or even bread dipped in vegetable curry!

What does it mean to "spoil your appetite"?

Eating a snack in the late afternoon makes you less hungry, so you're less likely to finish your dinner. Since your parents would rather you eat a nutritious dinner than a non-nutritious snack, they'll tell you to be patient and not to "spoil your appetite" with junk food.

Why do we eat three meals a day?

The easy answer to this question is that the human body needs a steady supply of energy—and having a meal early in the morning, around noon, and in the evening is a natural way to divide up the day. What's harder to figure out is how the tradition of a full breakfast, lunch, and dinner came about, especially since most people throughout history have had much more irregular eating habits.

For instance, in 17th- or 18th-century Europe, most ordinary folk ate a big meal around the middle of the day, usually skipping breakfast (the concept of which didn't really exist yet) and having a relatively small evening snack. Partly this was because of tradition, but partly it was because, until modern times, most families didn't have nearly enough to eat—in fact, the idea of eating three big meals a day would have been as alien to them as the idea of eating only one big meal a day would be to you!

So the second answer to this question is: since we live in more prosperous times, we can afford to have a substantial breakfast, lunch, and dinner (not to mention the occasional afternoon or before-bedtime snack).

What is the difference between supper and dinner?

Today, for all practical purposes, "supper" and "dinner" mean the same thing—the last meal of the day, served in the late afternoon or early evening. Until the 20th century, though, "dinner" referred to the biggest meal of the day, which usually was eaten in the early afternoon (or what lunchtime would be today), while "supper" was a much smaller meal served in the early evening. Any questions?

What is a smorgasbord?

It sounds like a kind of underwater creature, but a smorgasbord is actually a way of serving food that originated in Sweden. A smorgasbord consists of a variety of small dishes, from which guests assemble a plate of food and return to the dinner table to eat. If this sounds familiar, it's because Americans have adapted the traditional Swedish smorgasbord into the fully loaded buffet tables you sometimes see at weddings and other parties.

How was brunch invented?

The word "brunch" was devised in late 19th-century England to describe a leisurely late-morning meal that combined breakfast and lunch. Because most families at that time could afford only a small lunch, and barely ate breakfast at all, brunch was a privilege of better-off households, who could show off their wealth by serving large amounts of food.

Why don't we have dessert with breakfast or lunch?

In most families, dinner is the biggest meal of the day. It's also the last meal before bedtime, so most parents give their kids dessert as a reward for good behavior—which is why, if you've hit your little sister or refused to do your homework, you may not get any ice cream.

But that's only part of the reason you usually don't get dessert with breakfast or lunch. The idea of dessert was invented in 17th-century France, when guests would be served something sweet as the dishes were cleared away from the big meal of the day (usually dinner, served in the early afternoon). In fact, the word "dessert" is derived from the French word "desservir," which means "to clear the table." Since the biggest meal of the day is now dinner (served in the evening, not afternoon), the idea of dessert after dinner has persisted into modern times.

By the way, until recently, most desserts consisted of fruits, nuts, cheese, or the occasional pastry—so be thankful for that slice of chocolate cake!

Sandwiches

What is the difference between salami and baloney?

As you probably know from years of school lunches, salami tends to be thicker, saltier, and spicier than baloney (or, as it's properly spelled, bologna). Also, salami comes from Italy, while good ol' American baloney is a watered-down version of an Italian sausage called mortadella. By the way, the reason the word "baloney" is used to mean "nonsense!" is that some kinds of bologna are made from scrap meats (that is, what's left over from the cow or pig when all the good parts have been taken).

What did the Earl of Sandwich invent?

If this sounds like a trick question, that's because it is. For more than 200 years, people have given credit to John Montague, the Fourth Earl of Sandwich (an earl is a type of British noble, and Sandwich is the name of an English town), for putting a slice of roast beef between two slices of bread and thus inventing the dish that bears his name. Unfortunately, we only know this story from one source, and not a very reliable one at that—so it's possible that other aristocrats had been preparing "sandwiches" for years before the Earl came onto the scene in 1765.

More important, we know that people have been eating various combinations of bread and meat for thousands of years. For example, "trenchers"—slabs of meat served on thick slices of bread—were enjoyed by working people during the Middle Ages, and in the first century B.C. a rabbi devised the custom of eating chopped nuts and apples between two pieces of matzoh, or unleavened bread. The fact is, until the invention of knives and forks, eating meat was a messy affair, and it only made sense that somebody, somewhere, would get the bright idea of holding his dripping side of beef with a piece of bread!

Why does a piece of buttered toast always seem to land face-side-down?

A clever answer to this would be that, since the side of the toast with butter on it weighs slightly more than the side without butter, the force of gravity causes it to hit the floor first. Clever, but wrong. The fact is, if you accidentally flip a piece of toast off a table, it will usually have time for only half a rotation before it hits the floor—and since you set it on the table butter-side-up, it lands in a gooey mess butter-side-down.

What is the difference between white and whole-wheat bread?

Although little kids usually insist on white bread for their sandwiches, as you get older you'll discover that other types of bread—rye, whole-wheat, or multigrain—taste better and are a lot healthier. Plain white bread is made from processed wheat from which the outer shells have been removed; it goes down easy, but doesn't have much nutritional value. "Bumpier" types of bread like rye and whole wheat use more of the original grain and less chemical processing, so they're much better for you.

How was the peanut butter and jelly sandwich invented?

Oddly enough, this favorite sandwich of American kids seems to have been created during World War II by battle-hardened G.I.s. During the war, soldiers received rations of sliced bread and peanut butter, and added a ration of jelly to their peanut-butter sandwiches to make them more palatable (back then, peanut butter was much less sweet than it is today). When the war ended, these vets brought their taste for PB&J back with them, and a national craze was started.

Why is it called corned beef?

To the confusion of kids since time immemorial, the process of making corned beef has absolutely nothing to do with corn. In old England, the word "corn" was used to mean any small particle, whether that meant a tiny piece of corn or an even tinier grain of salt. Beef is "corned" by pumping it with seasoned brine (that is, salt dissolved in water), which produces the fragrant, crumbly, and very salty lunchmeat that's used in sandwiches.

While we're on the subject, corned beef is often mentioned in the same breath as pastrami, another popular sandwich meat served in delicatessens. The recipe for pastrami is a bit more complicated: a slab of beef is coated with salt, as well as a paste of various herbs and seasonings, including garlic, cinnamon, red peppers, and cloves. Then the meat is dried, smoked, cooked, and sliced. (We won't even mention an even more obscure sandwich meat, tongue, which can be made from the tongues of sheep, goats, pigs, and cows. Aren't you glad we spared you from that?)

Aging

Why do people grow old?

For gerontologists—scientists who study aging—this is the million-dollar question. As the reasoning goes, if we can identify the single biological mechanism that causes aging, we can invent a "cure" that will keep people young indefinitely.

Unfortunately, as matters stand today, it's unlikely that anyone in the near future will be able to take an anti-aging pill. Researchers are discovering that a large part of aging is programmed by our DNA, which contains a blueprint for how many times our cells can divide and how well they can continue to maintain and repair their own structure. The reason for this appears to be that life on earth could never have evolved if death wasn't an essential part of the natural cycle: the process of natural selection depends on older generations aging and dying, in order to clear space for new generations.

Since there's no way (yet, and probably ever) to reprogram our DNA, the best way to slow down the aging process, as far as anyone can tell, is to eat properly, get plenty of exercise, and stay out of trouble!

Why are people called "octogenarians" and "septuagenerians"?

If you want to impress your friends, try telling them that your 83-year-old grandfather is an "octogenerian." As complicated as this word sounds, it's simply a fancy way to describe a person who has lived into his eighth decade. There are comparable words for other ages: people between 70 and 79 are "septuagenerians," those between 90 and 99 are "nonagenerians," and folks lucky enough to live into their 100s are known as "centenarians."

What is Alzheimer's disease?

As some people age, a disorder of their brain cells causes them to slowly lose their memories (a condition once known as "senility"), as well as their ability to care for themselves. Over the past few decades, doctors have learned a lot about Alzheimer's disease, and it's possible they may one day be able to devise a cure—or at least an effective treatment that slows down the process and allows Alzheimer's sufferers to lead relatively normal lives.

What is a nursing home?

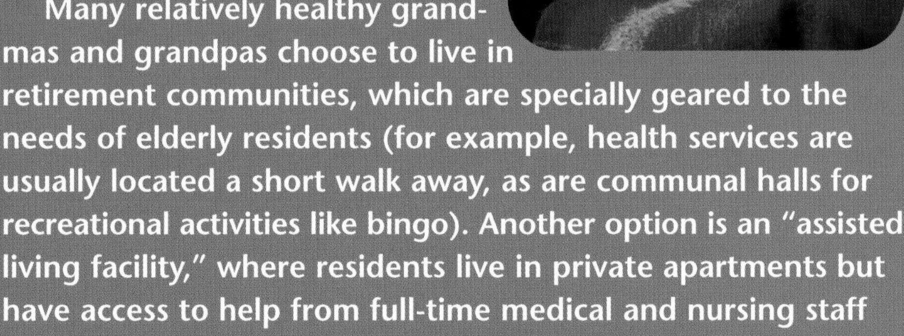

As people grow old, they can lose the ability to care for themselves on a daily basis: for example, severe arthritis can make it difficult even to walk to the bathroom. Fortunately, adults who can no longer live in their own homes have a variety of options, depending on the level of attention they need.

Many relatively healthy grandmas and grandpas choose to live in retirement communities, which are specially geared to the needs of elderly residents (for example, health services are usually located a short walk away, as are communal halls for recreational activities like bingo). Another option is an "assisted living facility," where residents live in private apartments but have access to help from full-time medical and nursing staff when needed.

Nursing homes are meant for elderly people who may, at one time or another, need continual medical care and attention. In some nursing homes, residents are "doubled up" in rooms (as in a hospital), but more expensive homes allow for more privacy. Today, hundreds of thousands of elderly people live in nursing homes all over America.

Why do women live longer than men?

In the U.S., most women tend to outlive most men by five or six years, a fact that has long puzzled doctors and scientists. No one is quite sure why this should be the case: it's possible that women are "programmed" by evolution to live longer, because they can help to raise grandchildren, while men are more disposable in this area. It's also possible that most women simply lead healthier, and less stressful, lives than most men, who succumb earlier to various aging-related diseases.

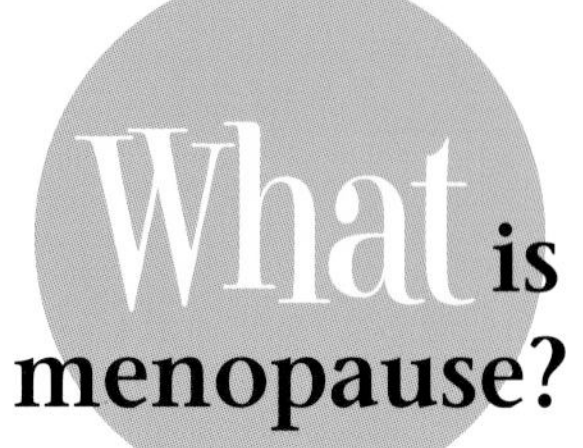

What is menopause?

Until she reaches her mid- to late 40s, a woman's ovaries produce eggs on a regular basis, which may or may not be fertilized by male sperm (resulting in a bouncing baby boy or girl!). Menopause occurs when a woman's ovaries stop producing the hormone estrogen, bringing these monthly cycles to an end. Oddly, there's no male equivalent of this process: a man can impregnate younger women well into his old age, but a woman's ability to have babies ends with menopause.

What is progeria?

An extremely rare genetic disease that occurs in about one of every five million newborn babies, progeria causes physical symptoms uncannily similar to aging: the affected child develops wrinkles, brittle bones, and heart problems, and usually dies of "old age" by the time he's in his teens! Doctors are especially interested in progeria because this disease may provide clues about the causes of "normal" aging.

Disabilities

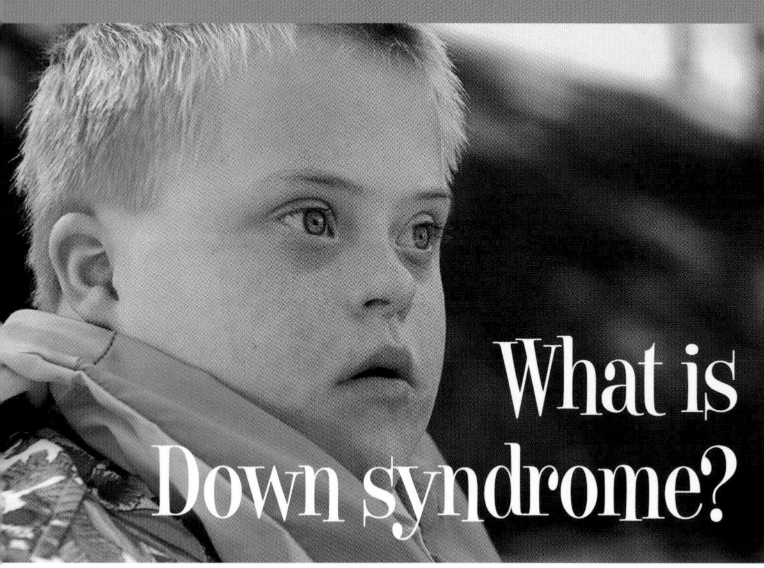

What is Down syndrome?

One of the most common birth defects, Down syndrome is a mutation of a specific gene in human DNA that results in mental impairment. Children with Down syndrome usually have almond-shaped, vaguely Asian-looking eyes (which is why this condition was once known as "Mongoloidism"), as well as shorter-than-average arms and legs and speech impairments. Although some people with Down syndrome are profoundly retarded (meaning they're barely able to feed or dress themselves), others are only mildly handicapped, and some have even gone on to earn college degrees!

It used to be that children with Down syndrome were sent to special schools, and pretty much kept separate from mainstream society. That's no longer the case: with the proper attention, most people with Down syndrome can function well, and it's not unusual for a Down child to be sent to a normal elementary school.

By the way, it has been shown that Down syndrome births occur much more often among older mothers: A mom in her 20s has less than a 1 in 1,000 chance of having a Down baby, but the odds shoot up to about 1 in 100 for moms over 40.

Why are handicapped parking spaces so close to the store?

Well, this one is easy to answer: it wouldn't be fair to ask a handicapped person to walk hundreds of feet to a restaurant or mall. While we're on the subject, you shouldn't necessarily jump to conclusions if you see a seemingly healthy person park in a handicapped space and walk out of his car. Many serious disabilities (such as chronic emphysema, which makes it difficult to breathe) aren't necessarily visible!

What is Marfan's syndrome?

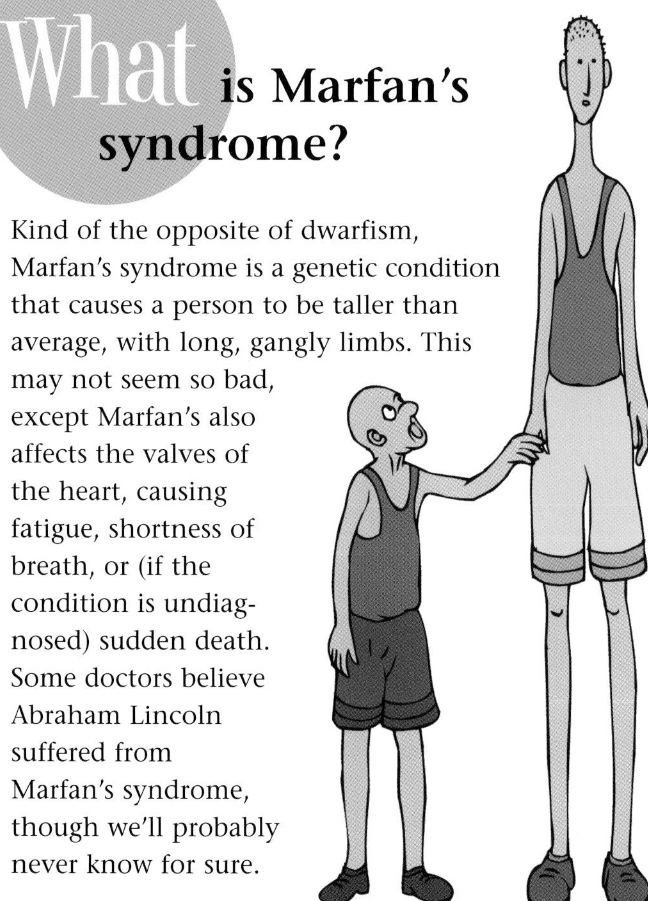

Kind of the opposite of dwarfism, Marfan's syndrome is a genetic condition that causes a person to be taller than average, with long, gangly limbs. This may not seem so bad, except Marfan's also affects the valves of the heart, causing fatigue, shortness of breath, or (if the condition is undiagnosed) sudden death. Some doctors believe Abraham Lincoln suffered from Marfan's syndrome, though we'll probably never know for sure.

How short are dwarfs?

First, let's use the proper terminology: most people who were once called "dwarfs" now prefer the name "little people." That said, the diagnosis of "dwarfism" is usually given to anyone who reaches an adult height of less than 4 feet 10 inches, with disproportionately short arms and legs compared to the trunk and head. Of course, many little people are much shorter than that, some times attaining a height of only two or three feet.

Why is it called "cystic fibrosis"?

Children born with cystic fibrosis have a genetic abnormality that causes their lungs to secrete thick, sticky mucus, causing infections and serious breathing problems (the reason the disease is called cystic fibrosis is because of its effect on the pancreas, rather than the lungs). Before the advent of modern medicine, most cystic fibrosis suffers didn't survive into adulthood, but many now live into their forties or even fifties and beyond.

What is the Americans with Disabilities Act?

Passed by Congress in 1990, the Americans with Disabilities Act prohibits discrimination based on "a physical or mental impairment that substantially limits a major life activity." Mostly, the purpose of the law is to prevent companies from firing (or refusing to hire) employees with severe disabilities, though its vague definition of what a "disability" is has caused some confusion in the legal system.

What is cerebral palsy?

Although cerebral palsy sounds like a single, specific disease, it's actually a term used to describe a wide range of symptoms, all of which can be traced to damage sustained by a baby during or shortly after birth. Generally, children with cerebral palsy suffer from a severe lack of coordination and muscle development, which can manifest itself as anything from mild twitching to complete paralysis of the arms or legs. Most such children (and adults) can walk only with the aid of crutches, and some are confined to wheelchairs. The majority of people with cerebral palsy aren't mentally retarded, though in about 20 or 30 percent of cases the two conditions go hand in hand.

Unlike Down syndrome (see the entry on the facing page), cerebral palsy isn't caused by a genetic defect. Usually, this condition can be traced to hypoxia (a lack of oxygen) during some part of the birth process, which causes damage to specific regions of an infant's brain (keep in mind that hypoxia itself has various causes, so it's more of a symptom than an explanation!). Cerebral palsy can also be caused by serious infections, such as encephalitis or meningitis.

Diseases

How does stress cause ulcers?

It doesn't! An ulcer is an open sore in the lining of the stomach, which is vulnerable to the powerful acids the stomach secretes to digest food. Recently, doctors discovered that ulcers are caused by a specific type of bacteria, and not by too much spicy food or excessive stress. For this reason, most ulcers nowadays are treated with doses of antibiotics, though a change of diet (and a calmer demeanor) certainly doesn't hurt.

What is arthritis?

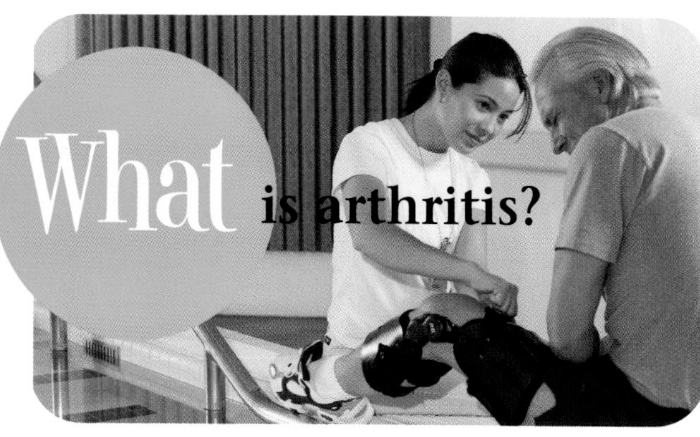

One of the most common diseases in the U.S., arthritis is a chronic inflammation of the joints, causing throbbing pain and restricted movement (usually in the hands, knees, and shoulders). Arthritis is most prevalent among the elderly, but has been known to affect children as well. This condition can't be cured, but it can be managed with physical therapy and anti-inflammatory medications.

What is a stroke?

In a way, a stroke is like a heart attack, except that the affected organ is the brain rather than the heart. Heart attacks happen when a blood clot blocks one of the arteries that nourishes the heart, causing damage to a portion of muscle (or causing it to die entirely). Strokes are also caused by blood clots, which lodge in one of the brain's numerous arteries and cause damage to the surrounding nerve tissue (small strokes can also be caused by burst arteries; a major burst is called a "cerebral hemorrhage").

Depending on where in the brain a stroke occurs, the victim can experience different symptoms. For example, many strokes occur in the "motor cortex" on the right or left side of the brain, which controls the opposite side of the body—so a stroke in the left motor cortex can cause paralysis of a person's right arm and leg.

The best way to treat strokes is before they happen. People at risk for strokes are usually given medications that inhibit the formation of blood clots and lower blood pressure (since untreated high blood pressure greatly increases the odds of a major stroke).

Why is it called Parkinson's disease?

In 1817, an English doctor named James Parkinson published a treatise called "An Essay on the Shaking Palsy," and his name has been attached to this condition ever since. Dr. Parkinson couldn't have known this at the time, but Parkinson's disease—which mainly afflicts middle-aged and elderly people—is caused by the slow destruction of the cells in a specific part of the brain, resulting in gradual loss of muscle control and, eventually, death.

What is diabetes?

The human body needs to carefully regulate its levels of glucose—the basic sugar from which it derives most of its energy. This is accomplished by means of the hormone insulin, which is secreted by the kidneys. The role of insulin is to regulate how much glucose is used by your body's cells: if you eat an ice-cream cone, your kidneys will secrete more insulin to manage the increased levels of glucose. If there's not enough insulin to process this excess glucose, the result is a disease called diabetes.

There are two main types of diabetes. Type I diabetes mostly affects kids (which is why it's known as "juvenile" diabetes), and is marked by the premature destruction of the kidney cells responsible for insulin production. Type II diabetes is called "adult onset" diabetes, because it occurs later in life, when the patient's peripheral tissues (that is, his hands, feet, and eyes) slowly become less responsive to the insulin secreted by his kidneys.

Type I diabetes can be kept under control with regular injections of insulin, while Type II usually responds to anti-diabetic drugs. It's also important for diabetes sufferers to follow a strict diet, which keeps their glucose levels from getting out of hand in the first place.

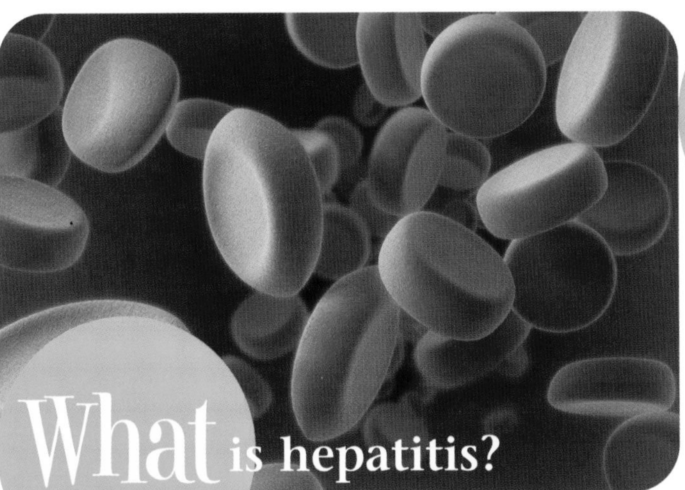

What is hepatitis?

The liver is one of the most important organs in the human body—it stores vitamins and minerals, synthesizes proteins, and filters toxic substances from the blood. Hepatitis is an infection of the liver, the severity of which depends on the type of virus involved: as unpleasant as it is, hepatitis A goes away fairly quickly, but hepatitis B and C are much more serious and can cause permanent liver damage.

What is angina?

"Angina pectoris," as it's called by doctors, is a condition in which the blood flow to the heart is restricted by narrowed arteries—resulting in chest pain and shortness of breath. Severe angina is often the prelude to a heart attack, in which a blood clot closes off an artery entirely. Angina is usually treated, and prevented, with medications that "dilate" (that is, widen) the blood vessels feeding the heart.

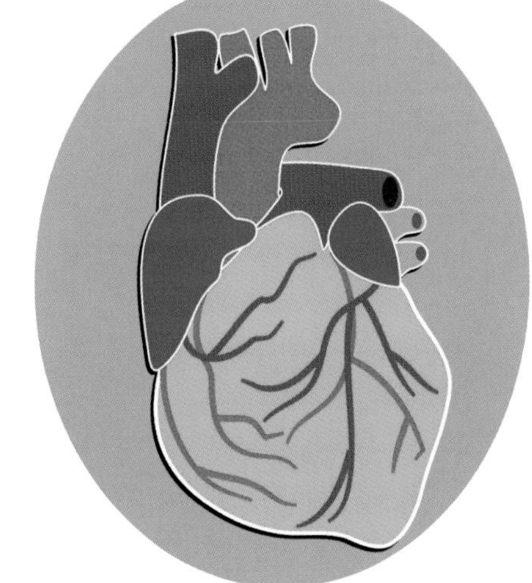

Why is it called a "cold"?

It has long been believed that what we call a "cold" is caused by cold weather (which is how it got its name), but it's not clear whether this is true. Although it's possible that cold, damp weather can wear down the body's immune system, making people more susceptible to the viruses that cause colds, what's more likely is that folks come down with more colds in the winter because they spend more time inside with other people, giving airborne (or fluid-borne) viruses an easy target.

Whatever the case, doctors have yet to come up with a reliable way to cure the common cold (which is odd, because they've managed to eliminate less widespread, but far more dangerous, diseases like smallpox and the plague!). Some people believe that taking large doses of vitamin C or herbal preparations like echinacea can get rid of colds, but doctors who have conducted careful studies say these pills have no effect. The fact is, a cold simply has to run its course, and the best way to recover is to get enough sleep and to drink plenty of fluids.

What is thrush?

Often, infants will develop a condition in which common yeast (the same stuff that causes bread to rise) infects their mouths and throats, causing them to develop painful, white patches (this happens because an infant's immune system isn't mature enough to combat this common microbe). As gross as it is, thrush can be easily treated with antifungal medicines.

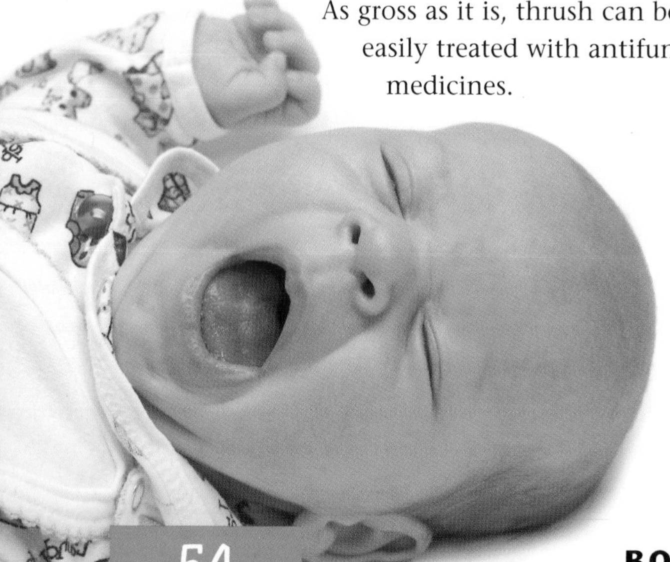

What is that little thing in the back of your throat?

It's called the uvula, and it's important for two reasons: first, it helps shape the sounds coming from your vocal cords (so you can speak clearly), and second, when you swallow, it blocks off the airways in your throat that connect to your nose, making sure the food goes down your esophagus into your stomach. And since you were about to ask: no, it can't be used as a punching bag!

Why do we have Eustachian tubes?

They may seem completely separate, but your ears, nose, and throat are all interconnected in important ways. For example, the insides of your ears are connected to the top of your throat by Eustachian tubes, small, hollow passages that equalize the pressure between your middle ear and the outside air. Eustachian tubes are what cause your ears to "pop" as an airplane takes off (or as you go up in a fast elevator), as they adjust to the sudden change in pressure.

What is the epiglottis?

If you've ever had a sip of juice "go down the wrong way," you can thank your epiglottis. This small but crucial piece of tissue blocks off your windpipe whenever you swallow, preventing food and drink from entering your respiratory system. Very occasionally, your epiglottis will become confused, and the result is a sudden cough as you try to clear the swallowed juice from the entrance to your lungs.

What is Strep throat?

Sometimes, when you have a bad sore throat, the cause is a kind of bacteria called *Streptococcus* (which is where the "Strep" in "Strep throat" comes from). Strep is most common in kids, and it can easily be cured with a few days of bed rest and a regular course of antibiotics. It's important not to let Strep go untreated, because, very occasionally, Strep bacteria can leave the throat and infect other parts of the body (like the lining around the heart!).

Why do we have sinuses?

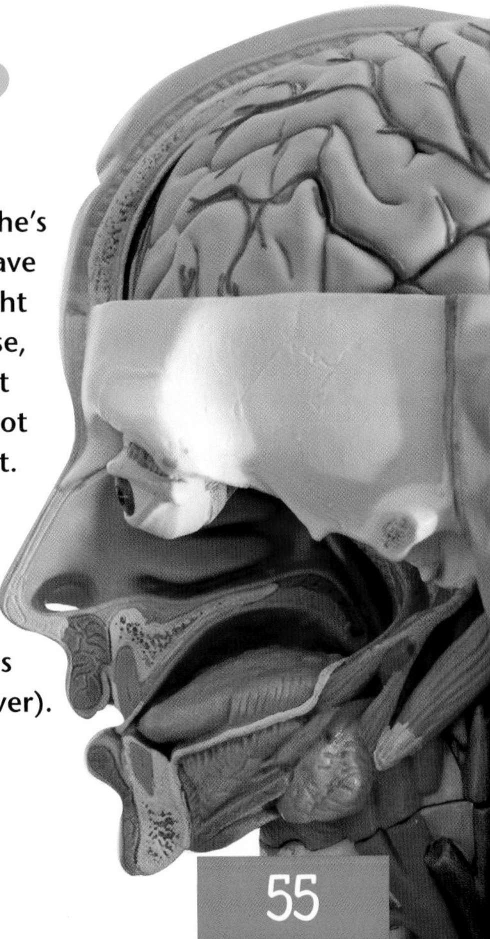

The next time someone says you have a hole in your head, tell him he's being too kind—the fact is, you (and everybody else in the world) have lots of holes in your head. These "sinuses," as they're called, are eight shallow pockets of air that reside behind your cheekbones, your nose, and your forehead. No one knows for sure why we have sinuses, but the most probable explanation is that these pockets of air weigh a lot less than solid bone or tissue, thus keeping our heads relatively light.

Most people don't even know they have sinuses until they become infected, which can result in a condition called sinusitis. A bad cold can cause your sinuses to become "stopped up" with mucus, so even after the cold in your nose has gone away, a residual infection can linger for days (or weeks) afterward in your sinuses (the usual symptoms are coughing, bad breath, and a low-grade fever). Sinusitis can usually be cured with antibiotics and nasal sprays, and don't worry, it's serious enough to keep you home from school!

How does smoking cause lung cancer?

You don't have to be a Nobel Prize–winning scientist to realize that human lungs haven't evolved to breathe cigarette smoke (or, for that matter, anything besides plain, ordinary air). Studies have shown that cigarette smoke contains about 4,000 chemicals, many of which have carcinogenic (cancer-causing) properties. Over the years, as they're absorbed into a smoker's lungs, these chemicals can slowly accumulate—and sooner or later, some of the lungs' cells sustain damaging mutations to their genetic material and become cancerous.

However, you should bear in mind that not all smokers develop lung cancer—and that smoking isn't the only cause of this disease. Every year, a few thousand people develop lung cancer from continual exposure to "second-hand" smoke (that is, from spending decades in close proximity to heavy smokers, in the home or workplace). And more than 1 in 10 cases of lung cancer are linked to radon—a colorless, odorless, radioactive gas that gradually accumulates in the basements of some homes, depending on where in the country they're located.

What is the difference between lungs and gills?

Lungs (which are found in land-dwelling creatures like birds, lizards, and mammals) and gills (which are found in ocean-dwelling creatures like fish and sharks) are designed to extract oxygen from the immediate environment. The difference, as you've probably guessed, is that lungs derive their oxygen directly from the air, while gills filter out the oxygen molecules that are dissolved in water.

Why do our lungs have alveoli?

The average person's lungs contain about three million "alveoli"—the tiny, balloon-like sacs that absorb oxygen and conduct it into the bloodstream. Because an alveolus has to be permeable to air, its surface is extremely delicate—about 50 times thinner than a sheet of tissue paper!

Unfortunately, this means that alveoli can also admit dangerous gases (such as carbon monoxide) into the bloodstream, along with the oxygen we need to live.

What is an iron lung?

Back in the 1940s and 1950s, an infectious disease called polio left many of its victims paralyzed and unable to breathe. Some of these people wound up in "iron lungs," large, tubular devices that mechanically force air into a patient's lungs by regulating the air pressure in the cabin. Today, iron lungs are rare, for two reasons: first, virtually nobody gets polio anymore, and second, doctors have since invented smaller, sleeker "ventilators" that don't take up an entire room!

What causes asthma?

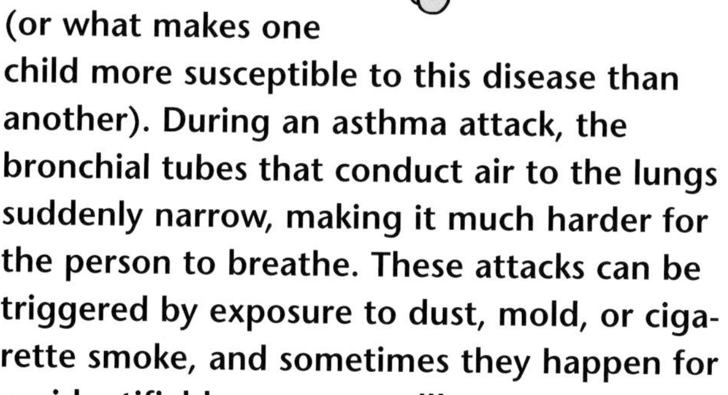

For such a common condition—about five million kids in the U.S. suffer from it, to one degree or another—doctors know surprisingly little about what causes asthma (or what makes one child more susceptible to this disease than another). During an asthma attack, the bronchial tubes that conduct air to the lungs suddenly narrow, making it much harder for the person to breathe. These attacks can be triggered by exposure to dust, mold, or cigarette smoke, and sometimes they happen for no identifiable reason at all!

There are two basic ways to treat asthma. Kids who have frequent attacks are prescribed medication that prevents the asthma from flaring up in the first place, while occasional sufferers usually carry an inhaler filled with medicine, which they spray into their mouths to lessen the attack's severity.

As to what causes asthma in the first place, that's a matter of controversy. Some people believe asthmatic kids have been raised in homes that are way too clean, so they haven't developed a resistance to common allergens—while other folks say asthmatic kids have been raised in homes that are way too dirty!

Why is your right lung bigger than your left lung?

Because our hearts are located on the left side of our chests, the human "body plan" is arranged in such a way that the right lung is slightly bigger than the left lung. The left lung is smaller because the heart takes up room on that side of the body. The right lung is divided into three "lobes" (that is, easily distinguished regions), while the left lung has only two.

What is pneumonia?

As with most other parts of your body, it's possible for the alveoli of your lungs (the tiny sacs that conduct oxygen into the bloodstream) to become infected by viruses or bacteria. Pneumonia, as it's called, is an especially serious infection because it can interfere with a person's ability to breathe. Most forms of pneumonia can be cured with antibiotics or antiviral medications, but "drug-resistant" pneumonias (which are thankfully rare) can be fatal.

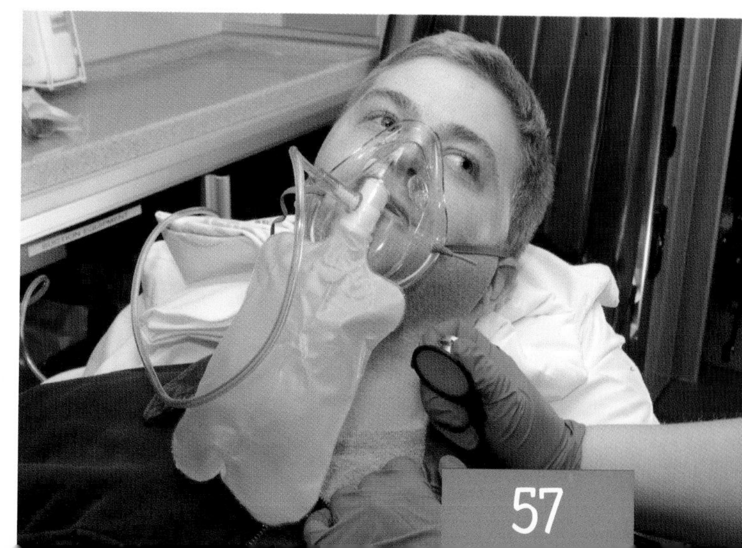

Why do psychiatrists have couches?

In the early days of psychiatry, it was standard practice for patients to lie down on a couch out of the therapist's sight, so they could talk freely about their feelings without taking cues from the doctor's facial expressions. While many therapists have maintained this practice, it has become increasingly common for patients to sit on a chair opposite the doctor and have a normal, one-on-one conversation. A good therapist will give her patients the option of lying on a couch or sitting on a chair, depending on their preferences.

What is OCD?

Obsessive-compulsive disorder, as it's called by psychiatrists, is a mental illness that causes a person to indulge in obsessive thoughts (for example, constantly imagining that his house is burning down) or engage in obsessive behavior (such as counting to 50 before he can touch a doorknob). Many people have mild forms of OCD, which are pretty much harmless, but severe cases have to be treated with medication.

What is schizophrenia?

It's commonly believed that people with schizophrenia (who are called schizophrenics) have "split personalities"—in fact, the word "schizophrenia" is derived from the Greek words for "split mind." This serious mental illness, which can be traced to an inherited abnormality in the brain, sometimes causes its victims to hear imaginary voices or experience wild mood swings, which is how it received its not-quite-accurate name. In fact, schizophrenics don't have two (or more) separate personalities; their brains are simply unable to process information in a normal way.

There are a few different types of schizophrenia, most of which manifest themselves in a person's teens or early twenties. For example, "catatonic" schizophrenics often stay in one place, not moving, for long periods of time, while "paranoid" schizophrenics may believe they are being plotted against (probably because of the voices they're hearing).

It used to be that most schizophrenics were left by themselves to roam the streets, or committed to institutions for their entire lives. Today, though, various medications can keep a person's schizophrenia under control, meaning that many sufferers of this disease are able to hold down jobs and lead relatively normal lives.

What is the difference between a psychologist and a psychiatrist?

Both psychologists and psychiatrists spend most of their time listening (and occasionally offering guidance) as their patients talk and try to work out their feelings. However, there's a major difference between these two professions: a psychiatrist is a fully licensed doctor who can prescribe medications, while a psychologist isn't an M.D. and doesn't have prescription privileges. Partly for this reason, psychiatrists are able to charge much more for hourly sessions!

That distinction aside, there are many different types of psychiatrists and psychologists. Some psychiatrists are strictly "Freudian"—that is, they treat patients according to the theories of Sigmund Freud, who believed people's behavior is strongly influenced by their subconscious desires—while other psychiatrists adhere to more modern theories. And in both professions, therapists have various specialties: for example, some psychologists work only with kids, others are marriage counselors, and yet others specialize in eating disorders or learning disabilities.

Why is it called manic depression?

The phrase "manic depression" sounds like a contradiction—after all, how can you be manic when you're also depressed? Victims of manic depression (also known as bipolar disorder) aren't happy and sad at the same time; they alternate between the two states, lapsing into a deep depression after a period of manic activity (say, going on a thousand-dollar shopping spree). Fortunately, medication can temper these wild mood swings!

What is group therapy?

Most people prefer to deal with their psychiatrist or psychologist on a one-on-one basis—that is, they talk with the therapist, alone, once or twice a week. But some psychologists specialize in group therapy, in which a dozen or so patients attend the same session and bounce their problems off one another. If any arguments arise, the therapist is there to maintain order and lead the discussion in a constructive direction.

Plastic Surgery

Why is it called plastic surgery?

The "plastic" in plastic surgery doesn't refer to the stuff dolls are made of; rather, it's derived from the Greek word "plastikos," which means to mould or shape. Essentially, that's what plastic surgeons do: they mould and shape human body tissue to produce a more pleasing appearance.

There are two main kinds of plastic surgery. Cosmetic surgery includes such procedures as facelifts and rhinoplasties (commonly known as "nose jobs"), which are meant to improve the patient's looks. Some people consider this type of plastic surgery frivolous, especially compared to far more serious reconstructive surgery, in which the surgeon tries to undo the visible damage caused by disease or injury (say, by sewing a missing finger back on, or piecing together a patient's face after a car accident).

Although cosmetic surgery is a relatively modern innovation, reconstructive surgery has been practiced since ancient times, when some doctors specialized in restoring mutilated ears or noses with the use of skin grafts.

How do surgeons reattach body parts?

Microsurgery—the procedure by which reconstructive surgeons can reattach a recently severed part of the body, such as a hand or foot—is one of the most amazing innovations in modern medical history.

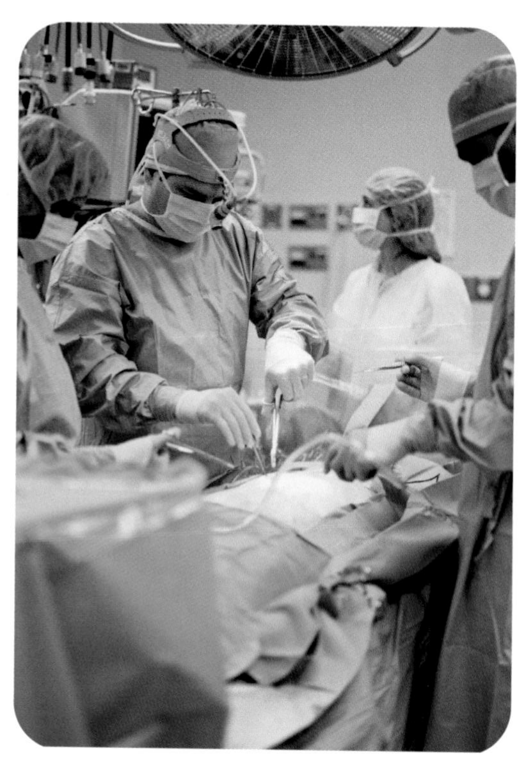

In the first step, the surgeon painstakingly reconnects (with the aid of a special kind of microscope) the tiny blood vessels that keep the missing body part nourished with blood. This is crucial, because a severed hand, say, can stay viable for only a certain amount of time before lack of oxygen causes irreparable damage. Once the circulation has been restored, the doctor can proceed to sew together all the other components that connect the hand to the wrist, including tendons, nerves, and skin—an operation that can take an entire day.

Although doctors can reconnect a missing hand almost seamlessly, it's hard to predict how "useful" this hand will be—that is, whether the patient will be able to type, point, or grasp objects. Usually, months or years of rehabilitation are required after surgery, just for the patient to learn how to move his fingers!

What is a "tummy tuck"?

It sounds cute and harmless, but a "tummy tuck" is a serious procedure in which a plastic surgeon removes excess skin and fat from the lower abdomen, and tightens the abdominal muscles (which is why this operation is technically called an "abdominoplasty"). Tummy tucks are most often sought by people with prominent "pot bellies" that don't respond to dieting or exercise.

What is liposuction?

A rather extreme weight-loss technique, liposuction is when a plastic surgeon sticks a special tube (known as a "cannula") into a patient and literally sucks out his fat cells using a very expensive vacuum cleaner called an "aspirator." A typical liposuction procedure only removes about 5 or 10 pounds of fat at a time—meaning a 300-pound person can't walk into a doctor's office and come out looking like a 98-pound weakling!

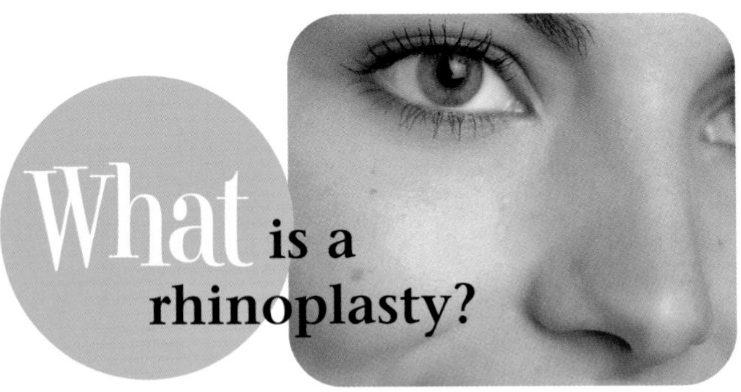

What is a rhinoplasty?

More commonly known as a "nose job," a rhinoplasty is when a plastic surgeon reshapes the cartilage of the nose to make it smaller or more symmetrical. Most rhinoplasties are done for appearance's sake, though some people have medical conditions (such as irregularly shaped nasal passages) that necessitate surgery. Like many things in medicine, getting a rhinoplasty used to be an involved procedure, but today some nose jobs can be performed in a single afternoon using only a local anesthetic!

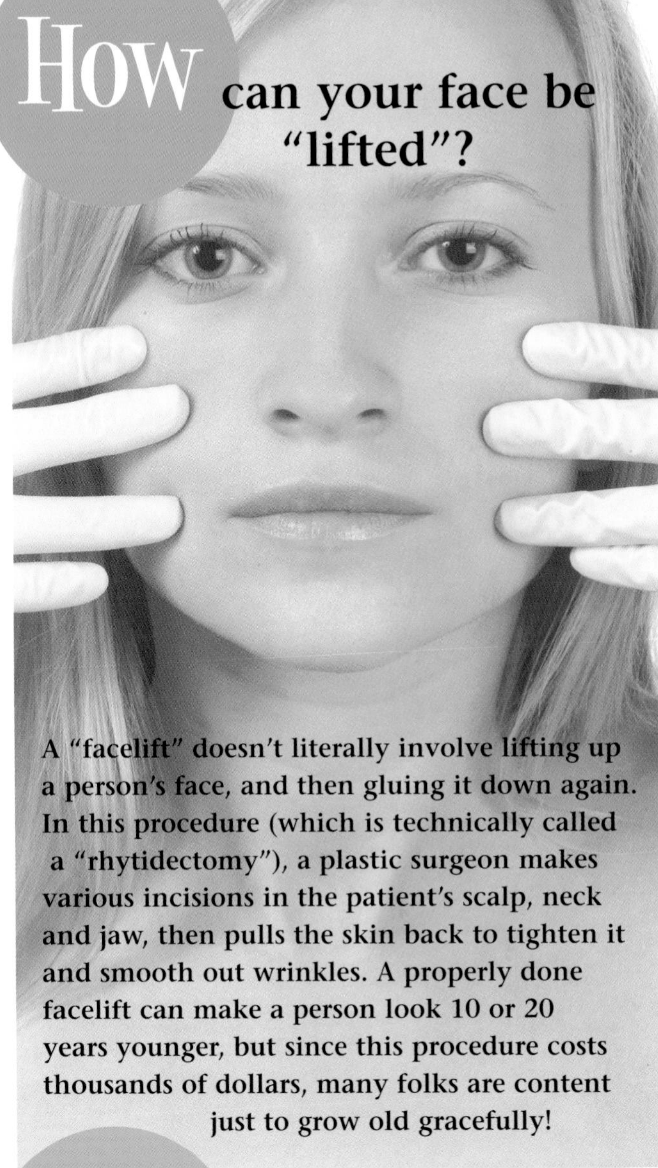

How can your face be "lifted"?

A "facelift" doesn't literally involve lifting up a person's face, and then gluing it down again. In this procedure (which is technically called a "rhytidectomy"), a plastic surgeon makes various incisions in the patient's scalp, neck and jaw, then pulls the skin back to tighten it and smooth out wrinkles. A properly done facelift can make a person look 10 or 20 years younger, but since this procedure costs thousands of dollars, many folks are content just to grow old gracefully!

What is a mastectomy?

Although it's not technically a kind of plastic surgery, a mastectomy—the removal of one or both of a woman's breasts as a treatment for breast cancer—is often followed by a procedure known as breast reconstruction. Usually, a natural-looking breast can be reconstructed using either skin and fat from another part of the woman's body or synthetic materials. Breast reconstructions are most often performed after single mastectomies, because many women are uncomfortable with having only one "natural" breast.

Pregnancy

What does a midwife do?

Giving birth in the hospital is a relatively recent innovation—before the 20th century, most women delivered their babies at home, with the help of midwives (specialized nurses who assisted with the delivery). Today, midwives are becoming popular again, as many mothers choose to give birth in the familiar surroundings of their homes rather than the sterile environment of a hospital. Today's midwives have to be licensed (meaning they meet minimum standards set by the government), and they're required to call a doctor if there are severe complications.

What is a preemie?

Moms are usually pregnant for nine months (give or take a couple of weeks) before they give birth. Occasionally, though, a baby can be born much earlier than that, after only six or seven months. These babies are called "preemies," after the word "premature," which basically means "not quite ready." Premature births can occur for a number of reasons, ranging from smoking and poor eating habits to medical conditions (like infections or abnormalities of the womb) that are out of the mother's control.

Before the 20th century, most severely premature babies (ones weighing less than two or three pounds) didn't survive for very long. The main problems facing preemies are that they don't have enough fat to maintain their body temperatures (which is why they're usually placed in heated incubators immediately after birth), and that their lungs are too immature to breathe properly. Thanks to modern medical advances, today, with proper treatment, even a two-pound preemie can survive and grow up to be a healthy child!

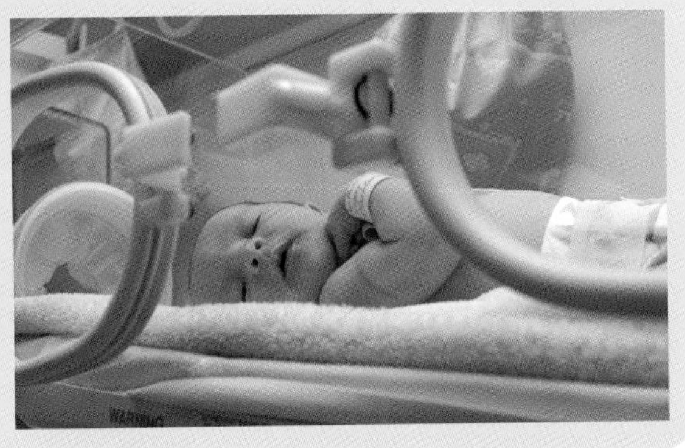

Why is it called a Caesarean?

Most people believe that a Caesarean (a procedure in which a baby is delivered by cutting through the mom's belly) is named after the Roman emperor Julius Caesar, who was supposedly born this way more than 2,000 years ago. This is doubtful, though, since Caesar's mother lived to see her son grow up, which would have been unlikely after having a Caesarean considering the state of medicine at that time. It's much more probable that "Caesarean" derives from the Latin word "caeder," which means "to cut."

Why do doctors slap a newborn baby?

Despite what you see on TV, a doctor will rarely slap a newborn baby on the behind hard enough to make an audible sound in the delivery room. The reason for the light slap (which is more like a pat) is to startle the baby into taking its first breath, since it's just spent the past nine months in the liquid environment of the womb. Many babies don't even need to be slapped, and start crying on their own as soon as they reach daylight!

Why does labor go on for so long?

It isn't called "labor" for nothing. Because a newborn's head is relatively big and its mom's birth canal is relatively small, delivering a baby can be a long, painful experience. Some moms are in labor for one or two days, though some others (especially if they've had children before) can give birth in only a couple of hours!

If a mom is having an especially painful delivery, the doctor may give her an "epidural"—an injection of local anesthetic (kind of like the Novocain you receive when you're having a cavity filled) that deadens the pain. Less often, she may be prescribed a general analgesic (kind of like a strong dose of aspirin). The problem with a general analgesic is that, up until the moment it's born, a baby is still attached to its mother's bloodstream, so a small amount of this painkiller may find its way into the newborn's body.

In the last few months of their pregnancies, many women take "Lamaze" classes, which teach various relaxation techniques and breathing exercises that they can use to distract themselves during delivery. Lamaze is especially popular with women who can't, or who would prefer not to, receive drugs during childbirth.

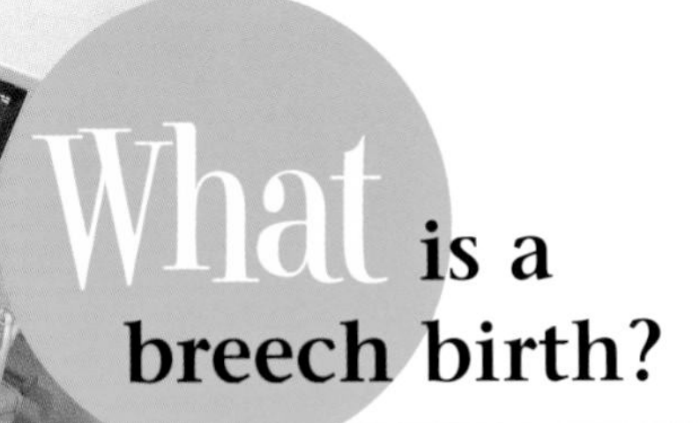

What is a breech birth?

Babies are meant to be born head first, since the hardest part of delivery is squeezing the baby's head through the mom's birth canal—once that's done, the rest of the kid slides out like a watermelon seed. A "breech birth" is when the baby comes out feet or behind first, so its head is liable to get stuck. Today, most breech births can be avoided by checking the position of the baby beforehand with an ultrasound scan, and eithergetting the baby to change its position before birth or performing a Caesarean (that is, cutting through the mom's belly rather than having her deliver the normal way).

Speech Impediments

Why do some kids stutter?

You might think most kids stutter because they're shy, or because they're uncertain about what they want to say. But as far as doctors can tell, stuttering is hard-wired into the brain—that is, kids stutter because there's a "short-circuit" between the part of the brain that produces speech and the muscles that control the mouth and tongue. It's not unusual for a stutterer to say "I think things faster than I can say them" or "what I'm trying to say just won't come out right"—in other words, there's nothing wrong with a stutterer's intelligence, just his speech patterns!

Severe cases of stuttering—in which the speaker gets "stuck" on certain words for long periods of time—may require treatment. Usually, stutterers receive behavioral therapy, which teaches them how to relax while talking, or how to use improved breathing patterns to get the words out faster. While there's no 100 percent cure for stuttering, the goal of therapy is to reduce the speaker's stress and anxiety to improve this condition (and if therapy doesn't work, medication can be an option too).

What is Tourette's syndrome?

What doctors call a "tic" is a constant, involuntary muscle spasm, which can range from a slight fluttering around one of a person's eyes to jerky movements of his arms or legs. Tourette's syndrome is a neurological condition that causes a variety of tics, including some that affect speech: a small percentage of Tourette's sufferers have a tic that causes them to blurt out curse words or inappropriate remarks. Fortunately, Tourette's can be kept under control with the appropriate medication.

What is a deviated septum?

Occasionally, kids are born with a very small defect that causes their nasal septum—the ridge of cartilage that separates the nasal cavity leading up from the two nostrils—to deviate slightly to the right or left, which can cause a nasal-sounding voice, snoring, or breathing difficulties. Most deviated septa are completely harmless, but surgery may occasionally be required for cases that cause serious discomfort.

Why do some kids need speech therapy?

Aside from those kids with relatively serious conditions like stuttering (see the question elsewhere on this page), most children in kindergarten or grade school who receive speech therapy simply have trouble pronouncing certain sounds: usually, "r"s and "l"s cause the most trouble. A speech therapist is a professional who teaches kids how to pronounce these difficult sounds correctly, before this mispronunciation becomes a habit!

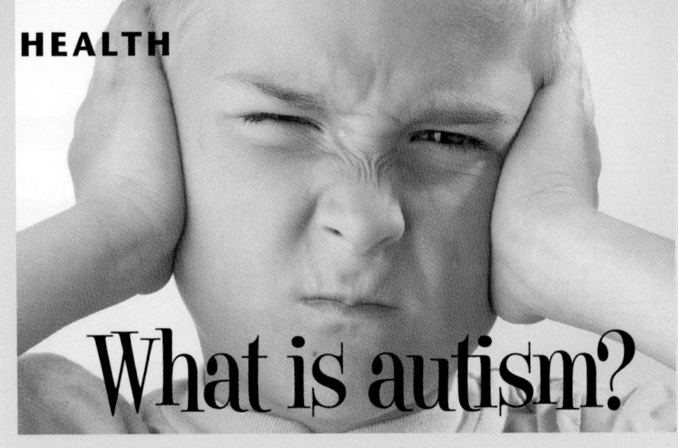

What is autism?

Sometimes, children are born with a developmental disorder that causes them to have difficulty interacting with other kids, expressing theiremotions, or even speaking at all. This condition is known as "autism," and it affects different children in different ways. Some kids with mild autism can function in a regular classroom, but severely autistic kids (who can be prone to sudden tantrums, or exhibit inappropriate behavior like shrieking or flapping their arms) usually don't have this option.

One of the unfortunate things about autism is that it often doesn't show itself until a toddler is old enough to speak (or not to speak!), at which point parents are more likely to notice their child's unusual behavior. Because there's no single test that can detect autism, a doctor will first try to rule out other causes of this behavior, such as undiagnosed deafness. Because autism can't be cured (at least not yet), most kids diagnosed with this disorder receive intensive therapy designed to teach them how to deal with other people and behave in an appropriate way.

What is a cleft palate?

One of the most common—and also one of the most easily treated—birth defects, a "cleft palate," is a deformity of the upper lip where the bone beneath it (in the most severe cases) leaves it cleaved completely in half. In most cases, doctors correct cleft palates surgically within six months of birth. In poorer countries, people who can't afford this surgery may be saddled with cleft palates for their entire lives—which severely affects their ability to speak.

What causes lisps?

There are a few different kinds of lisp, all of which are marked by difficulty pronouncing the letter "s" (or sometimes "z"), which come out in the lisper's speech as "th," "sh," or "zh" sounds. Lisping is caused by the protrusion of the tongue between or behind the teeth, and can usually be corrected with speech therapy (though some people retain slight lisps throughout their entire lives).

Teeth

What are dentures made from?

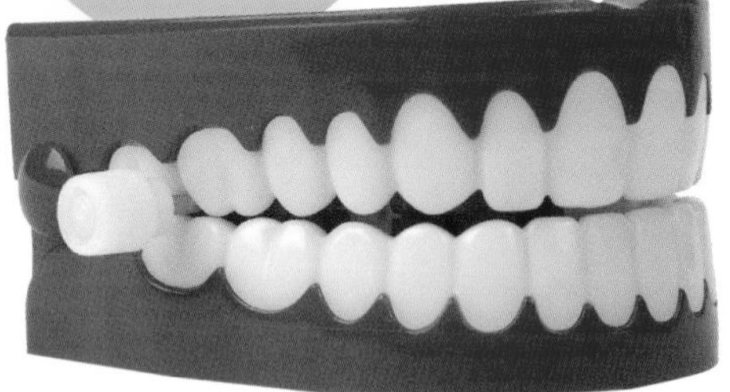

We've come a long way from George Washington's wooden teeth. Today, dentures—that is, removable false teeth—use a combination of plastic and metal for the base, and a type of plastic called "acrylic" for the teeth. Despite their increased comfort and durability, modern dentures can't be used around the clock—they have to be removed before the wearer goes to sleep.

What is gingivitis?

The technical name for your gums is "gingiva," so "gingivitis" translates as "inflamed gums." Unlike other –itises (like, say, appendicitis), most people have gingivitis to one degree or another, usually caused by poor brushing technique or not flossing after meals. Mild gingivitis can be treated with a good cleaning by a dental hygienist, but more serious cases may require a trip to the periodontist, a doctor who specializes in gums.

How do they put the stripes in toothpaste?

Despite what you may think, toothpaste isn't striped when it's inside the container. A tube of striped toothpaste actually contains two side-by-side compartments, one containing one color of toothpaste, and the other containing the second. When you squeeze the tube, a special nozzle in the opening swirls the two colors onto your toothbrush in a striped pattern.

How was orthodontia invented?

Up until the 19th century or so, the most insignificant problem people had with their teeth was that they wouldn't grow in evenly—generally, folks were more concerned with toothaches and gum disease, which could result in serious health problems, than with having a nice, smile. However, this didn't mean that the concept of orthodontia was completely unknown: archeologists have unearthed ancient mummies with metal bands wrapped around their teeth, which may have been intended as crude braces.

The first professional association of orthodontists was created in the U.S. in 1900, and since then, the art of fitting kids with braces has become much more streamlined (not to mention much less painful). For kids in the 1960s and 1970s, going to the orthodontist could be a protracted, multi-appointment ordeal, resulting in ugly-looking, metallic braces that caught bits of food and made it difficult to speak. Today's braces are much more comfortable and much less noticeable, so if an orthodontist decides you need treatment, just be glad you don't have to go through what your parents did!

How was dental floss invented?

There are no references to "flossing" as such in ancient texts, but this practice seems to have existed for as long as people have. Grooves made by a floss-like substance have been found in the teeth of prehistoric humans, and folks have always been using toothpicks after meals. That said, modern dental floss can be traced to a New Orleans dentist named Levi Spear Parmly, who recommended regular flossing to his patients back in 1815.

Why is it called a retainer?

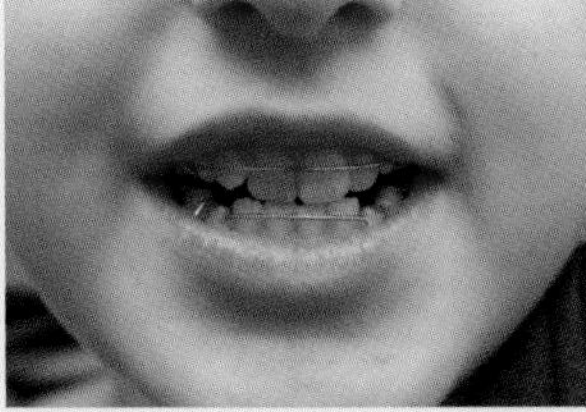

After a teenager has her braces removed, the job is only half done: her teeth are straight, but the gums and bones surrounding them haven't yet adjusted to their new position. A retainer "retains" the teeth in the correct configuration until the gums and bones have completely caught up. Most kids are told to wear their retainers (usually at night) for a few years, a good investment to make if you want a straight smile as an adult.

What is a root canal?

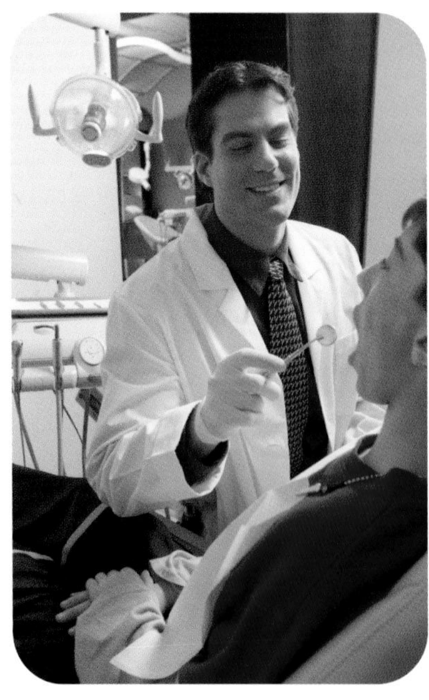

Technically, the term "root canal" refers to the hollow interior of a tooth, where the tooth's nerve (that pesky thing that causes toothaches) is nestled inside a bed of soft "pulp." But "root canal" also describes the procedure in which a dentist drills inside a tooth to remove pulp that has become infected (and that has been pressing against the nerve, causing pain). Or, to put it another way: drilling and filling an ordinary cavity is like digging a small hole and covering it over again, but having a root canal is like digging a big hole and throwing in a stick of dynamite!

As ghastly as it sounds, for most people, having a root canal is just as painless (albeit much more involved and expensive) than having a cavity filled. Since the main cause of root canals is neglected cavities—which expose the tooth's pulp to infection—your best bet for avoiding a root canal is to take good care of your teeth and to have regular checkups. (Still not convinced? You don't even want to know what happens if you ignore a tooth in need of a root canal—your entire jaw can become severely infected!)

Eastern Medicine

Why do people meditate?

Although there are various types of meditation, the basic technique is the same. Usually, when meditating, a person will sit on a chair (or cross-legged on the floor) and close her eyes. Some schools of meditation advise clearing the mind of all thought, while others prescribe a "mantra" that's repeated over and over. Whatever the technique, meditation can be a good way to ease anxiety and even to lower your blood pressure!

What is tai chi?

Kind of a cross between a martial art and a meditation technique, tai chi involves a series of rigorous slow-motion exercises (if you've ever seen a person in the park slowly raising his arms above his head, with a look of intense concentration on his face, he's probably practicing tai chi). Tai chi is especially popular with senior citizens because it has been known to ease the aches and pains of old age.

How does acupuncture work?

As with many practices associated with Eastern medicine, there are some Western experts who believe acupuncture doesn't work at all. But because this ancient healing art has been practiced in China for thousands of years, there's a feeling (even among some skeptical scientists) that there must be something to it.

According to Chinese medicine, the human body is crisscrossed by "meridians" that affect a person's health and well-being. By sticking tiny needles into key points on these meridians, an acupuncturist can (supposedly) relieve pain and ease various conditions, such as arthritis or shortness of breath. What makes acupuncture so strange to Western observers (besides being stuck with needles like a pincushion!) is that the needles often aren't placed anywhere near the affected part of the body—headaches, for instance, can be treated by sticking needles into the patient's hands.

So far, there isn't sufficient evidence one way or the other to prove that acupuncture works. But because acupuncture patients believe it does—and respond well to treatment—that's pretty much the only thing that matters!

What is the difference between Eastern and Western medicine?

Before we answer this question, it's important to make one thing clear: when a person has a heart attack in China, he's taken to a hospital and treated with medication (and sometimes surgery), just as he would be in the U.S.

Although medicine all over the world is increasingly being "Westernized," subtle differences exist in the way doctors approach their patients. In the countries of the Far East, there's a tendency to take more of a "holistic" approach, meaning a doctor will consider a patient's emotional state and cultural beliefs when prescribing a course of treatment. By contrast, in the West, physicians usually take a more "disease-centered" approach, concentrating on physical symptoms and attacking the disease at its core with medicines and surgical techniques.

Until recently, there was a tendency to see Western medicine as "modern" and Eastern medicine as tainted with superstition. However, as researchers in the West have examined the "placebo effect"—that is, the ability of patients to "believe" themselves into good health—the lines between Eastern and Western practices have become much more blurred.

What are yin and yang?

According to traditional Chinese medicine, all things (including a person's health) are in a constant state of change, as determined by the complementary qualities known as "yin" (which translates roughly as "shady") and "yang" (which means "sunny"). However, despite what many Westerners believe, yin and yang don't correspond to "good" and "evil"; they're both necessary for the healthy functioning of the body!

What is yoga?

In ancient India—where it originated—yoga was (and is) more of a spiritual practice than a form of exercise. There are many different types of yoga, but the one most often practiced in the West is "hatha yoga," which involves holding various painful-looking poses. Most Western adherents practice yoga because it keeps the body limber, and it has also been known to improve concentration and self-discipline.

What is herbal medicine?

Ever since ancient times, people have believed that specific herbs can cure or alleviate specific diseases—sometimes for a good reason (as modern scientists have discovered by isolating active chemical agents from plants) and sometimes out of superstition. Today, herbal medicine has millions of adherents all over the world, but its efficacy is rarely backed up by scientific evidence. For instance, folks still believe the herb echinacea can cure the common cold, but a recent study shows that's not the case!

Eye Medicine

Why does an ophthalmologist put drops in your eyes?

If you've ever been to the eye doctor, you've probably had your eyes "dilated." In this procedure, the doctor administers eye drops that cause your pupils—the round, black spots in the middle of your eyes—to open wide, either by stimulating the muscles that open the iris or inhibiting the muscles that cause it to close. Once your pupils are dilated, it's much easier for the doctor to shine a tiny flashlight and examine your retinas, the light-gathering organs in the back of your eyeballs. Unfortunately, your pupils usually stay wide open for a few hours after the exam—which is why you need an adult to guide you back home!

By the way, ophthalmologists aren't the only physicians who check pupils. When a patient is admitted into the emergency room of a hospital, doctors will usually examine his eyes, because unevenly dilated pupils (say, the pupil of the left eye is more dilated than the pupil of the right eye) can be a sign of a serious brain injury. Also, if a patient has suffered a drug overdose, the doctor can sometimes diagnose this by his extremely small (or extremely dilated) pupils.

How do polarized sunglasses work?

When light reflects off a flat surface—a highway, say, or a field of ice—most of the photons of which it's composed take on a different orientation, or "polarization," causing painful glare. Polarized sunglasses are made of a substance that blocks this bothersome polarization of light, and greatly reduce (but won't totally eliminate) the glare.

What does it mean to have 20-20 vision?

A person with good eyesight can stand exactly 20 feet away from a standard eye chart and tell the optometrist exactly what it says, which means he has "20-20" vision. If you have 20-60 vision, on the other hand, this means you'd have to stand 20 feet away from the chart to see it as clearly as a person with 20-20 vision standing 60 feet away.

Confused yet? Well, get this: it's possible to have better than 20-20 vision, which means you can make out details at 20 feet that an ordinary person could only see at 10 feet! This is called 20-10 vision.

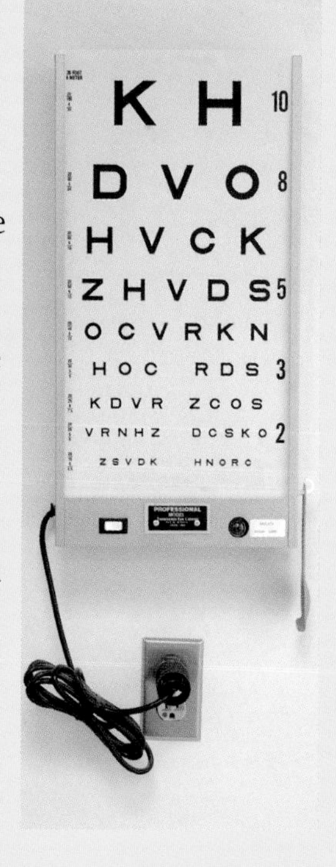

Why are they called bifocals?

As people get older, they usually have a harder time reading small print (which is why you may see your dad take off his ordinary glasses and hold small lettering right up to his eyes). The "bi" in "bifocals" denotes the number "two," and it refers to the fact that these glasses have two different kinds of lenses joined together horizontally: higher magnification on the bottom for close-up viewing, and lower magnification on top for ordinary viewing.

What is the difference between an optometrist and an ophthalmologist?

Well, for one thing, "ophthalmologist" is a lot harder to say! Beyond that, though, an ophthalmologist is a medical doctor who can perform operations and prescribe medicine, while an optometrist is only allowed to examine your vision and prescribe corrective lenses for your eyes (glasses or contacts). Often, optometrists and ophthalmologists work together in the same office, so they can easily refer patients to one another.

What is glaucoma?

The human eyeball isn't solid, like a golf ball—it's filled with a thick, jelly-like substance called "aqueous humor" (not because it's funny, but because "humor" is a Greek word meaning "substance"). Normally, this aqueous humor is constantly draining into and out of the eye, but in some people the drainage channel becomes blocked, causing the humor to build up to dangerous levels and exert damaging pressure on the eyeball—a condition known as glaucoma.

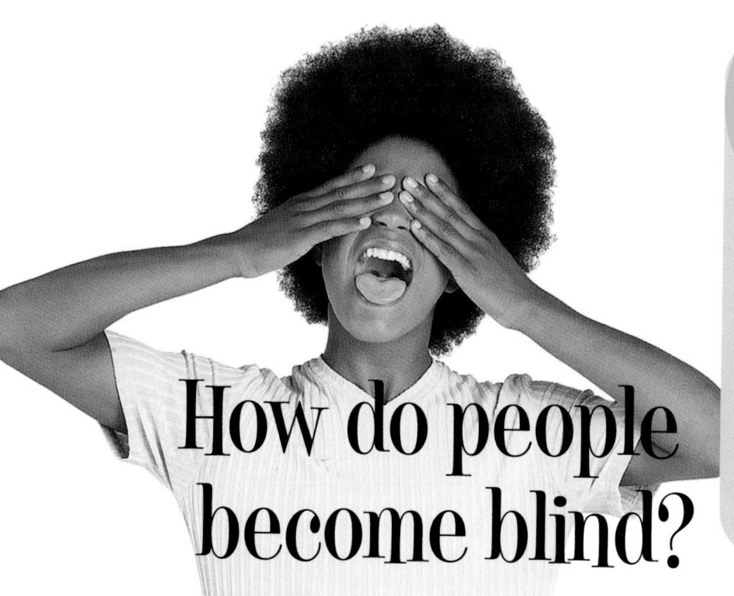

How do people become blind?

Basically, there are three causes of total blindness. The first (and most common) occurs in the womb, when a rare genetic abnormality causes a baby's brain to be unable to process visual information. Apart from this "congenital blindness," as it's called, people can also go blind from accidents (such as explosions or car crashes), or, later in life, in the final stages of slow, degenerative diseases like "retinitis pigmentosa" or "macular degeneration."

Because total blindness (which is sometimes called NLP, for "no light perception") is relatively uncommon, the word "blind" is usually used to refer to people who have seriously impaired vision, but who are still able to (for instance) distinguish between night and day. Many people qualify as "legally blind," which simply means that they can't see an object clearly from 20 feet away and so are not legally allowed to drive a car without glasses or contact lenses.

Today, life for totally blind people is much easier than it was 50 or 100 years ago. For example, computer programs exist that read text out loud, as well as send "spoken" e-mails back and forth over the Internet!

Health Insurance

What is an HMO?

A "health maintenance organization" is a network of doctors and hospitals affiliated with an insurance company. The reason people belong to HMOs is that, because these networks are supposed to manage their expenses, they can provide affordable health insurance. The main drawback of an HMO is that you have to use doctors in the HMO's own network—if your family physician isn't a member, you'll have to pay your own expenses.

What is preventive medicine?

Most diseases are easier (and less expensive) to treat when they're in the earliest stages, rather than full-blown. For this reason, most insurance companies encourage patients to get regular check-ups, so doctors can detect and treat any conditions they find early on (for example, it's cheaper—and much less painful—to take medicine every day for heart disease, than to suffer a heart attack ten years down the road and wind up in the hospital!).

How does health insurance work?

Getting sick can be an expensive proposition—the common cold or flu is no big deal, but treating a case of cancer costs hundreds of thousands of dollars, and even something as simple as breaking your arm on the playground can result in a big hospital bill. For this reason, most people in America have some kind of health insurance, meaning they pay an insurance company a few hundred dollars a month in return for having their expenses covered in case of illness.

Until recently, most companies automatically provided health insurance for all employees. (This practice started after World War II as a way for these companies to attract and keep skilled employees.) Unfortunately, health care costs have been rising so fast that many of these firms can no longer afford to provide cheap health insurance, so they either drop their coverage entirely or require their employees to pay more of the costs. That, combined with the fact that many people have no health insurance at all, is why so many politicians talk about "fixing" the health-insurance system before it breaks down completely.

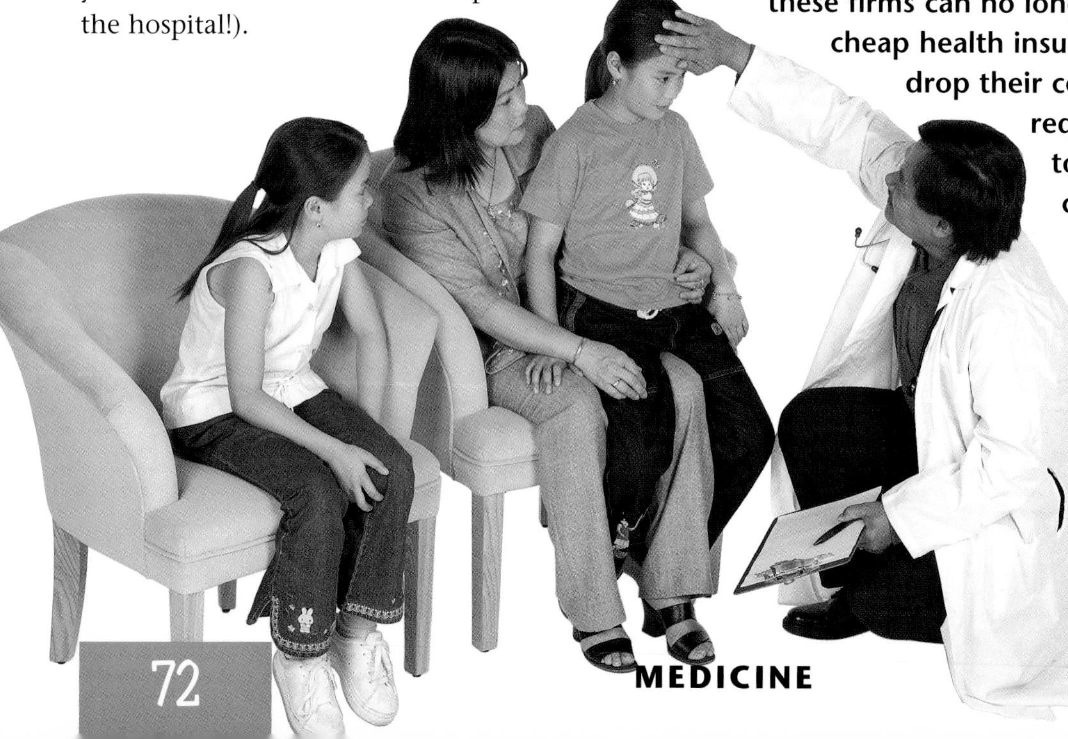

Why is health insurance so expensive?

Not too long ago, a decent health insurance plan for an entire family might cost only $100 a month. There were two main factors that made this possible: first, expensive medical procedures used to be performed much more rarely than they are today, and second, most employers paid a large part (or all!) of the monthly premiums in order to keep their employees happy.

Today, it's a different story. Most individual health-care policies charge at least a few hundred dollars per month, and insuring a family with children can cost more than $10,000 per year. While many companies still pay a portion of these expenses, others can't afford to take on this burden and leave a larger percentage of the monthly premiums to be paid by their employees.

Basically, what has made health insurance so expensive is that, as medicine becomes more and more sophisticated, common medical procedures cost more and more money. So the best way to reduce health insurance premiums is to somehow bring these spiraling medical costs under control!

What is national health insurance?

In some countries, health insurance is provided by the government, rather than by private companies (as in the U.S.). Some people believe that a national health insurance system would be a good way to provide affordable health insurance for all U.S. citizens, but others think it's a better idea to let private insurance companies compete with each other to offer the best rates. In any case, national insurance isn't perfect—in Canada, for instance, patients with certain conditions have to wait months to see a doctor!

What is Medicaid?

It'll be a long, long time before you're eligible, but you may have heard your grandparents talking about something called Medicaid. This is a government-sponsored health plan for people over 65, which keeps down medical expenses at a time in life when many people have chronic diseases. Medicaid is also offered to children from poor families, as well as various people with disabilities.

What is a deductible?

Even though health insurance can be expensive, it won't necessarily pay all of your medical expenses. Most plans have what's called a "deductible," which means you have to pay the first $500 (or $5,000) of your medical bill before the insurance kicks in. Needless to say, the cheapest plans usually have the highest deductibles!

Hospitals

Why is it called the emergency room?

Basically, hospitals have two kinds of patients: those who have been admitted in advance by their doctors (as you would be if you were, say, having your tonsils removed) and those who are acutely ill or have been in accidents. The second type of patient is taken to the emergency room (or, sometimes, walks or drives there herself), where doctors are on call 24 hours a day to provide help.

However, just because a patient has been taken to the ER doesn't mean a doctor will see her right away. First, a "triage nurse" will decide who needs immediate care, and who can afford to wait for a few hours. For example, if you've been hit by a bus, the triage nurse will have a doctor see you right away, but if you've reported to the ER in the middle of the night because you have a runny nose, you might have to wait awhile.

If a patient is in especially serious condition, she may be taken from the ER to the intensive care unit, also known as the ICU. Here, she can be closely monitored around the clock by doctors, nurses, and various machines.

How does an ambulance decide which hospital to go to?

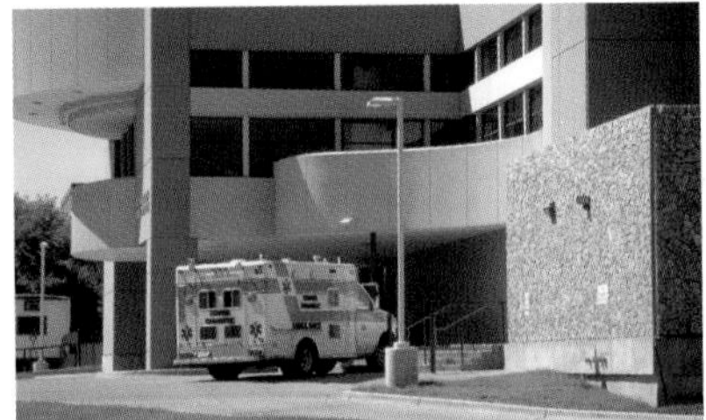

Most of the time, an ambulance will take a patient straight to the nearest hospital. In big cities, though, it's not quite that simple: some hospitals refuse to accept new patients, either because they're filled to the brim or because they're not equipped to treat the person's condition. Part of the job of the ambulance crew is to decide what the best hospital is for the patient, and to get him there as quickly as possible.

Why are you required to use a wheelchair inside a hospital?

After you've been admitted to the hospital, you're not allowed to walk around wherever you like—even if you're just being treated for a broken arm, a nurse or orderly pushes you from one room to another in a wheelchair. This isn't because you're weak from your injury and need to recover your strength; it's because the hospital is concerned that if you slip and fall, your parents will file a lawsuit!

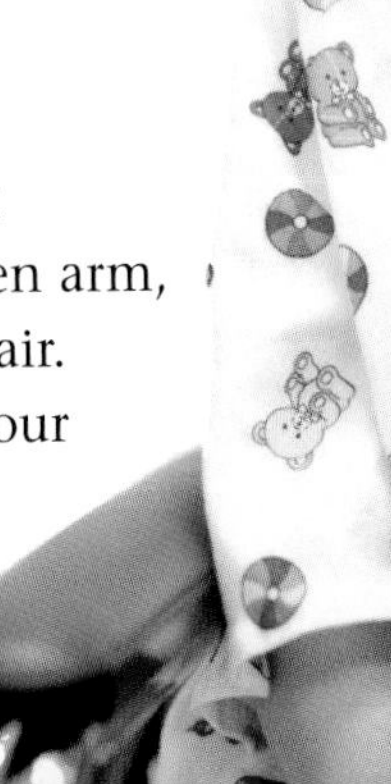

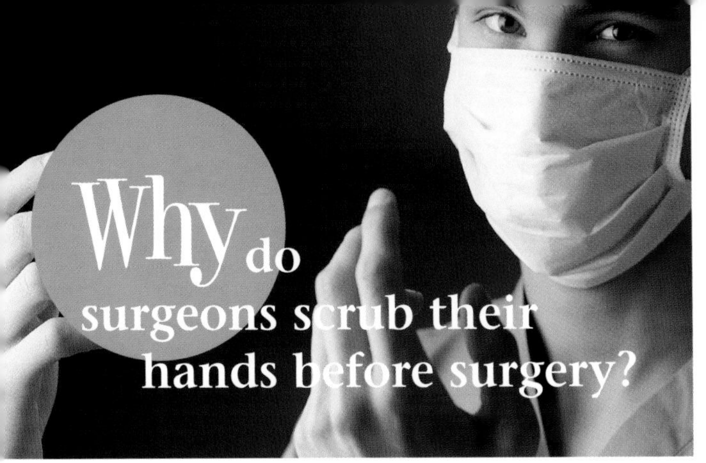

Why do surgeons scrub their hands before surgery?

Look at it this way: you wash your hands before eating, so wouldn't you want your doctor to wash his hands before he does something more serious, like taking out your appendix? In a hospital, it's especially important for doctors and nurses to stay clean and sterile, because the sick people they treat (and operate on) are susceptible to infections.

What is a nosocomial infection?

This may sound like an odd word, until you learn that the Greek word for hospital is "nosokomeion"—so "nosocomial" refers to an infection that a patient picks up while staying in the hospital (and that has nothing to do with the reason he was originally admitted). Nosocomial infections mostly affect older and sicker patients, and they can be difficult to treat, since they're usually caused by bacteria that have developed a resistance to antibiotics.

Why are people "admitted for observation"?

Most of the time, doctors can examine a patient and decide right away whether she needs to be admitted to the hospital. When a patient is admitted for observation, that means she looks okay for the time being, but is at risk of developing a serious condition within the next 24 or 48 hours. An example would be someone who has fallen down and hit her head: she may seem perfectly fine, but the doctor will want to watch her for a day or so to make sure she hasn't suffered a more serious injury.

What does "critical condition" mean?

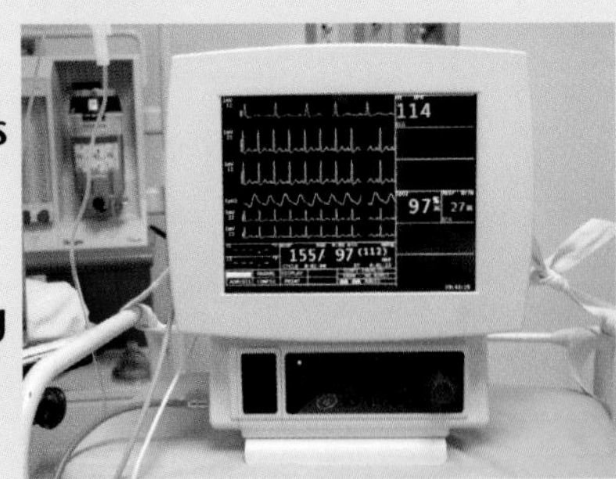

If you watch lots of medical shows on TV, you've probably heard doctors referring to patients as being in "critical" or "stable" condition. Since newspapers and TV news shows also use these terms when referring to people being treated in the hospital, it's helpful to know exactly what they mean.

"Critical" is the worst condition a patient can be in; usually, it means he's at risk of dying within the next 24 hours. Compared to this, being in "serious" condition is actually an improvement; it means the patient has been moved out of the intensive care unit but still requires close observation by doctors. Hospitals sometimes describe a patient as "critical but stable" or "serious but stable"; this means his condition hasn't improved, but it hasn't gotten any worse, either.

By the way, despite what you see on those TV shows, real doctors and nurses almost never talk among themselves about a patient being in "critical" or "serious" condition. Instead, they use specific medical terminology to describe the patient's condition, which imparts much more information than simply saying he's "stable."

Medication

Why do some medicines make you drowsy?

In some medications, the same active ingredient that produces the desired effect (say, drying up your runny nose) also has the unintended effect of making you sleepy. For kids, this isn't much of a problem—as long as you're taking the day off from school, you may as well take a nap. But for adults who have to work, it can be a major inconvenience, which is why some anti-allergy medications (for example) are specially formulated not to make users drowsy.

How do antihistamines work?

One of the most commonly taken drugs in the U.S., next to pain killers, antihistamines keep the cells of the respiratory system from secreting chemicals called "histamines," which are responsible for the stuffy, wheezy misery of allergies. There are many different kinds of antihistamines, so it's important to read the package to make sure the type you're taking is appropriate for your age and has no unwelcome side effects.

What is an over-the-counter drug?

Pharmacies sell two kinds of drugs: prescription drugs that can be obtained only with a doctor's permission (usually a written prescription slip that your mom hands to the pharmacist), and "over-the-counter" drugs (like aspirin or cough medicine) that you can buy as easily as a bag of potato chips. Most health insurance plans pay some of the costs of prescription drugs, which can be very expensive, but you're pretty much on your own when it comes to over-the-counter drugs.

While we're on the subject, a close relative of over-the-counter drugs are generic drugs. When a drug company invents a new type of medicine, its patent lasts for a set period of years (during which time it's the only company that can legally sell the drug). After the patent expires, though, another company can develop a "generic" version of the drug, which contains the same active ingredients. Since generic drugs are much cheaper than brand-name drugs, many insurance companies will pay for only the generic version if it happens to be available.

Why do some adults take an aspirin every day?

No, it's not because they have headaches they can't get rid of. Medical studies have shown that daily doses of aspirin "thin" the blood, inhibiting the formation of the clots that cause strokes and heart attacks. For this reason, many doctors prescribe an aspirin (or two) per day to their older patients, whether they have any bothersome aches and pains or not.

What is the difference between aspirin and acetaminophen?

If you're a kid, the main difference between aspirin (which is sold under the brand names Bayer, Bufferin, Anacin, etc.) and acetaminophen (which is mostly sold under the brand name Tylenol) is that you're much more likely to receive the latter if you have a headache or fever. This is because aspirin can (very) occasionally cause a serious side effect in children under 16 called Reye's syndrome, which can cause sudden paralysis and even death.

Other than that, though, aspirin and acetaminophen reduce pain in two different ways. The active ingredient of aspirin, salicylic acid, is an "anti-inflammatory," meaning it reduces the swelling and inflammation that cause pain. While it's known that acetaminophen doesn't have anti-inflammatory qualities, how it does work is still something of a mystery, but it probably has something to do with the suppression of a specific protein involved in the pain response.

By the way, aspirin and acetaminophen aren't the only widely available pain medications. For example, another anti-inflammatory drug, ibuprofen, is often used to treat arthritis (a painful inflammation of the joints that's most common among older people).

How does cough syrup work?

Despite what you may think, cough syrups don't instantly suppress your cough by coating and soothing that sore area in the back of your throat (though swallowing a heaping teaspoon certainly doesn't hurt). It's after you actually ingest these medicines that they go to work, as the chemicals they contain travel to the nerves of your throat and respiratory tract and reduce your urge to cough.

Why is it called a "booster shot"?

By the time they're a year or two old, most infants have been inoculated against—that is, given a shot that protects them from—diseases like measles, polio, and whooping cough. However, this first shot doesn't confer lifetime immunity; every few years, it's necessary to "boost" the child's resistance with a new inoculation, or "booster shot."

(But don't worry, that needle isn't nearly as big as it looks!)

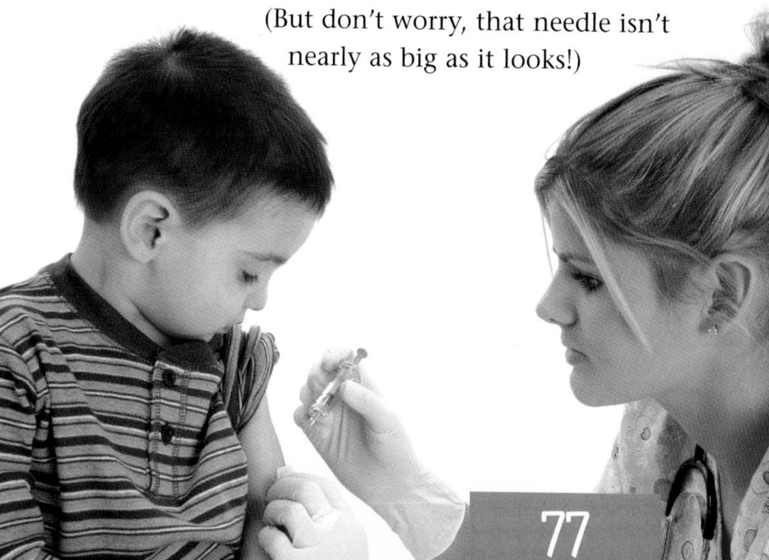

Pain & Painkillers

What are endorphins?

About 30 years ago, doctors discovered that the human brain secretes powerful, pain-killing chemicals in times of stress. These "endorphins," as they're called, are chemically similar to morphine, but scientists haven't yet figured out a way to get the brain to release them "on cue," which might eliminate the need for artificial painkillers.

What is laughing gas?

Despite what you see in cartoons, laughing gas (which is technically called nitrous oxide) won't reduce a roomful of people to helpless giggles, although it has been known to cause spontaneous laughter. What nitrous oxide does do is give you a pleasant, tingly, light-headed feeling, which helps distract you from, say, a dentist filling a cavity in your mouth. By the way, the earth's atmosphere contains small amounts of nitrous oxide, though not enough to affect you one way or the other.

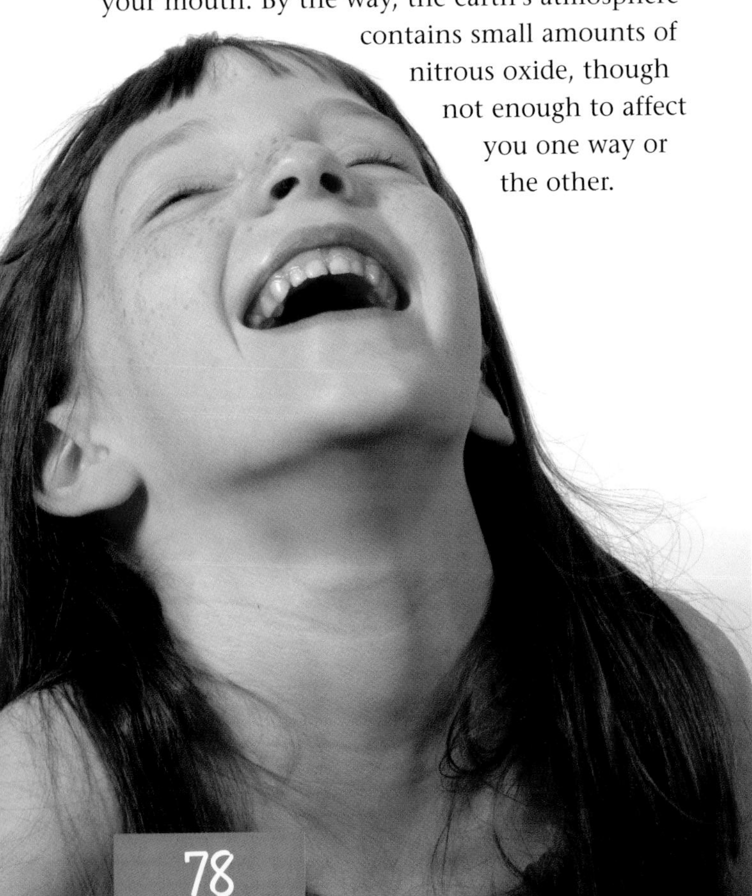

Why does the body feel pain?

If you've ever had a bad toothache or headache, you know just how much of a, well, pain it can be to be in intense pain. But even though pain isn't much fun, it serves an important function, either alerting you to danger (say, that you've just been bitten by a large dog) or letting you know that a part of your body isn't working properly (or, more likely, has been strained from overuse).

Pain is caused by the stimulation of specialized nerve cells that can be found all over the body (except in some internal organs, like the brain). There are different kinds of cells that respond to mechanical stimuli (that is, being hit or bitten), thermal stimuli (putting your hand on a hot stove), and chemical stimuli (swelling and inflammation—the most common cause of pain—which is caused by substances released by your own body).

Most pain is classified as either acute or chronic: an acute pain hurts really, really badly for a few minutes or hours, while chronic pain is somewhat less severe and can last for days or weeks. There's also such a thing as "psychosomatic" pain, which can't be traced to any physical cause but exists only in the sufferer's mind!

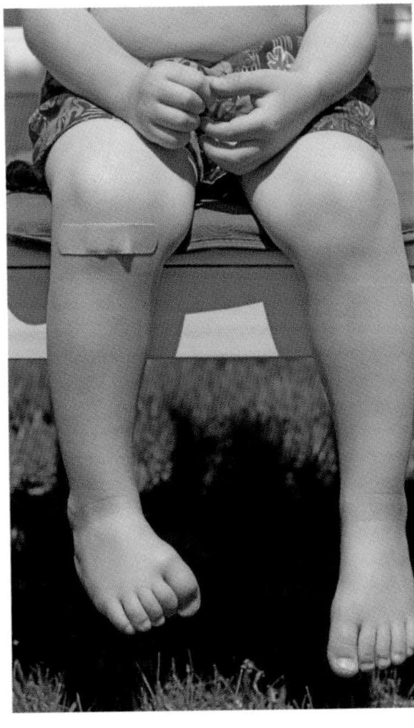

How was anesthesia invented?

Although the word "anesthesia" (from the Greek roots meaning "unable to feel") was coined only in 1846, the concept has existed for thousands of years, dating back to the ancient Greeks. Before the modern age, however, it was uncertain whether a crude anesthetic of opium or alcohol could be counted on to knock a patient out cold, and even if it did, it might wind up killing him in the process. Generally, the best a surgical patient could hope for was something that muffled the pain slightly as the doctor sawed off his leg!

Anesthesia started to become a science in the 19th century, when physicians discovered the painkilling properties of nitrous oxide (otherwise known as laughing gas) and, especially, ether. Ether was the first anesthetic that could reliably put a person to sleep, but its dangerous side effects (not to mention its tendency to catch fire in the presence of a lit candle) prompted doctors to move on to the more dependable chloroform. Today, there are many different kinds of anesthetic, which can be safely mixed and matched to suit the needs of individual patients.

What is the difference between a pain and an itch?

The most honest answer to this question is that doctors know a lot more about pain (and how to prevent it) than they do about itching, which is formally known as "pruritus." We do know that itching is related to the release of chemicals called histamines, but beyond that, its causes and mechanisms are largely unknown.

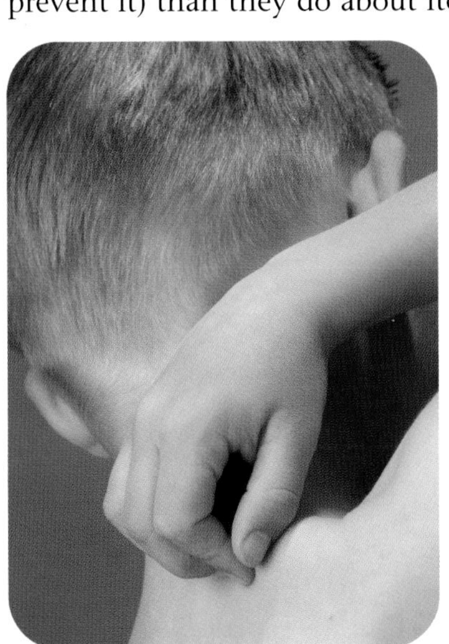

What is CIPA?

Very, very rarely, a child can be born with the inability to feel pain, because of a "short-circuit" between his brain and the pain receptors in his body. This condition, known as CIPA (congenital inability to feel pain), may seem like a sweet deal, but it's not: because they don't react to pain like normal people, children with CIPA are susceptible to burns and serious injuries, and need to be supervised constantly.

How does Novocain work?

Novocain is an example of a local anesthetic, that is, a substance that deadens the pain receptors when injected into a specific part of the body (usually the mouth), without putting the patient to sleep. Although people use the word "Novocain" generically, most dentists actually use lidocaine, which is chemically similar to Novocain but works faster and lasts for a longer time (and causes fewer side effects as well).

Sports Medicine

Why is it called tennis elbow?

Well, for one thing, this condition's medical name ("lateral epicondylitis") isn't quite as catchy. Basically, tennis elbow is a painful inflammation of the muscles and tendons in the elbow, caused by repetitive movement like swinging, throwing, or hammering. It probably earned its name because "tennis elbow" is an easy phrase for doctors and patients to remember, which is odd, because most people with this condition have never played tennis!

What is a hip pointer?

This is one of those injuries that's often alluded to by sportscasters, but rarely explained. Most common in football, a hip pointer is a bruise to the "iliac crest," the part of your hip bone that juts out just above your beltline. Unless the bone is actually fractured, the best way to treat a hip pointer is with pain medication and a long time-out away from the field.

How does arthroscopic surgery work?

The word "arthroscopic" is a combination of the Greek words for "joint" and "look," so that may give you some idea what this advanced surgical procedure is all about. During an arthroscopic procedure, a doctor makes a small incision near the joint being operated on (usually the knee or shoulder), then snakes in a microscopic-sized camera attached to a fiber-optic cable, which supplies light, as well as miniaturized surgical tools. Then, the doctor starts clearing away torn cartilage (the usual cause of soreness and pain in athletes) while looking at an enlarged image of the inside of the joint on a computer monitor.

Before arthroscopy was invented, a pitcher with a sore shoulder would have to undergo a full surgical procedure, involving anesthesia, a stay in the hospital, and a long recovery time—meaning he was likely to miss the entire season. Today, though, many simple joint problems can be cured in a matter of weeks, though more extensive injuries (or injuries to smaller joints, like the elbow, that are more difficult to treat arthroscopically) may still require a long period of convalescence.

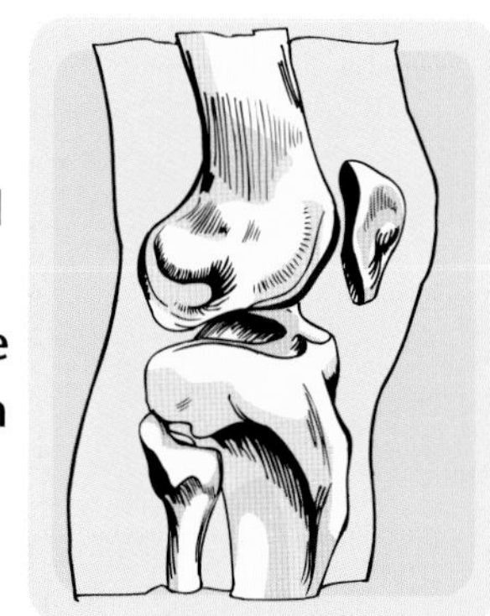

What is the Achilles tendon?

You may have heard the phrase "Achilles' heel," meaning the one vulnerable spot of an otherwise invincible opponent. The Achilles tendon is a strong slab of tissue that connects your heel bone to the muscles of your calf. An inflamed Achilles tendon makes it nearly impossible to walk (much less run), and a ruptured tendon can lay an athlete flat on his back for months!

Why does pitching cause so many injuries?

Few things in sports are as unnatural as repeatedly throwing a baseball at speeds of 80, 90, or even 100 miles per hour. Because pitching puts enormous strain on the arm, shoulder, and elbow—and because reliable pitchers are essential to any team hoping to reach the World Series—major-league pitchers are some of the most well-looked-after athletes on the face of the earth. Coaches will carefully count the number of pitches a starting pitcher throws during a game, and pitchers are the only baseball players who get to rest for three or four days between starts.

One of the most dangerous injuries a pitcher can face is a torn rotator cuff. Although it sounds like something you'd find on a jet plane, the "rotator cuff" is what doctors call the tendons that surround the shoulder joint (that is, the place where the upper arm attaches to the shoulder). Because pitchers generate most of their strength by way of their shoulders, not only is a torn rotator cuff painful, but it can greatly diminish pitching speed and effectively end a pitcher's career.

What is a shin splint?

It sounds like a kind of dance, but a shin splint is actually a painful injury of the lower leg, most common in runners. Oddly, though, "shin splint" is a very non-specific phrase; it can refer to anything from soreness in the muscles surrounding the shin to an actual fracture of the shinbone itself. Unless there's a broken bone involved, most shin splints are treated with anti-inflammatory medications and, of course, by staying off the affected leg!

How do athletes become dehydrated?

When you're in the middle of a bruising game of football or basketball, it can be easy to forget to replenish your bodily fluids—and because athletes sweat so much from physical exertion, they need to drink lots of water (or "electrolytic" fluids like Gatorade) in between plays. That's why, whenever you watch a football game on TV, nearly all the players on the sidelines can be seen drinking from paper cups.

Culture &

WHAT is a "cold case"? HOW does the stock market work? WHY don't we get mail on Sundays? Here's where you'll find answers about the everyday institutions that keep society running, as well as how law and order are maintained by police, firefighters, and other professionals.

Government

Hats

Why do people wear hats?

This may seem like an odd question—you may as well ask, why do people wear pants? But the fact is, unlike shirts or socks or underwear—all of which serve a specific function, such as keeping your feet warm—hats are pretty much disposable. (The exceptions, of course, are summer hats and winter hats, which keep you from freezing or broiling!)

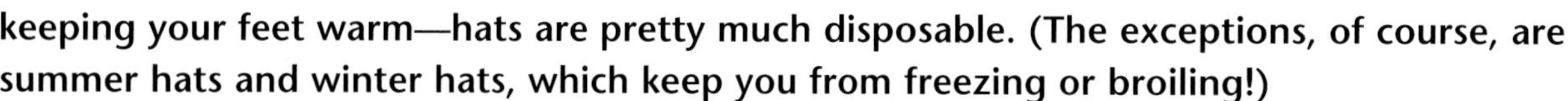

Throughout history, hats have been worn primarily as emblems of status or authority. Medieval kings and religious leaders tried to outdo each other with bejeweled headgear, and it was fashionable for ladies of the court to wear gigantic, plumed hats that set them apart from the common people.

Until about 50 years ago, most men and women in the U.S. wouldn't be caught dead outside without wearing a hat. Fashions have a way of coming and going, though, so it's possible that hats will once again become a popular item.

Why did colonists wear three-cornered hats?

The three-cornered hats ("tricorns," as they're sometimes called) that you see in historic paintings—don't really have any symbolic meaning; they just happened to be wildly popular toward the end of the 18th century. At the peak of tricorn mania, this distinctive hat was worn by ordinary civilians as well as soldiers, but fell out of fashion shortly after the American Revolution.

What is a mitre?

One of the most elaborate pieces of headgear you're likely to see, the mitre is a tall, cone-shaped hat worn by senior officials of the Catholic church: popes, cardinals, and bishops. Like other aspects of Catholicism, the mitre has a long and illustrious history: some historians say a mitre-like cap was worn by the early apostles, in the second or third century A.D. It's more likely, though, that the first recognizable mitre appeared in Rome (the seat of the Catholic church) a few hundred years later.

Why do we take off our hats indoors?

Hats were once as commonly worn as shoes, so there are a large number of rules (mostly ignored today) about the proper times and occasions to put on or remove one's hat. Learning the rules of "hat etiquette" won't do you much good in the schoolyard, but who knows—it might really impress your grandma!

Up until the early 20th century, it was customary to tip one's hat when meeting a lady, or as a non-verbal way to say "thank you" to someone who did you a favor. Gentlemen would also tip their hats as a quick way of saying hello to people they passed on the street. This may have had something to do with the military salute, though soldiers usually only touch their hats rather than remove them.

The most important rule, though, was to remove your hat inside someone's home or (if there were ladies present) inside an elevator. "Doffing" (or removing) one's hat was considered an important sign of respect, and your host might be mortally insulted if you deliberately chose not to do so.

How was the baseball cap invented?

Probably the most common piece of headgear in the world today, the modern baseball cap was first introduced in the 1940s (players had worn hats before that, of course, but not in any standard style). The reason a baseball hat has a solid brim, or visor, is to shield the player's eyes from the sun while he's up at bat or trying to catch a fly ball.

How tall was a stovepipe hat?

It's easy to picture Abraham Lincoln wearing a three-foot-tall hat, but in fact, the average stovepipe hat (or, as it's also called, "top hat") was only about a foot high. These hats were introduced around the year 1800 and soon became wildly popular, although today the only folks you're likely to see wearing stovepipe hats are magicians or people in tuxedos.

Why do French people wear berets?

Despite what you see in cartoons, it's not true that every Frenchman has a soft, floppy beret perched on top of his head. These hats were first used by the French army in the 19th century, for two main reasons: unlike a stiff military hat, they could be easily folded and stuffed into a pocket, and they were easy (and cheap) to manufacture in large quantities. Today, different varieties of beret are worn by soldiers (and civilians) all over the world.

Holidays

How was Valentine's Day created?

Although some cynical people believe Valentine's Day was created by American greeting-card companies as a way to boost sales, the fact is that this holiday has a long and venerable history. Ever since ancient times, the middle of February has been a time to celebrate love and courtship (probably because it's so cold and bleak otherwise!), and somehow this tradition became associated with the medieval Catholic holiday celebrating St. Valentine (there were three different St. Valentines, by the way, and not much is known about any of them).

What day does Kwanzaa fall on?

Over the past few years, the African holiday of Kwanzaa has been observed by an increasing number of African- American families in the U.S. It takes place from December 26 to January 1 (putting it square in the middle of the Christmas–New Year's Day extended school holiday), and it's usually celebrated with food, music, and exchanges of gifts.

Why are Jewish holidays celebrated on different dates every year?

It can be confusing for non-Jewish people—and even for some Jewish people as well!—but holidays like Passover and Yom Kippur are celebrated according to the ancient Jewish calendar, not the modern calendar. The Jewish calendar dates back more than 6,000 years, and it's extremely complicated, involving an entire leap month that's inserted every few years. The result is that a major holiday like Rosh Hashanah can be celebrated anywhere from October 4 to September 23.

To be fair, many non-Jewish holidays are celebrated on different dates as well. This is because certain federal holidays aren't designated for the exact same date every year, but by formulas such as the first Monday in October (for Labor Day) or the fourth Thursday in November (for Thanksgiving). For this reason, if you were born on December 25, Christmas will always be on your birthday—but if you were born on November 26, Thanksgiving Day might coincide with your birthday only once every few years.

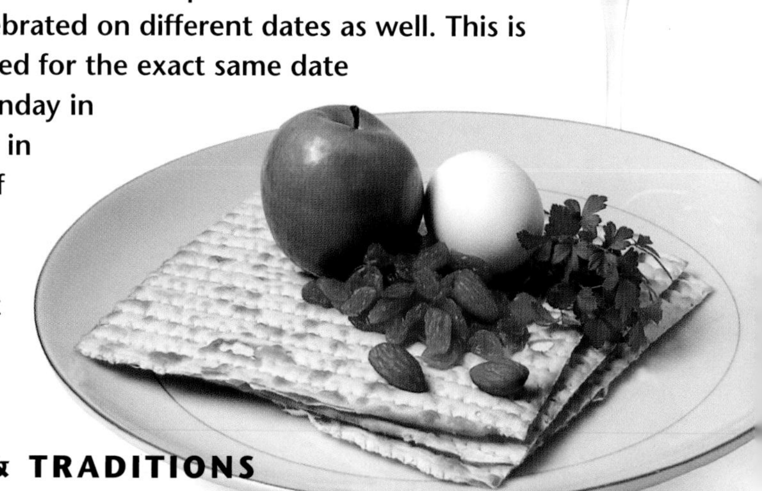

Why isn't there a Children's Day?

Think about it—we celebrate Mother's Day in May and Father's Day in June, so why isn't there a Children's Day? Well, if you ask most parents, they'll probably say something like "every day is children's day"—but if it makes you feel better, in 1954 the United Nations drafted a resolution recommending a "Universal Children's Day" to be celebrated on November 20 all over the world. Unfortunately, this holiday hasn't quite caught on yet!

What is Arbor Day?

One of those holidays that used to be a lot more popular a couple of decades ago than it is today, Arbor Day is meant to celebrate the nation's trees and forests—which is why it used to be widely observed (and sometimes still is today) by planting trees. In case you want to mark it on your calendar, Arbor Day is celebrated on the last Friday in April, and no, you don't get the day off from school.

What does it mean to be a federal holiday?

Dozens of holidays are celebrated every year, in various parts of the country, but the "big" holidays are recognized by the federal government, meaning banks, schools, and post offices are closed and government employees have the day off. The official list of federal holidays includes New Year's Day, Martin Luther King Day, Washington's Birthday, Memorial Day, Independence Day, Labor Day, Columbus Day, Veterans Day, Thanksgiving, and Christmas Day.

Just because government offices are closed, though, doesn't mean your parents will necessarily get the day off as well. While practically all businesses close for Christmas and Thanksgiving, many remain open for "minor" federal holidays like Washington's Birthday or Columbus Day.

It can take a lot of work to get a holiday recognized by the government. For instance, Martin Luther King Day (celebrated on the third Monday in January) was resisted by various states, which didn't want to give their residents another day off, and was only fully accepted as a national holiday in January 2006!

Why are some holidays three or four days long?

Technically, Christmas and Thanksgiving are only celebrated on a single day, December 25 and the fourth Thursday in November. However, it's traditional for businesses to give adults an extra day off before or after Christmas Day, as well as the Friday after Thanksgiving (leading into the weekend, which makes for a four-day break). Holidays like Memorial Day and Labor Day, on the other hand, are always celebrated on Mondays, resulting in much-needed three-day weekends.

Names

What do "Mr." and "Mrs." mean?

As you may have guessed, the word "mister" (which is abbreviated as "Mr.") derives from "master," a respectful way to address men in bygone times. "Miss" and "Missus" (abbreviated as "Mrs.") come from the equally old-fashioned "mistress." "Miss" is traditionally used to address unmarried women, while "Mrs." is reserved for married women or widows.

The abbreviation "Ms." (pronounced "mizz") has a more recent history. As you may have noticed in the paragraph above, there are two terms of address for women depending on their marital status, while that same distinction doesn't apply to men—that is, addressing someone as "Miss Smith" automatically tells everyone in the vicinity that she's unmarried, while "Mr. Smith" is completely neutral. "Ms." was invented as a counterpart for "Mr.," though it hasn't yet come into wide usage.

By the way, most languages have abbreviations similar to Mr. and Mrs. In Spanish, for instance, a woman is addressed as *Señora* (Sra.), while a man is called *Señor* (Sr.) and an unmarried woman is a *Señorita* (Srta.).

Why are they called nicknames?

The word "nickname" is derived from the Old English word "ekename." Since "eke" meant "also" or "extra," an ekename was a person's "second" name. As to why people have nicknames in the first place, that's easy: if you have a multi-syllabic name like "Nathaniel," it's much simpler for your friends to call you "Nat" in everyday conversation.

What country has the most people with no last name?

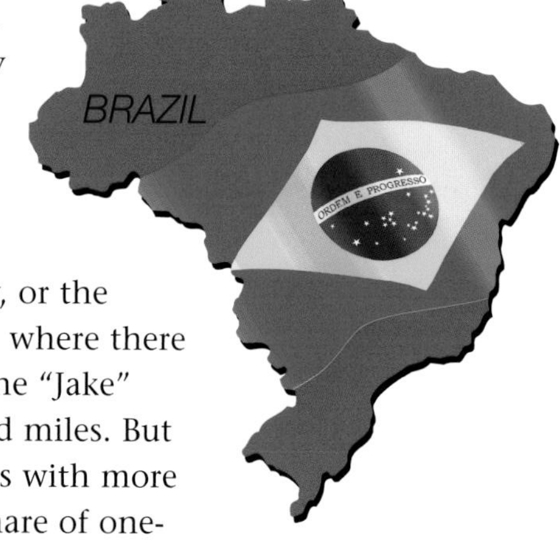

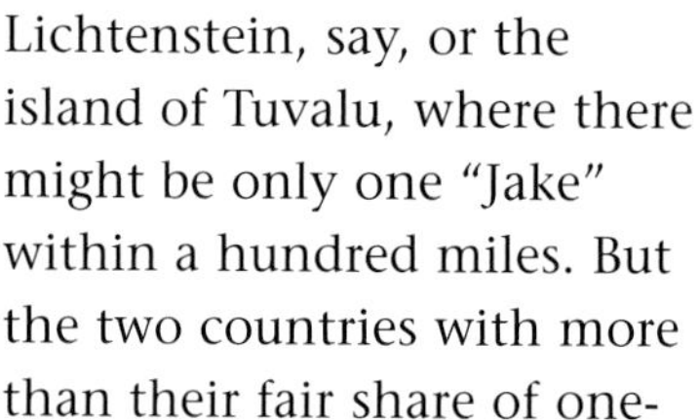

You might think people with only a first name would live in relatively tiny countries—Lichtenstein, say, or the island of Tuvalu, where there might be only one "Jake" within a hundred miles. But the two countries with more than their fair share of one-named inhabitants are Brazil and Indonesia, which both have hundreds of millions of people. This might seem like a recipe for disaster, but most of the one-named people in these nations are identified by both their name and the town in which they live, eliminating any confusion.

Why do Chinese people put their last names first?

In China (and most countries in the Far East, for that matter), it's traditional to put your family name first and your given name second—rather as if you introduced yourself to people as "Smith John." This is one of those cultural differences that's simply a matter of convention—in fact, our naming system probably seems as strange to Chinese people as theirs does to us!

How hard is it to change your name?

Not as hard as you might think, though there's a lot of paperwork involved. Legally changing your name usually involves visiting a courthouse and signing various forms and documents. There are some rules, though: you can't change your name to a legal trademark, say, or deliberately copy the name of a famous person. And, in most cases, you have to be an adult—though some kids are allowed to change their names after their parents divorce.

Why do we have middle names?

The tradition of giving children middle names is most prevalent in North America and Anglo-Saxon countries like England and Australia, though there are various countries in Southeast Asia (like Vietnam) that also observe this practice.

Most often, the purpose of a middle name is to allow your parents to honor a relative (say, a great-grandfather) in a discreet way, or to give you a second name they happen to like but which might be too "old-fashioned" for everyday use (the middle name of this book's author is Frederick, and he's sure glad he didn't bring that with him into the first grade!).

Most people simply abbreviate their middle names to the first initial, if they don't forget them altogether, but some folks grow up and discover that they like their middle name more than their first name. In this case, they might abbreviate their first name to an initial and use their complete middle name (if your name is Hubert James Peartree, for instance, you might just call yourself H. James Peartree).

How did Jack become a nickname for John?

This is a difficult question to answer. "Jack" has been a nickname for "John" since the Middle Ages, but it's unclear why this is so. The most likely explanation is that "Jack" was adopted from the French name "Jacques," which was used to address random strangers (kind of like how people today will say "Hey, Bud!" to someone walking down the street). Since "John" was a common English name, it's possible that people called folks named "John" "Jack." Got that, Mack? Probably the most famous John/Jack was President John F. Kennedy.

Weddings & Marriage

Why do brides wear white dresses?

As with so many other things at weddings, the bride wears a white dress for purely symbolic reasons: technically, it means that she's pure and virginal (that is, that she hasn't been with another man). If a woman divorces (or is widowed) and marries a second time, she'll often forgo the white dress, which some people consider more appropriate for first-time brides.

What is a civil ceremony?

Not all couples decide to get married in a religious ceremony attended by guests. It's also possible to have a simple civil ceremony, in which the bride and groom exchange vows in front of a civil servant (usually a court clerk), who legally registers the marriage. A civil ceremony isn't quite as romantic as a church or temple ceremony, but it's every bit as "official" in the eyes of the law.

Why is rice thrown at weddings?

In ancient times, grain was a symbol of fertility—that is, the ability to have lots and lots of kids. Since marriage back then was as much a matter of having children as of spending the rest of your life with the person you loved, spectators at weddings would throw wheat as a way of blessing the new couple. When wheat became too expensive in medieval England, revelers took to throwing rice instead, a tradition that has persisted to the present day.

Fertility is also the explanation behind another wedding custom, the bride's bouquet of flowers. In ancient Rome, brides and grooms wore garlands of flowers around their necks, which symbolized youth and the ability to have children. Throwing the bouquet, though, seems to be a uniquely American tradition: turning her back to her female guests, the bride tosses the bouquet over her shoulder, and whoever catches it is supposed to be the next to marry.

What does a "best man" do?

In a modern wedding, the best man (usually the husband-to-be's brother or best friend) has a prominent place in the ceremony, in return for which he's supposed to help the groom with various details, such as catering or transportation. In ancient England, though, the best man had a much more exciting job: he'd accompany his friend to a nearby village in search of a bride, and use his sword to fight off anyone who objected! (Another possibility is that the "best man" originated in duels, in which combatants would have "seconds" who handed them their pistols. Who thought weddings had such violent origins?)

At least the maid of honor—who assists the bride in pretty much the same way the best man assists the groom—derives from a gentler tradition. In medieval England, daughters of wealthy families were accustomed to being attended by servants, and a special "maid of honor" would be appointed to help the bride-to-be in the days leading up to her wedding. Even today, most maids of honor take their responsibilities much more seriously than most best men (who would probably rather be somewhere else, sword fighting!).

How did the Bridal March originate?

If you've ever been to a wedding, you've probably heard the "Bridal March" played as the bride walks down the aisle ("Here comes the bride, all dressed in white . . . "). Considering how ancient other wedding traditions are, this tune is of surprisingly recent origin: it's from the wedding scene of the 1848 opera *Lohengrin*, by the German composer Richard Wagner.

What is the difference between a separation and a divorce?

It's not the kind of thing you want to read about on a page devoted to marriage, but couples do get separated and divorced—so it helps to know what these terms mean. A separation is when a husband and wife declare their intention (legally) to no longer live together, but the door is still open for them to get back together later on. A divorce is more final: it's the legal termination of the marriage, after which the man and woman are free to marry other people.

What is an annulment?

Divorce isn't the only way to end a marriage. If it can be shown that the marriage was fraudulent—say, because the groom already had a wife and didn't quite get around to telling the bride—the marriage can be declared "null and void" by a court. There are other, more complicated reasons for annulment, which you're too young to read about here, but "bigamy" (already being married) is far and away the leading cause.

British Royalty

What is the difference between a duke and an earl?

Sorting out the various gradations of British royalty can be a bit like collecting butterflies—if you don't know what you're doing, it's easy for things to get out of control.

The peerage, as it's called, is a system by which the king confers honors on "noble" individuals (or, as we'd say, the upper crust of society). There are five broad categories of peers, in descending order of importance: dukes, marquesses, earls, viscounts, and barons. In ancient times, these ranks brought significant benefits (like huge estates bequeathed by the king), though today they're more ceremonial in nature. (If this system seems baffling to you, keep in mind that the "classless" society of the U.S. can be equally baffling to Britons!)

By the way, once he's been raised to the peerage, it's traditional for an honoree to cease using his given name and start calling himself after his place of origin: "The Duke of Marlborough," "The Earl of Queensberry," etc., which can be a bit confusing for American kids studying British history.

Why is the king or queen's son called the "Prince of Wales"?

In 1301, King Edward I celebrated his conquest of Wales (a province on the west coast of lower England) by naming his son the Prince of Wales. (According to one story, he told a crowd of angry Welshmen that they would be ruled by "a prince born in Wales, who did not speak a word of English," then tricked them by holding up his new-born son!) Since then, the heir to the throne hasn't had any special relationship to Wales, but the name has stuck.

What is the Royal Family?

As you might have guessed, the British Royal Family comprises all the people most closely related to the reigning monarch—sons and daughters, brothers and sisters, wives or husbands, and grandchildren and in-laws (though sometimes not aunts and uncles). Most members of the Royal Family are entitled to small privileges, such as using the designation HRH (for His Royal Highness or Her Royal Highness) in front of their names.

How long has England had royalty?

Like most of the other nations in Europe, it took nearly a thousand years for England to become united under a single king: the island had various rulers and warlords as far back as Roman times, but they only commanded the allegiance of individual tribes. It wasn't until long after the Romans left, in about A.D. 800, that the first recognizable major kingdom appeared: the Kingdom of Wessex, ruled by Alfred the Great. Even then, Wessex had to compete with other, smaller kingdoms in southern England.

Over the next few hundred years, a line of kings gradually emerged who could claim uncontested rule of the lower part of England (the upper part of the island, Scotland, was a separate kingdom until 1707). Today, England is one of the few modern countries to have a king or queen, although now the position is completely ceremonial—that is, the monarch isn't allowed to pass laws or set policy.

What does it mean to be knighted?

In medieval times, becoming a knight involved owning your own horse, knowing how to joust, and employing a page. Today, though, knights are created in a simple ceremony presided over by the British sovereign, in recognition for outstanding achievements in art, music, government, or other fields. Being knighted allows the recipient to use the word "sir" in front of his name (or "dame" if she's a woman), but not much more.

What is an OBE?

Like the British peerage system, being honored for one's accomplishments in England is a complicated process with various subtle gradations. An OBE, or Officer of the British Empire, is an honor bestowed by the king or queen that doesn't quite rise to the exalted level of "knight." It's also possible to earn a less prestigious title, an MBE (or Member of the British Empire).

Why did Edward VIII abdicate the throne?

When he became King of England in 1936, Edward VIII was involved in a relationship with a married woman, Wallis Simpson. Although Simpson was willing to get a divorce so she could marry Edward, Edward was prohibited by court protocol from marrying a divorced woman. Partly for this reason, he resigned from the throne—the only British monarch ever to do so voluntarily—and spent the rest of his life married to Wallis as a private citizen.

What is the electoral college?

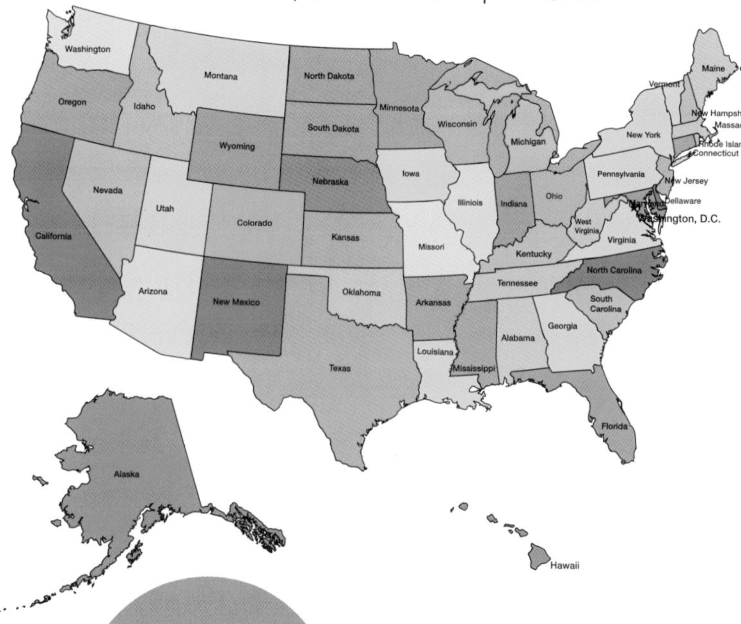

The electoral college is one of those institutions that has baffled kids—and most adults—ever since it was outlined in the U.S. Constitution. Technically, when your parents vote for president, they're actually casting ballots for their state's electors, who then go on to cast official votes for one of the presidential candidates. There is a total of 538 electors in the U.S., with a proportionate amount for each state (New York has 31 electors, for instance, while Louisiana has only 9). A candidate has to receive at least 270 electoral votes to become president.

By this point you may be asking: why not just have direct elections for president, and skip the electoral college entirely? Oddly enough, no one knows for sure why the Founding Fathers decided on the electoral system. It's possible that it was designed to protect smaller states from the influence of larger ones, or (more likely) that it was meant to restrict the ultimate power of electing the president to a relatively small group of prosperous (and, presumably, level-headed) individuals.

Why are ballots kept secret?

Look at it this way: if you were voting for class president, would you prefer to quietly write the candidate's name on a slip of paper and drop it in a box, or run up onto the stage of your auditorium and shout it to the entire school? The reason ballots are kept secret is to protect people from intimidation and allow them to vote their conscience, with no chance of unpleasant repercussions afterwards.

Why are voting machines set up in schools?

In many communities, schools are the only public buildings spacious enough to accommodate hundreds of voters at a time. That's part of the reason Election Day is a school holiday: while you get to stay home and watch TV, your parents (and the other people in your town or neighborhood) head to your school and vote, usually on machines set up in the lunchroom or auditorium.

Why are most candidates Democrats or Republicans?

The U.S. Constitution has nothing to say about the number of political parties allowed to put candidates up for election. However, as things have evolved over the past 200 years, most people are content to vote either Democratic or Republican, meaning the U.S. essentially has a two-party system. Every few years, "independent" parties of one type or another pop up (usually during presidential elections), but they have yet to establish themselves as firmly as the two mainstream parties.

Why don't we have electronic voting?

Since most people today are comfortable using computers, it makes sense to explore the possibility of "electronic" voting—that is, allowing folks to vote by clicking on a Web site at home, or by using touch-screens at a public polling place. The reason electronic voting hasn't caught on yet is concerns about security: it's hard to keep an ordinary computer safe from hackers, so there's a slim possibility that a technical wizard could manipulate the results of an election in favor of the candidate of his choice!

How often are elections decided by one vote?

That depends on the office in question. If the election is for sheriff of a small town, and there are only 50 eligible voters, the odds of a candidate winning by one or two votes are relatively high. Those odds decrease in congressional elections (in which candidates bring out tens or hundreds of thousands of voters), and are even smaller in presidential elections, in which votes are counted in the tens of millions.

Now for the "but." There are two reasons every adult should vote, no matter how big or small an election is. First, although some people will talk themselves out of voting on the premise that "one vote won't make any difference," if everyone thought that way, major elections would be decided by a couple of dozen people! And second, even presidential elections sometimes come down to individual votes, as happened in the 2000 contest between Al Gore Jr. and George W. Bush. In that election, the state of Florida was so evenly split that every vote had to be counted with extreme care, with the outcome determining who became president.

What is an exit poll?

In major elections, it takes at least a few hours to tally the votes and announce the winner. For that reason, many news organizations set up "exit polls" in polling places, and ask people who've already cast their ballots to reveal which candidate they voted for. Based on the results of these polls, a TV news network can reliably project the winner of an election before the "official" results are released.

U.S. Government

What is the separation of powers?

Two hundred years ago, when the founding fathers were drafting the Constitution, they faced a tricky situation. Historically, governments around the world had a serious flaw: one person (the king, say, or his prime minister) could accumulate a huge amount of power, then impose his will on other, supposedly independent bodies like the courts or the police. To avoid this situation, the framers of the Constitution divided the U.S. government into three main components: the executive (the president and his staff), the judiciary (the Supreme Court), and the legislature (the Senate and the House of Representatives).

In theory—and usually in practice—each branch of government is supposed to keep a check on the other two. For example, the president has the power to name nominees to the Supreme Court, but these nominees have to be approved by the Senate—and, in turn, the Supreme Court has the ability to override legislation proposed by the president and enacted by Congress. Remarkably, the separation of powers has held up pretty well over the course of U.S. history, thanks to the wisdom and foresight of people like Thomas Jefferson and James Madison.

How long can a Supreme Court justice serve?

The reason it's such a big deal when the president nominates a candidate for the Supreme Court is that this is a lifetime appointment: while a senator has to be re-elected every six years, and a congressperson every two years, a Supreme Court justice can stay on the job until the day he or she dies. (It's legally possible for Congress to impeach—that is, remove—a sitting justice, but this has never happened.)

Why does the Supreme Court have nine justices?

Oddly enough, the Constitution doesn't specify an exact size for the Supreme Court, leaving that decision up to Congress. When it was founded in 1789, the court had six justices, and a congressional act in 1869 set the official size at nine. The one attempt to change this law was initiated by President Franklin D. Roosevelt, who wanted to "pack" the Supreme Court with judges sympathetic to his views. If his plan had been approved by Congress, the court could have had as many as 15 members!

Why is it called "lobbying"?

Often, businesses have a direct stake in laws passed by Congress. To make their views known, corporations hire "lobbyists," whose job it is to sway lawmakers to the business's point of view. The reason it's called "lobbying" is because, since these hired guns aren't allowed in the inner chambers of Congress, they once had to collar senators and representatives in lobbies (though today most lobbying is done over expensive dinners at fancy restaurants!).

What is the difference between the House and the Senate?

A whole book can be written about the way Congress operates, but the difference between the House and Senate boils down to this: the House is a proportional body (meaning more populous states, like New York, get to have more congresspeople than less populous states, like Montana), while every state, no matter how big or small, can send only two people to the Senate. The reason for this difference was the desire of the founding fathers to protect smaller states from unfair "majority rule" imposed by larger states.

Because the Senate has fewer members—and because senators are elected for six-year terms, compared to only two years for congressmen—there's a certain sense in which one senator is more powerful than any one congressperson. This difference was even more pronounced before 1913, when senators were elected by state legislatures rather than by the people who resided in the state.

Although the House and Senate have different duties, each body has to approve important legislation by a majority (or two-thirds) vote before it becomes law. That's why, over the course of history, many laws approved by the Senate have been turned down by the House, and vice-versa!

Why does the president have term limits?

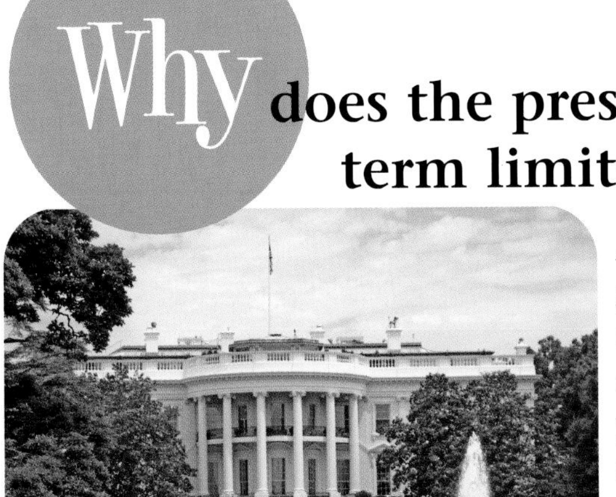

A senator or a congressperson can be reelected to an indefinite number of two- or six-year terms, but by law, the president is allowed only two consecutive four-year terms. The reason for this is that, after Franklin D. Roosevelt was elected to four consecutive terms starting in 1932 (he died in office in 1945), Congress grew uneasy about allowing any single person to hold the presidency for that long, and enacted term limits to prevent this from happening.

Why is it called "impeachment"?

For such a serious act—the removal of a sitting president by Congress—"impeachment" is an awfully funny-sounding word. No, peaches have nothing to do with it: this word is derived from the Latin verb "impedicare," which means to catch or entangle. "Impedicare" became "empechen" in medieval England, and from there it turned into the modern "impeachment."

United Nations

How many countries are in the U.N.?

At the latest count, the U.N. had 191 member states, ranging from big hitters like the U.S. and China to tiny island nations like the Maldives and the Seychelles. (Interestingly, the U.N.'s membership has practically quadrupled since its founding in 1945, when it had 51 members.) Two nations, Palestine and Vatican City, have "observer" status, meaning they can participate in debates in the General Assembly but aren't allowed to vote.

What organization did the U.N. replace?

After the end of World War I—which was almost as destructive as the Second World War twenty years later—U.S. President Woodrow Wilson proposed a "League of Nations" that would settle disputes between countries and maintain global peace and security. Because the league didn't have the means to enforce its resolutions, it could only stand by helplessly as Germany and Japan invaded neighboring countries in the 1930s and started World War II.

What does the U.N. secretary-general do?

Basically, the secretary-general is the public face of the U.N.—in much the same way that the president (to other nations) is the public face of the United States. Besides issuing statements about global matters, it's the secretary-general's job to administrate the vast workings of the U.N., a task that involves everything from mediating disputes between representatives to helping raise money for U.N. causes.

Why was the United Nations founded?

After the end of World War II in 1945—in which tens of millions of soldiers and civilians were killed and entire nations (like Japan and Germany) practically destroyed—the last thing anyone wanted was another global conflict. The United Nations (U.N.) was founded as a forum in which two hostile countries could settle their differences, or a small country could seek protection from other members against aggression by a larger, more hostile neighbor.

Unfortunately, for much of its history, the U.N. didn't quite live up to its mission. In its first few decades, its proceedings were dominated by the politics of the cold war—countries aligned with the Soviet Union or China would vote against measures proposed by non-Communist countries like the United States, while nations aligned with the U.S. would do likewise when it came to the interests of Communist countries. It has been only in the past few years that the U.N. has functioned pretty much as it was intended to—for instance, by sending peacekeeping forces (composed of soldiers from various nations) to war-torn countries like Serbia.

How many translators does the U.N. employ?

You can do the math: not only does the U.N. have six "official" languages (English, French, Russian, Chinese, Spanish, and Arabic), but it also employs translators competent in 20 or so additional languages, such as Thai, Japanese, and Turkish. So on a busy day in the General Assembly, hundreds of translators are working to convey the proceedings to representatives!

Why is the U.N. in New York?

By the end of World War II, the U.S. was the world's reigning superpower, so it seemed natural to erect the U.N. building in New York (though San Francisco was also in the running). However, the U.N. building doesn't technically belong to the U.S.—it has "extraterritorial" status, meaning it's the property of all the member nations of the U.N. In some situations, the laws within the U.N. building take precedence over the laws outside—but this doesn't mean that representatives can get away with murder.

How is the U.N. organized?

Because it's meant to represent all the nations of the world, the U.N. has a fairly complicated structure. Apart from its committees—of which there are way too many to list!—the two most important bodies are the Security Council and the General Assembly.

You may be familiar with the General Assembly from TV: that's the huge amphitheater where representatives of all the member nations of the U.N. sit behind nameplates identifying their countries. The General Assembly is a forum for freewheeling debate, which often results in non-binding resolutions—"non-binding" because member nations (and the U.N.'s leadership) aren't obliged to follow the assembly's vote.

As important as the General Assembly is, the real power of the U.N. resides in the Security Council. This is composed of five permanent nations—the U.S., Russia, China, France, and Great Britain—and ten elected nations that rotate in and out over the course of two years. Unlike the General Assembly, the resolutions of the Security Council are binding and must (at least in theory) be followed by all the U.N.'s members. Also, each of the five permanent nations has veto power, meaning it can block any resolutions it doesn't like.

Why is there a West Virginia?

Up until the Civil War, Virginia was one state, the biggest of the original thirteen from which the United States was founded in 1776. However, it included a natural barrier, the Allegheny Mountains, which separated the eastern and western parts of its territory.

As its population grew in the early 19th century, Virginia took on two very different personalities. The eastern part of the state was dominated by slave owners with large cotton plantations, while the western, more industrial part was settled largely by the inhabitants of northern states like Pennsylvania and Ohio. Since the economy of western Virginia wasn't suited to slavery, this created serious tension when the Civil War started in 1861.

Virginia held itself together for a couple of years, but in 1863, Abraham Lincoln recognized a petition from representatives of the western part of the state to secede and become West Virginia. So the new, relatively small state of West Virginia returned to the Union, and what was left of Virginia continued to fight for the Confederacy until the war ended in 1865.

How did Texas become a state?

In 1823, a group of 300 American families emigrated to Texas, which was then a territory belonging to Mexico. As the American population grew, it came into increasing conflict with the Mexican government over such issues as slavery (the American Texans were all for it, but Mexico had made the practice illegal). In 1836, over Mexican objections, Texas declared itself a separate country, and in 1845 it was admitted to the United States as a slave state.

Why isn't Arkansas pronounced like Kansas?

Kansas is pronounced with an "s" sound at the end, but as you may know, the correct pronunciation of Arkansas is "Arkansaw." The reason for this is that the state of Arkansas was originally settled by the French, whose pronunciation of the name lingered long after they left. The state of Kansas was also named by French settlers, but unlike in Arkansas, the English inhabitants adopted the English pronunciation of the name after the French departed.

What is often called the "51st State"?

Ever since it became an American territory in 1898 (during the Spanish-American War), the island of Puerto Rico has hovered on the verge of official statehood, though this has become less likely as an increasing number of Puerto Ricans prefer complete independence. Unofficially, though, many U.S. citizens consider Puerto Rico to be the "51st State," though some folks in Canada also use this term (humorously) to describe their own country.

Why do some states have straight borders?

Looking at a map, you might notice that most states in the eastern and southern parts of the U.S. have irregular borders, while most of those in the western and middle parts (like Wyoming, Nevada and South Dakota) are carved out of straight lines. This is because, as the U.S. acquired huge swaths of territory in the 19th century, it was easier for the government to divide states by artificial lines, rather than the natural, craggy boundaries (such as mountains and rivers) that divided states in the East.

What does the "D.C." in "Washington, D.C." stand for?

The Founding Fathers were concerned that no one state should have control of the capital of the United States of America (since this might change the balance of power among the 13 founding states). For this reason, a special territory called the "District of Columbia" was created on the border of Virginia and Maryland, and this area was officially named Washington in 1791, the only time in history that such an important region was named after a still-living president.

Although the location of Washington, D.C., was an acceptable compromise to the northern and southern states of the U.S., when the Civil War broke out, it turned into a liability for the Union. Because the nation's capital was so close to the Confederate border, it was in constant danger of attack, which greatly affected Union strategy. There was even a time, early in the Civil War, when it seemed as though Maryland might join the Confederacy—and if it had, the war's outcome might have been very different!

Why do so many states have strange names?

Compared to New Jersey, New Hampshire, and Georgia, states like Mississippi, Wisconsin, and Minnesota seem to have much more interesting names. This is because the original thirteen states derived their names from English places and people (such as York and Jersey), while most of the other states are named after their original Native American inhabitants. For example, the name Oklahoma is derived from the Choctaw phrase for "red people"!

Banks

What does a bank do?

You might think banks were invented so people could have a safe place to store their money. But that's only part of the story: while it's nice not to have to keep your life savings stashed under your mattress, the real purpose of banks is to create a "pool" of money that can be tapped as a source for loans.

When you deposit your money in a bank, it's not as if a big white bag with a dollar sign painted on the side is suddenly dropped into the bank's vault. Rather, your savings—and the savings of thousands of other depositors—exists as a big pile of "virtual," or electronic, cash. The bank lends out this money to other customers—say, if they want to start a business or buy a house—and makes a profit by charging them interest on the loans.

If all this strikes you as slightly reckless, there's no need to worry. Any depositor who wants his money back can pull it out of the bank whenever he wants—and thanks to the Federal Deposit Insurance Corporation (FDIC), which automatically insures bank deposits, even a bankrupt bank can't wipe out its customers' life savings!

What is an investment bank?

The type of bank in which your parents invest their money (and have checking and savings accounts) is known technically as a commercial bank. Investment banks don't deal with everyday customers: rather, they work with companies (and some wealthy individuals) to raise hundreds of millions of dollars for investment purposes. Usually, when you hear about one company buying another, the money has been raised by a group of investment banks working together.

What is the difference between a checking and a savings account?

Most bank customers maintain two separate accounts: a checking account (from which they remove money to pay their bills and other expenses), and a savings account. The main difference between these accounts is that a savings account usually pays more interest—which is why, if they can, most people choose to keep the bulk of their money in savings accounts.

Why is it called a "bank run?"

To a large extent, banks are based on trust: depositors trust the bank to look after their money, and the bank repays this trust by (in theory) not using its customers' money for foolish purposes. A "bank run" is when customers are concerned about a bank's financial health (or the health of the economy in general), and they all run to pull out their money at the same time. The reason this is a problem is because, on any given day, a bank has usually loaned out more money than it has on hand—so it can't satisfy all its depositors!

The worst bank runs occurred during the Great Depression, when so many people tried to reclaim their savings that President Franklin D. Roosevelt declared a four-day "bank holiday" in order to stabilize the economy. Since that time, bank runs have largely been averted by the creation of the Federal Deposit Insurance Corporation, which insures peoples' savings accounts up to $100,000 each. (However, FDIC insurance doesn't cover the contents of safe-deposit boxes, in which bank customers can store important documents or small, valuable items like jewelry.)

What is the difference between an ordinary bank and a savings & loan?

Technically, "savings & loans" ("S&L"s for short) have a much narrower focus than commercial banks: all they're supposed to do is open savings accounts for customers and make mortgage loans (that is, lend customers money so they can buy houses). The S&L crisis of the 1980s—in which thousands of these institutions failed, losing investors more than $100 billion—was mainly caused by the expansion of S&Ls into other, riskier types of loans, which weren't insured by the U.S. government!

Why is it called a PIN?

The initials PIN stand for "personal identification number," which is a bit of a misnomer since many PINs contain letters as well as numbers! A PIN is the equivalent of an online password: it's the sequence of buttons you push on an automated teller machine (after you slide in your bank card) in order to remove cash from your account. Because a PIN is necessary to withdraw money, a criminal who steals your bankcard won't have much luck without it!

What is an overdraft?

Every now and then, people write checks when they don't have enough money in their checking accounts to cover the balance. Usually, this is an honest mistake, but the bank still penalizes the "overdraft" by imposing a penalty (say, about $50 or so). However, people who habitually overdraft can get into serious trouble, since writing "bad checks" is a federal crime punishable by long prison sentences!

College

Why is it called the Ivy League?

The "Ivy League" consists of eight of the most prestigious colleges in the U.S.: Brown, Columbia, Cornell, Dartmouth, Harvard, Princeton, Yale, and the University of Pennsylvania. Yes, it's named after the ivy plants that grow on the outside of old, historic buildings, but since many other colleges also have ivy, the real reason these eight schools are grouped together is because they belong to the same division of the NCAA (the National Collegiate Athletic Association).

What is the difference between a college and a university?

When you're only in grade school, college and university sound equally far away. But though these words are often used interchangeably, they have slightly different meanings. In the U.S., a college is usually an institution that grants students a four-year degree (say, a Bachelor of Arts). Universities also bestow four-year degrees, but students there can go on to earn a more advanced "postgraduate" degree like an M.A. or Ph.D. Over the years, this distinction has blurred, so many institutions with "college" in their names are technically universities.

What was the first university in the U.S.?

Although it's not clear whether it's the oldest university in the technical sense (see the definition elsewhere on this page), there's no question that Harvard is the oldest institution of higher learning in America. In fact, Harvard predates the U.S. by 140 years—it was founded in Boston in 1636, and the Declaration of Independence wasn't drafted until 1776.

Just to show how times have changed, Harvard is named after the minister John Harvard, who willed the two-year-old school a small amount of money and a library of a few hundred books. Today, just getting a university to name a single building after you requires a gift of millions of dollars!

Harvard is probably the single most prestigious university in America and has produced no less than seven American presidents (including Franklin D. Roosevelt and John F. Kennedy). Every year, thousands of hopeful high-school students apply for admission, but only a small percentage wind up being accepted.

What are fraternities and sororities?

You may have overheard your mom or dad reminiscing about the good ol' days at "Beta Theta Phi" or "Phi Delta Theta." These aren't planets in another galaxy, but examples of college sororities and fraternities, which traditionally name themselves using Greek letters. Sororities (based on the Latin word for sister, "soror") are campus organizations for college women, while fraternities (from the Latin word for brother, "frater") are for college men.

However, a fraternity or sorority is much more than an exclusive club. Usually, members live together in a special house located off campus, and band together for social activities like parties and pep rallies. Traditionally, the hardest part about "Greek" life is getting into the sorority or fraternity of your choice: pledges have to complete a series of (often unpleasant) tasks to prove that they're worthy of inclusion. In the past, some fraternities would subject pledges to physically abusive "hazing" (like being swatted repeatedly on the rear with a whiffle bat), but most colleges and universities have banned this practice.

What is graduate school?

Most college students are content to earn their four-year degrees and venture out into the working world. Others, however, want to pursue more intensive study in their chosen field, and go on to earn a Ph.D., or "doctor of philosophy," degree (despite the name, Ph.D. candidates aren't limited to philosophy; they can study anything from biology to psychology to literature).

A graduate school is an institution of higher learning that bestows Ph.D.s, as well as other advanced degrees.

Why do schools offer athletic scholarships?

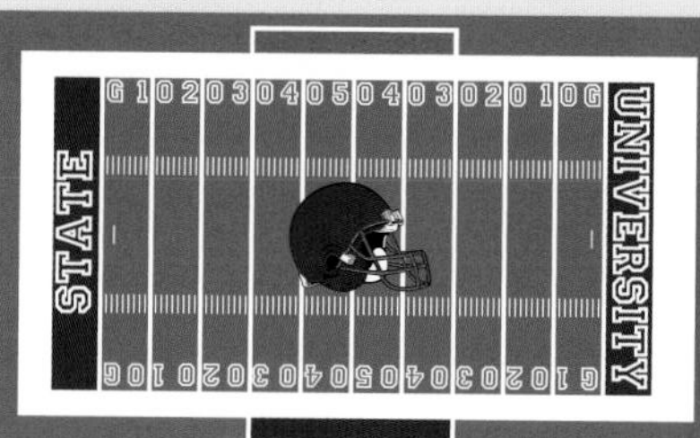

The performance of a college's football or basketball team can have a direct bearing on its prestige: winning teams receive more attention from the media and attract more applicants and financial donors. That's why schools award scholarships—that is, free four-year educations—to the very best high-school athletes.

What is a major?

If you have an older brother or sister going to college, you may have heard talk about having to choose a "major." A major is the subject on which a college student spends most of her time: biology majors, for example, mostly take biology classes in their junior and senior years. College students can also have "minors," a secondary, less intensive course of study in another field (so a biology major can have a minor in, say, English literature).

What was the first newspaper?

Because all written materials had to be laboriously copied out by hand (or etched in stone!), it's a safe bet that there were no newspapers before the middle of the 15th century, when Johann Gutenberg invented the printing press. After that, the correct answer to this question depends on how you define the word "newspaper." For instance, a letter from Christopher Columbus was set in type and circulated in the Spanish city of Barcelona in 1493, and that certainly qualified as news—and during the 16th and 17th centuries, it was common to print up sheets and pamphlets devoted to specific events, though these usually had a very small print run.

However, if you define newspapers as widely circulated publications covering multiple news events, the first weekly specimens appeared in Germany in 1609, after which the idea spread quickly to other cities in Europe. In America, the very first newspaper appeared in Boston in 1690, bearing the literal title "Public Occurrences, both Foreign and Domestic." Amazingly, the first edition of this paper had a story about the day of "thanksgiving" that had recently been celebrated by the Indians in Plymouth Colony!

Why are newspaper comics smaller than they used to be?

Up until the 1950s, most newspapers (especially on Sundays) printed comics in large, lavish, full-page format, and wouldn't stint on the size of daily strips, either. Unfortunately, the rising cost of newsprint over the years has prompted newspaper editors to print comics in smaller and smaller sizes, so today you can find as many as two dozen strips crammed onto two pages! (Since most people believe today's comics aren't nearly as good as they used to be, that may not be much of a loss.)

What was the first advice column?

Today, practically every newspaper has one, but when a young reporter named Marie Manning wrote the very first advice column in 1898 (in the *New York Evening Journal*), it created a huge sensation. Manning's column was called "Dear Beatrice Fairfax," and the first installment answered questions from proper young women seeking advice about dating. By the way, because the column was written under a pseudonym (that is, a fake name), "Beatrice Fairfax" became famous, while most people wouldn't recognize Marie Manning if they bumped into her on the street!

Why are some newspapers bigger than others?

Basically, all newspapers in the U.S. come in two sizes, "tabloid" and "broadsheet." In most major cities, the newspapers are broadsheets—these are the ones you buy folded in half, with sections inside sections, kind of like an onion (examples are *USA Today* and *The New York Times*). A tabloid paper is slightly smaller and unfolded; a good example is the *New York Daily News*. (You may have heard the phrase "tabloid journalism," which implies that tabloids are less devoted to the truth than broadsheets. This may once have been the case, but not anymore!)

Why does newsprint rub off on your hands?

When a newspaper is hot off the press, its ink (and the paper it's been printed on) hasn't quite dried yet. This is because most newspapers are printed with cheap, air-dried ink that isn't designed to last for decades (unlike, say, the ink used to print books and magazines). Because there's still some moisture in the paper, in the ink, and on your fingertips, you're likely to find your hands smudged after you read your morning paper.

Why is it called "yellow journalism"?

In the late 1890s, the American newspaper publisher William Randolph Hearst wanted the U.S. to go to war with Spain over the island of Cuba. In order to drum up public support for the war, Hearst instructed one of his newspapers, *The New York Journal*, to run sensational (and usually exaggerated) stories about mistreatment of Cubans by Spanish colonists. There's even a story (which may or may not be true) that Hearst told a reluctant photographer, "You supply the pictures, and I'll supply the war!"

So where does the color yellow come in? *The New York Journal* was known for running a full-page comic strip called "The Yellow Kid," and the term "yellow" attached itself to Hearst's brand of journalism. Today, "yellow journalism" refers to any newspaper (or magazine or TV show) that deliberately misstates or exaggerates the truth in order to inflame the public or accomplish a specific political goal. This can be as obvious as putting a shocking photo on the cover with a huge headline, or as subtle as reporting only one side of a story (and not seeking comments from people who hold a different view).

Post Office

How many people work for the Postal Service?

Let's put it this way: if the U.S. Postal Service were an army, other countries would be very, very worried. This huge organization employs about 700,000 people, not to mention almost 200,000 vehicles (mostly trucks, plus some airplanes). As you might have guessed, the bulk of this activity is funded by the cost of stamps, with some additional subsidies provided by the U.S. government.

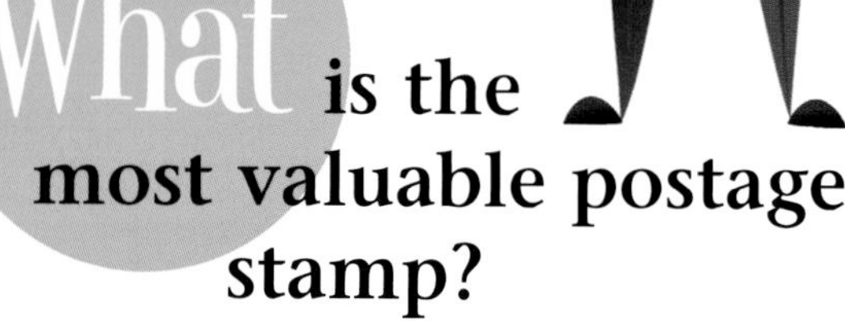

What is the most valuable postage stamp?

Like rare paintings, rare postage stamps can command astronomical prices from collectors. The most expensive stamp in the world is the one-cent "black on magenta," which was issued in British Guiana in 1856; the only copy ever found sold in 1980 for close to a million dollars. In the U.S., the champ is a stamp issued in 1867 bearing a portrait of Benjamin Franklin (the founder of the U.S. Postal Service). Only two copies of this stamp are known to exist, and each is worth only slightly less than the one-of-a-kind "black on magenta."

Why is it called a "ZIP code"?

As hard as it may be to believe, ZIP codes weren't widely used until the early 1960s—and even then, they weren't mandatory until the 1970s! Basically, the Postal Service started assigning ZIP codes for the same reason phone companies hand out area codes: there are simply too many people receiving mail, in too many different parts of the country, for local post offices to route mail correctly without additional information besides the recipient's name, address, city, and state.

As for the "ZIP" in ZIP code, that stands for "Zone Improvement Plan"—though it didn't escape the Postal Service's notice that the acronym "ZIP" conjures up an image of especially speedy and accurate mail delivery.

Today, in many big cities, even a five-digit ZIP code isn't enough to reliably get mail to its destination. That's why people can choose to use a nine-digit "ZIP + 4" code, which isn't mandatory (yet) but may eventually become so as the U.S. population continues to grow.

Why is some mail second-class?

An ordinary letter bearing an address and a stamp is what's known as first-class mail. Second-class mail isn't really mail at all, but the name that the U.S. Postal Service gives to periodicals (that is, magazines and newspapers) that can be mailed at a lower postage rate. Because it doesn't want companies to take unfair advantage of this system, the Post Office has very strict rules about what qualifies as second-class mail.

Why isn't there any mail on Sundays?

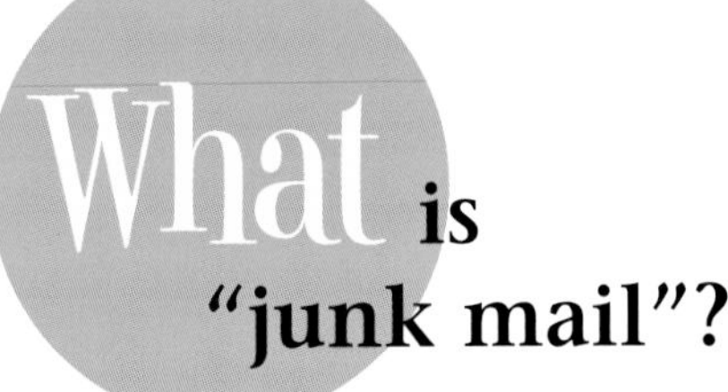

Since most government offices are closed on Sundays, not to mention all schools and a large proportion of stores, it's no surprise that the post office doesn't operate on that day. The real question here is: why do we get mail on Saturdays?

Ever since the U.S. Postal Service was founded (by Benjamin Franklin in 1755), it has operated as a monopoly—that is, it's the only organization allowed to deliver first-class mail. Long before the days of overnight carriers like UPS or Federal Express, it made sense to schedule Saturday delivery, since the Postal Service was the only means of mailing important documents—and if a crucial letter didn't arrive on Friday, the recipient often couldn't afford to wait until the following Monday.

In recent years, government officials have suggested eliminating Saturday delivery, citing the increased availability of overnight delivery services and e-mail (not to mention the prospect of lowering the Postal Service's huge budget). However, this measure has yet to pass, largely because of opposition from junk mailers and the postal unions representing letter carriers.

What is "junk mail"?

More properly (and less insultingly) known as "bulk mail," what most people call "junk mail" refers to all those menus, coupons, circulars, and credit-card solicitations that wind up in your mailbox every day. Advertisers like bulk mail because the post office grants them a discount for sending out huge amounts of these materials, most of which are thrown out without being opened!

How many letters are mailed each day?

According to the U.S. Postal Service, billions of letters are mailed every day—but since there are only 300 million people in the United States, the majority of that mail is clearly of the "junk" variety (defined elsewhere on this page). The fact is, the use of e-mail for friendship, romance, and business has pretty much ended the practice of sending handwritten letters via "snail mail," so the Post Office doesn't handle nearly as many of these letters as it used to!

How were sewers invented?

There's an old saying that necessity is the mother of invention, and that helps to explain why sewers of one type or another have been around since a few thousand years B.C. After all, would you rather let the waste accumulate each time you went to the bathroom, or find a way to discharge it into a deep underground cesspool or a faraway river or creek?

Although the Romans were famous for their aquatic engineering—which included networks of sewers connecting homes, from which waste was flushed into underground passages, and aqueducts that transported clean water from rivers—the Indus civilization of Mohenjo-Daro (in modern Pakistan) had the Romans beat by a couple thousand years. The houses in this ancient city had surprisingly modern bathrooms, which discharged waste directly into channels in the street that tilted down to the local river.

Oddly enough, the more "advanced" European cities of the Middle Ages often neglected to build sewers at all—which not only offended people's sense of smell, but made them more susceptible to infectious diseases.

What is a septic tank?

Since homes out in the country aren't connected to the sewer systems of towns and cities, they need a reliable, safe way to dispose of waste. A septic tank is a specially designed container that's usually buried underground, in the yard. As the waste drains into the tank from the home's bathrooms, the heavier portions float to the bottom where they're digested by bacteria, while the cleaner water on top is slowly absorbed into the soil.

Why is it called a toilet?

In 18th-century France, noblewomen lined their dressing rooms with toile, a kind of soft, fancy cloth. Eventually, the process of getting washed and dressed became known as a lady's "toilet," a name that somehow attached itself to the flushing contraption we use today. (By the way, in England toilets are called "loos," probably because sailors used to urinate over a ship's leeward side, that is, away from the wind.)

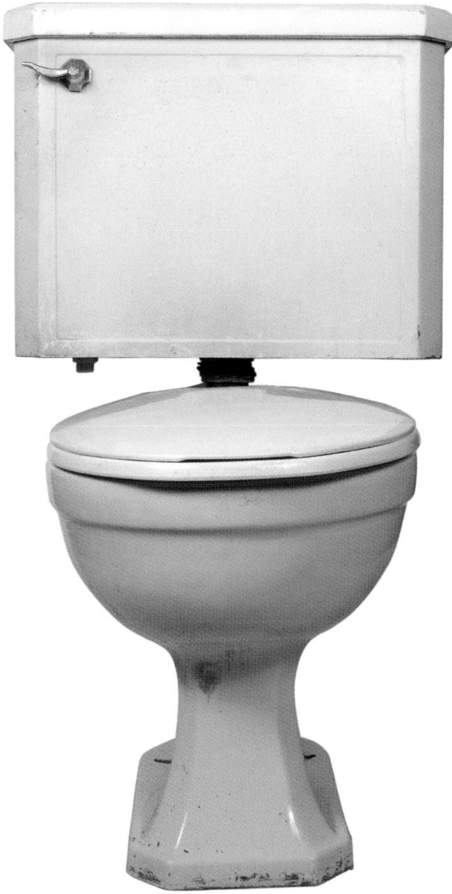

How does a sewage treatment plant work?

Big cities produce much, much more in the way of sewage than the environment can safely handle. A sewage treatment plant is a large installation in which most of the raw sewage is converted into a liquid "effluent," which can be safely discharged into a river or ocean. The remaining solid "sludge," though, has to be disposed of more carefully, often by drying it in big blocks and burying it underground.

Why did people once refuse to take baths?

During the Middle Ages in Europe, it was possible for an enterprising peasant to visit a public bath (since practically no one had running water at home) and get reasonably clean. However, after the Black Plague in the 14th century—which killed about one-third of Europe's population—Europeans developed a superstition about bathing, believing this practice helped spread disease by opening up the pores of the skin. (They also believed the Earth was flat, so you can get a pretty good idea of the state of knowledge around this time.)

Rather than take life-threatening baths, wealthier Europeans developed the practice of dousing themselves with heavy perfumes (and not a tiny dab, either, like your mom uses—more like emptying an entire bottle over your head!), while peasants didn't even bother to mask their odor. This lack of personal hygiene, combined with the lack of sewers, made cities like Paris so unbearable in summer that visitors never went there unless it was absolutely essential.

What is a chamber pot?

Before modern times, only a few civilizations had perfected the use of running water for toilets. Those that didn't—such as the European nation-states of the middle ages—had to rely on chamber pots, large bowls in which a person did his business (if he lived in a particularly filthy town, he might simply heave the contents out the window). One good thing about chamber pots was that they were democratic—everyone had to use them, whether a king or a peasant, though you can bet the king's was much nicer and he didn't have to empty it himself!

Stock Market

How does the stock market work?

In order to function properly, companies need "capital"—that is, reserves of cash that can be used to pay employees, invest in factories, or even buy other companies. For this reason, many firms sell "shares" of their operations to ordinary people, by means of what's known as a stock exchange. This allows the company to raise money it wouldn't ordinarily have, and it allows folks to invest their spare money in a promising company, in the hopes that the company will make a profit and its stock price will rise.

A firm can't just list itself on the stock market, rake in tons of cash, and do whatever it pleases. A publicly owned company has specific obligations set by the U.S. Government: for instance, it has to issue annual reports that show how it's been spending its investors' money, and it has to allow stockholders to vote on important issues, such as mergers with other companies. Assuming it meets these standards, the company's shares can be bought and sold in a stock exchange, along with the shares of hundreds (or thousands) of other firms.

What is a mutual fund?

Many investors don't like to tie up all their money in one company—because if that company goes bankrupt, their life savings could be wiped out! For this reason, most everyday investors prefer to buy "mutual funds," which own shares of dozens (or even hundreds) of companies at any one time. This way, if one company happens to go under, the price of the fund as a whole will drop only a little bit, if at all.

What is the difference between a recession and a depression?

There's an old wisecrack to the effect that a recession is when your friend's father loses his job, but a depression is when your father loses his job. Technically, a recession occurs whenever the U.S. Gross National Product (a measure of total spending) stops growing for a few months in a row. As painful as they can be for some people, most recessions are relatively mild. A depression, on the other hand, is an unusually severe recession that puts millions of people out of work and does serious damage to the nation's economy.

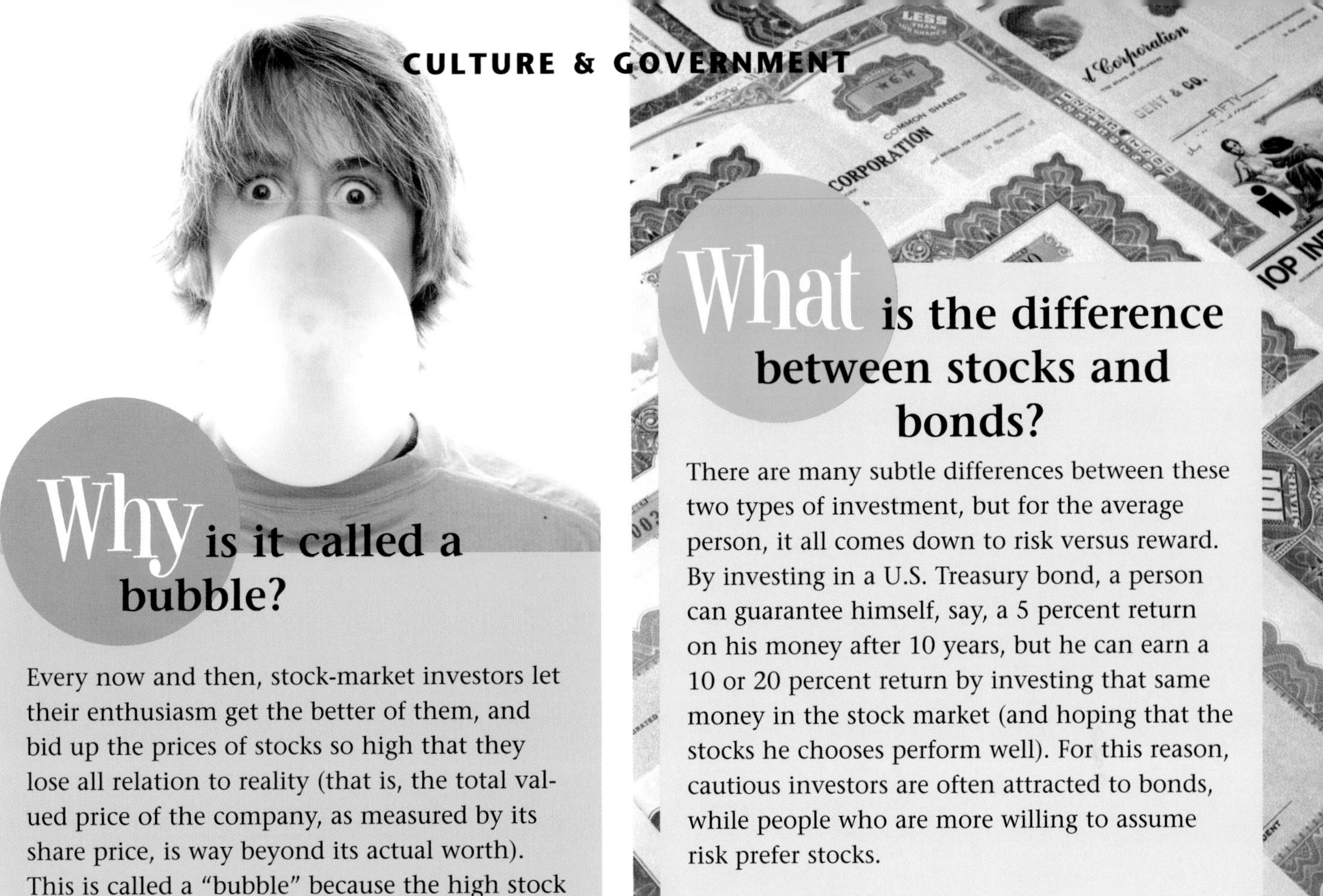

Why is it called a bubble?

Every now and then, stock-market investors let their enthusiasm get the better of them, and bid up the prices of stocks so high that they lose all relation to reality (that is, the total valued price of the company, as measured by its share price, is way beyond its actual worth). This is called a "bubble" because the high stock prices are like balloons filled with hot air that deflate shortly afterward, causing lots of people to lose lots of money!

What is the difference between stocks and bonds?

There are many subtle differences between these two types of investment, but for the average person, it all comes down to risk versus reward. By investing in a U.S. Treasury bond, a person can guarantee himself, say, a 5 percent return on his money after 10 years, but he can earn a 10 or 20 percent return by investing that same money in the stock market (and hoping that the stocks he chooses perform well). For this reason, cautious investors are often attracted to bonds, while people who are more willing to assume risk prefer stocks.

What was Black Friday?

In the financial world, the adjective "black" applies to any day in which the price of stocks takes a sudden, sharp turn for the worse. Although most people associate "Black Friday" with the stock market collapse of 1929 (which was followed by the Great Depression), Friday was only one of a number of "black" days that October, coming smack between "Black Thursday" and "Black Monday." By the end of 1929, stocks had lost nearly half their value, wiping out millions of investors.

You may be surprised to learn that the largest one-day drop in the stock market happened not in 1929, but as recently as 1987. On that day (remembered, of course, as "Black Monday"), the Dow Jones Industrial Average—a measure of the value of large, commonly held stocks—plunged more than 500 points, or almost 25 percent. As you can guess, the 1987 crash precipitated a severe economic downturn, though not a depression, shortly afterward. (There have been big one-day point drops since then, but a 500-point loss is less painful when the Dow Jones is at 10,000 than when it's at 3,000!)

What is an audit?

Want to have fun with your parents? The next time you bring in the mail, sneak up behind them on the couch and yell, "tax audit!"

Although they're less common than they used to be, audits are an extremely stressful experience for people of all income levels. What triggers an audit is the belief of the Internal Revenue Service (the government agency responsible for collecting taxes) that a taxpayer has either paid less in taxes than he's supposed to, or is earning more income than he has declared (that is, has officially reported) to the government. (Some tax returns, honest or dishonest, are also audited randomly as part of the government's Taxpayer Compliance Measurement Program.)

Usually, an audit involves going down to the local IRS office and proving (with the appropriate documents) that your tax return has not been conjured up out of thin air. As you can guess, audits are targeted far more often at people earning more than $100,000 per year, since there are fewer opportunities for low-wage earners to cheat the government.

What are dependents?

The federal government doesn't require all people who earn the same income to pay the same amount of federal taxes. To lessen the tax burden on families, taxpayers are allowed to claim children as "dependents," which lowers the taxable part of their income by a few thousand dollars per child. So the next time your mom punishes you for breaking a piece of furniture, remind her how much money she's saved by having you!

Why do some states have higher tax rates than others?

As a general rule, highly populated states with a wide range of social programs and benefits (such as California and New York) impose higher taxes than smaller states like Nebraska or Rhode Island. There are some important exceptions, though: Texas (the second biggest state in the union) has no state income tax at all, while Montana, with only about a million people, has the highest income tax (for residents with high incomes) of any state in the union!

Why are taxes progressive?

It stands to reason that people who earn more money have the resources to pay more taxes. For this reason, most taxes in the U.S. are progressive, meaning that folks who earn, say, a million dollars a year pay a higher percentage of their income in taxes than people who earn $20,000 a year. (That's what your parents mean when they talk about the "tax bracket" they're in.)

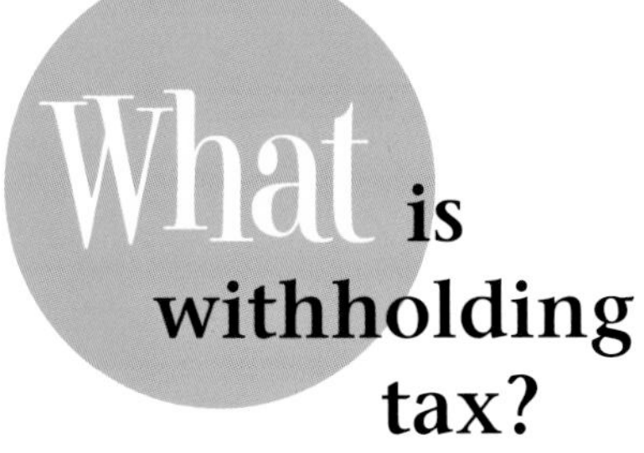

What is withholding tax?

Although all U.S. citizens are subject to federal income tax, few actually have to write out a check. Instead, the government requires businesses to "withhold" a certain portion of an employee's paycheck for tax purposes, meaning a job that technically pays $1,000 per week is only worth about $700 when the paycheck arrives. The reasoning behind the withholding tax is that it reduces tax evasion, since workers might be tempted to (illegally) keep a larger portion of that $1,000 check.

Why do we pay taxes?

It's true that the government of the United States is run by and for the people, but it has to be *paid for* by the people, as well. Not only is the government responsible for national defense (a hugely expensive proposition, even when no major wars are going on), but it has to invest in public infrastructure (such as repairing dams and interstate highways), programs like Social Security (which maintain workers' living standards after they retire), and the national debt (the interest of which amounts to hundreds of billions of dollars every year!).

Although the federal government claims the biggest chunk of the average person's tax bill, your parents usually pay state taxes and sometimes a city tax as well. There are also real-estate taxes, sales taxes, and "hidden" taxes that show up almost unnoticed in your phone and cable bills.

As unfair as all this sounds, though, citizens in the U.S. actually get off pretty lightly compared to other countries. Most Europeans, for instance, pay about half of their incomes in taxes, while we pay anywhere from 10 to 40 percent in this country.

How long has there been an income tax?

Although taxes of various kinds had been collected long before, the federal government began taxing income only in 1913, after Congress passed the 16th Amendment to the U.S. Constitution. Even today, some people insist that the government doesn't have the constitutional power to tax its citizens, but (as you can imagine) their arguments have fallen on deaf ears!

Tests

What does an IQ test measure?

Ever since it was developed by Alfred Binet in 1905, the IQ (intelligence quotient) test has been a lightning-rod for controversy. This test consists of multiple-choice questions that measure verbal comprehension, perceptual skills, and other quantities that (according to psychologists) are directly related to intelligence. The majority of people in the U.S. have IQ scores ranging from 85 to 115; a score of 150 or above is considered genius level, and anything under 70 may indicate mental retardation.

Theoretically, a person's IQ is a direct indication of how smart he is; the problem is what's meant by the word "smart"! When he first devised his test, Binet only meant to identify grade school students who needed extra help, not to classify huge segments of the population according to their IQ scores. Today, many people believe the classic IQ test really measures only one, very specialized kind of intelligence, and ignores the "street smarts" that most people use in their daily lives.

What does it mean to be "graded on a curve"?

Some tests are graded against an objective standard: for example, if you get 15 questions right out of a total of 20, your grade is a 75 (meaning you answered 75 percent of the questions correctly). When a test is graded on a curve, that means you're being compared to your classmates rather than to a list of correct answers—so if you get only 15 questions right, but that's the best performance in the class, your grade would be 100!

What is cramming?

If you know you have to take a big test in two weeks, there are two ways to prepare: by studying a little bit every day, or by trying to memorize everything all at once on the night before the test, which is known as "cramming." Although cramming is popular among high-school and college kids, it's not nearly as effective as slowly and surely learning the subject you're being tested on!

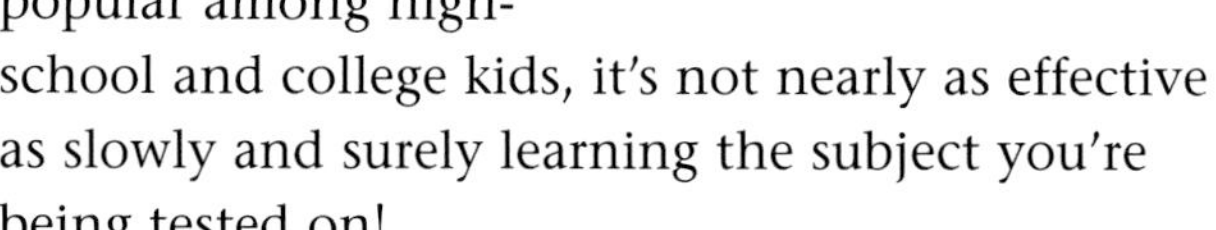

How do teachers know the answers to tests?

As hard as it may be to believe, your science teacher doesn't necessarily know all the answers to that science quiz right off the top of his head (especially if he pulled it out of a textbook and didn't think up the questions himself). That's why most school textbooks have "teacher's guides," a special teachers-only edition that provides the answers to all those problems listed at the ends of chapters!

What is the "Nation's Report Card"?

Every year, the U.S. Department of Education tests a national sample of public- and private-school kids in the 4th, 8th, and 12th grades, in order to measure their performance (and the performance of the U.S. educational system in general). This test, the results of which are sometimes called the "Nation's Report Card," often makes headlines, especially if it shows that U.S. kids are falling behind their counterparts in other countries.

Why are tests standardized?

A "standardized" test consists mostly of multiple-choice or true-or-false questions that have only one right answer (and can be graded by computer), as well as the occasional essay question that has to be evaluated by an actual person. The reason tests are standardized is so their results can be compared from school to school and region to region, as a measure of how well (or how badly) students are performing.

Why do high-school students take SATs?

If your older sister has been especially tense lately, it may be because she's preparing to take the Scholastic Aptitude Test, or SAT. This "standardized" test gauges a student's knowledge of math, science, and English, and its scores are considered by colleges when they decide which applicants to accept. There's also a "preliminary" SAT, or PSAT, which determines the winners of the National Merit Scholarship (but, for most students, really just amounts to a "practice" SAT).

Until recently, the SAT consisted mainly of multiple-choice questions in English, math, and science. In 2005, though, an essay section was added to the test, on the premise that high-school students should be judged on their ability to write, not just to answer multiple-choice questions!

Because the SAT is so important, many high school students take SAT preparation courses, which promise to raise their scores by a few percentage points. Although these courses can be effective, when it comes right down to it, there's nothing like paying attention in school and doing your own studying to get a high score on the SATs!

What is globalization?

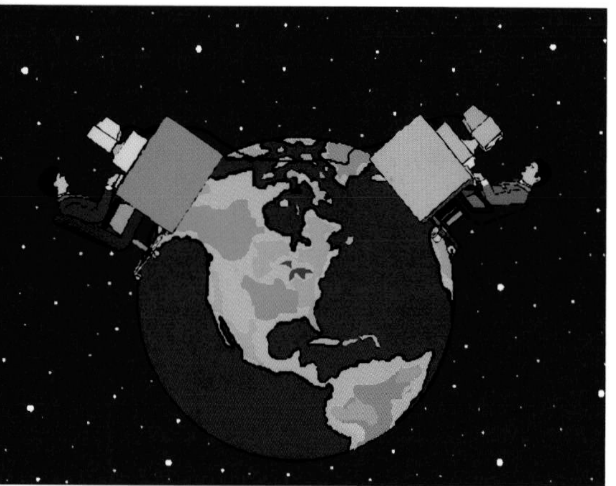

By itself, "globalization" is a fairly harmless word—it simply refers to the fact that the economies of all the world's nations are much more interconnected (and dependent on each other) than they used to be. The reason you may have heard your parents talking about globalization, or read stories about it in the newspaper, is that to most ordinary people "globalization" means the increasing tendency of American companies to "outsource" jobs to countries where workers don't have to be paid as much money.

This outsourcing has two effects, one positive and one negative. On the positive side, it gives the citizens of countries like India and China the chance to improve their standard of living (as low as their weekly wages might seem to us, that money goes a long way in the places these workers live!). On the negative side, though, the result can be a loss of jobs for American workers, or a decrease in pay as wages "even out" around the globe.

As painful a process as it can be, the fact is that globalization, in one form or another, is here to stay—the big question is what the governments of the world do to meet this challenge!

What does it mean to be a "most favored nation"?

Countries that trade with one another like to know that they're not being taken advantage of—or, at the very least, that they're not being taken advantage of any more than any other country! When a country is granted "most favored nation" status, it means that it receives all the advantages of other trading countries, and not that it's somehow "special" and entitled to receive better terms than anyone else.

What is the trade deficit?

A country's "balance of trade" is calculated from the amount of goods it exports (that is, sells to other countries) and the amount of goods it imports (that is, buys from other countries). A trade deficit results when a country imports many more goods than it exports. The U.S. has a trade deficit of a few hundred billion dollars, but experts disagree about whether this is a good or bad thing.

What is NAFTA?

Signed into law in 1994, the North American Free Trade Agreement is a trade treaty among the U.S., Mexico, and Canada. Basically, NAFTA is meant to eliminate trade barriers (such as tariffs) and create one big North American market without any unfair rules or impediments. What makes NAFTA controversial is that some people believe it encourages U.S. corporations to move their factories to Mexico, where labor costs are much cheaper.

Why are tariffs so controversial?

They may sound dull, but tariffs—that is, taxes imposed on goods imported from other nations—are among the most potent weapons a country has, short of actual guns and bombs!

Usually, a country will impose a tariff in order to protect its own industries. For example, a high tariff on imported cotton goods has the effect of shielding that country's cotton growers from competition: an imported cotton shirt that would cost $10 without the tariff may cost $15 with the tariff, making a "home-grown" shirt a better buy for consumers. Needless to say, these tariffs wouldn't be popular among countries that export cotton, which may feel they're being unfairly excluded from a profitable market.

Tariffs are closely intertwined with the issue of "free trade." Ideally, some economists believe, tariff barriers will become a thing of the past, and all the countries of the world will learn how to trade with one another on an even playing field. As logical as it sounds, though, free trade could have a devastating impact on workers in certain countries, so it has to be implemented very carefully!

Why are they called sweatshops?

In some countries, workers are crammed into small, hot factories and paid ridiculously low wages for long hours of labor (usually, these are nations that lack basic worker-protection laws, such as a minimum wage). You often don't hear about these "sweatshops" unless a large company happens to buy merchandise from one and sells it at extremely low prices—which basically amounts to taking advantage of other people's misery!

What is a multinational corporation?

Today, most big, brand-name companies are multinational: that is, they maintain headquarters in various countries around the world, and sell their products around the globe (McDonald's is an especially large multinational, as are Honda, Toshiba, and Coca-Cola). Amazingly, the budgets of the biggest multinational firms dwarf those of most small countries!

U.S. Cities

Why are they called the Twin Cities?

Technically, "twin cities" are any two cities—usually separated by a river—that have grown steadily over the years and intertwined with each other. In the U.S., the term "Twin Cities" refers to Minneapolis and St. Paul, in Minnesota, whose downtown areas are about 10 miles apart. Probably the most famous twin cities in the world are Buda and Pest in Hungary, which are better known to non-Hungarians as the single city of Budapest.

Why are so many state capitals in small cities?

It's not always the case that a state's biggest, most prominent city is also its capital—for example, the capital of New York state is Albany (about 300 miles north of New York City), and the capital of California is Sacramento, which is a long way from either San Francisco or Los Angeles. Partly, this is for historical reasons: Sacramento, for instance, was made California's capital in the mid-19th century, long before those other cities experienced their growth spurts.

But there's another, more subtle reason that some state capitals are located in smaller cities. Take New York as an example: because New York City already accounts for 40 percent of the state's population, the citizens who live upstate may not be particularly eager to locate the state legislature there, since this would give New York City even more power over non-city residents. In fact, many non-city residents prefer their state capitals to be located in smaller towns, since this (at least theoretically) gives them more of a say in issues that affect the entire state.

What is the oldest city in the U.S.?

You probably think the answer to this question is New York (or maybe Boston), but you have to remember that the English and Dutch weren't the first people to explore the New World. In fact, the oldest city in the U.S. is St. Augustine, Florida, which was founded by the Spanish explorer Juan Ponce de Leon in 1513—about a hundred years before New York was settled by Dutch colonists!

Why is it called New York?

As you may have learned in history class, the city we call New York was originally known as New Amsterdam, after the Dutch settled the island of Manhattan in 1613. The burgeoning city remained in Dutch hands until 1664, when it was conquered by the British, who promptly renamed it "New York" after the Duke of York, a prominent British nobleman. (There are still many Dutch place names in New York—for example, the borough of Brooklyn was named after the Dutch town "Breukelen.")

Until the 1800s, most of New York City remained crowded on the southern part of Manhattan; pretty much everything above 14th Street was undeveloped farmland (that's about two-thirds of the island, and all of midtown, for those of you unfamiliar with the city). Today, New York City—which includes the island of Manhattan as well as the other four boroughs of Brooklyn, Staten Island, Queens, and the Bronx—has more than 8 million residents, making it the biggest (and most densely packed) city in the U.S.

How did the Chicago Fire of 1871 start?

Only three times in American history has a major U.S. city come close to total destruction: the San Francisco earthquake of 1906, the "Great Chicago Fire" of 1871, and Hurricane Katrina in 2005, which flooded New Orleans. For a long time, it was believed that this fire—which left 90,000 people homeless out of a total population of 300,000—was caused by a cow kicking over a lantern into a pile of hay. In 1893, though, a reporter confessed to making up this story, so the exact cause of the fire is still a mystery!

What is the biggest city in the U.S.?

There are two ways to answer this question: by population, or by total area. In terms of population, the clear winner is New York, with a whopping 8 million residents. But in terms of total area, New York isn't even close: with less than a million residents, Jacksonville, Florida, has a total area of 874 square miles, compared to about 300 square miles for New York. In other words, you couldn't walk from one end of Jacksonville to the other even if you wanted to!

How did Philadelphia get its name?

Philadelphia is one of the few U.S. cities whose name is completely made up, rather than borrowed from a famous person or Indian tribe. William Penn, the founder of Pennsylvania and a strong believer in freedom and religious tolerance, named his capital city after the Greek phrase for "brotherly love." And it's a good thing, too—the Indian name for the Philadelphia region was the much less poetic-sounding "Shackamaxon."

What is telecommuting?

Workers today have a powerful tool that didn't exist 20 years ago—the Internet. At more and more companies, employees are allowed to work from home for one or two days a week, since they can easily communicate with colleagues over the phone and by e-mail. One of the big advantages of "telecommuting" is that a stay-at-home worker doesn't have to do any real commuting, which can eat up a couple of hours every day.

Why is it called a "job"?

Most 9-to-5 toilers would probably enjoy this explanation: in Old English, the word "jobbe" was derived from "gobbe," which means "mass" or "lump" (that meaning still persists today, as in a "gob of spit"). Beginning in the 16th century, people in England did "jobbes of work," which gradually shortened into just "job." (And no, since you were about to ask, the word "job" has nothing to do with the biblical figure Job.)

Why are people "fired?"

Usually because they haven't been doing a good job! Seriously, though, the phrase "you're fired" is derived from "fired out," a slang term of the late 1890s which meant "ejected" (as in, shot at high speed from a cannon). In the mid-20th century, employees often found out they were fired when they received a dreaded "pink slip" in their interoffice mail—though it's not clear how the color pink came to be associated with this bad news.

Why are they called "freelancers"?

In medieval times, most knights were attached to the estates of particular lords, and served that nobleman exclusively (usually by fighting in wars with other nation-states). Some knights, though, offered their services to the highest bidders, and became known as "free lances" after the sharp spears they carried.

Today, the life of a typical freelancer has very little to do with medieval chivalry. A freelancer isn't employed full-time by a specific company, but offers her services to a stable of clients that hire and pay her for specific projects. The upside to being a freelancer is the freedom to tackle interesting jobs and make lots of money; the downside is having to live from project to project, since a freelancer can't count on a regular weekly paycheck from an employer.

Thanks to the Internet (which enables people to work from home) there are many more freelancers in the U.S. than there used to be. Years ago, most freelancers were writers or designers, but now you can find freelancers in all fields, ranging from finance to computer programming to law enforcement.

What does it mean to "get a promotion"?

In a lot of ways, the working world is like the army: when you first join a company, you're a lowly private, but if you work hard and show ambition, you may be made into a corporal or major. In most companies, a promotion to a more important job (say, from salesperson to district sales manager) means three things: a bigger salary, increased responsibility, and more people to supervise.

Why do some companies have dress codes?

As a general rule, companies have dress codes—suits and ties for men, dresses for women—for two reasons: a dress code helps maintain a businesslike environment, and it pleases clients who may drop by unexpectedly (and who want to see that the lawyers they've hired aren't dressed like slobs!). However, even firms with dress codes may have a "Casual Friday" every week, on which employees can dress however they please (within limits, of course).

How many prisoners have escaped from Alcatraz?

Officially, the number is zero, though some people think otherwise. When Alcatraz, located on a small island in the middle of San Francisco Bay, was turned into a U.S. prison in 1933 (before then it had been a disciplinary barracks for the U.S. Navy), it quickly acquired a reputation as being impossible to escape from. First, even if an inmate somehow found his way out of the prison, he had to escape the island by swimming to the mainland across the freezing-cold bay. Second, as a maximum-security penitentiary, Alcatraz had a relatively small number of inmates (only about 250) and a large number of guards.

Even so, about three dozen prisoners tried to escape from Alcatraz until it was shut down in 1963; most of them were shot by guards or presumed drowned in San Francisco Bay. The most elaborate escape attempt was in 1962, when three inmates tunneled their way out of their cells and were never heard from again. Searchers never found the men's bodies, but because no one popped up years later claiming to be one of the escapees (which would have resulted in instant fame), it's most likely that they drowned.

How does parole work?

Unless he's been convicted of an especially serious crime like murder or armed robbery, the average prisoner doesn't have to serve his entire sentence. After a certain number of years, he becomes eligible for parole—that is, if he has behaved well in prison, he's released on the condition that he checks in regularly with a parole officer and gets a regular job. If a released prisoner is caught violating his parole, he can be sent back to jail without a trial.

Why is it called Sing Sing?

It sounds like the kind of place you'd go to hear a musical, but Sing Sing is the informal name for the maximum-security federal prison in Ossining, New York (about an hour's drive north of New York City). One of the oldest penitentiaries in the country, Sing Sing first opened for business in 1828—and back then it was known by an even more misleading name, Mount Pleasant!

What is probation?

Not all convicted criminals are packed off to jail. Depending on the nature of the offense, some judges will order probation instead, meaning the person has to report regularly (say, once a week or once a month) to a probation officer and agree to stay out of trouble. Violating the terms of your probation means a one-way ticket to the stony lonesome.

How was the electric chair invented?

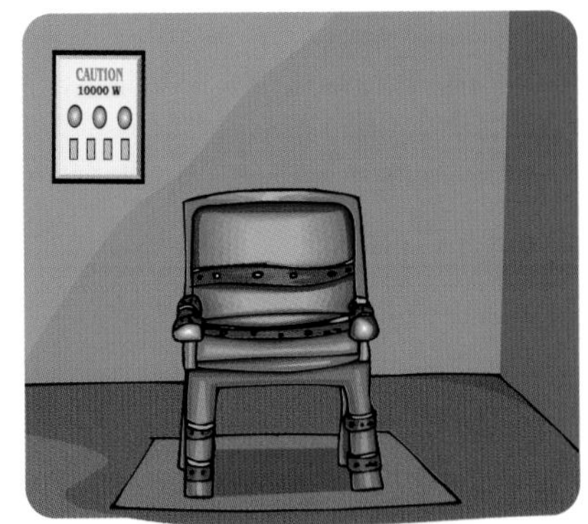

Like the guillotine—the fiendish device used during the French Revolution to cut off people's heads—the electric chair's day has pretty much come and gone. Early in the 20th century, though, "the chair" was widely feared by prisoners on death row, who considered it an especially horrible way to go.

In the 1880s—when large parts of the U.S. were still being electrified—an inventor named Harold Brown realized that electric current could be used to execute prisoners (he came to this conclusion after reading about the accidental death of a boy who had touched a downed power line). At that time, prisons were looking for a better means of capital punishment than hanging, which was unreliable. So Brown teamed up with Thomas Edison, the inventor of the light bulb, to come up with a better solution.

Unfortunately, it took a long time—and a lot of experimentation—to come up with a working electric chair. In order to convince prison officials that his invention was the way to go, Edison arranged to have a circus elephant killed by a jolt of AC current—not a high point in the great man's career!

What does it mean to post bail?

When a person is arrested for a crime, he doesn't necessarily have to stay in prison until he goes to trial. Depending on the nature of his offense, the judge may decide to assign bail—meaning the accused criminal has to put up a certain amount of money (say, $5,000) for the privilege of remaining free. If the defendant "skips bail" by running away before his trial, he loses his bail money—but if he cooperates, it's returned in full.

What is the difference between a felony and a misdemeanor?

In the broadest terms, a felony is a serious crime like murder, armed robbery, or arson, while a misdemeanor is a lesser offense like vandalism or petty theft. Most felonies are punishable by prison terms, but it's rare to have to go to jail for a misdemeanor—usually you just pay a hefty fine and receive a lecture from the judge.

What was Enigma?

At the start of World War II, the Nazis had what they thought was an insurmountable edge over the Allies: a coding machine called "Enigma." This device, about the size of a typewriter, used rotating wheels to encrypt messages in a sophisticated way that changed with every keystroke. Unfortunately for the Germans, they underestimated the ability of allied code breakers, who slowly, painstakingly cracked the Enigma code, partly with the help of primitive computers.

As crucial as it was to the war effort, cracking Enigma presented the allies with a thorny problem. If they acted on all the messages they intercepted—say, by tracking down and sinking every U-boat in the Atlantic Ocean—the Germans would realize that Enigma had been compromised, and would switch to a newer, possibly even harder-to-break code. By exploiting Enigma in a strategic way, though, the American and British intelligence services kept Germany completely in the dark: even as late as 1945, the Nazis were still sending Enigma messages, confident that they could never be broken!

What is quantum cryptography?

Since the beginning of history, people (mostly for military purposes) have tried to develop unbreakable codes. The science is way too complicated to go into here, but quantum cryptography is a system that causes a transmitted message to vanish, never to be retrieved, if it's intercepted (or eavesdropped on) by an unauthorized party—making it 100 percent secure!

What were the earliest codes?

Until modern times, most military codes involved substituting one letter for another—so that, say, the word "division" might appear in code as "aqcqdqof." However, these primitive codes were soon rendered obsolete by the practice of "frequency analysis." For example, analysts know which letters occur most frequently in the English language, so an entire page written in substitution code can be cracked fairly easily by matching the frequency of a code letter's appearance to the real letter it represents.

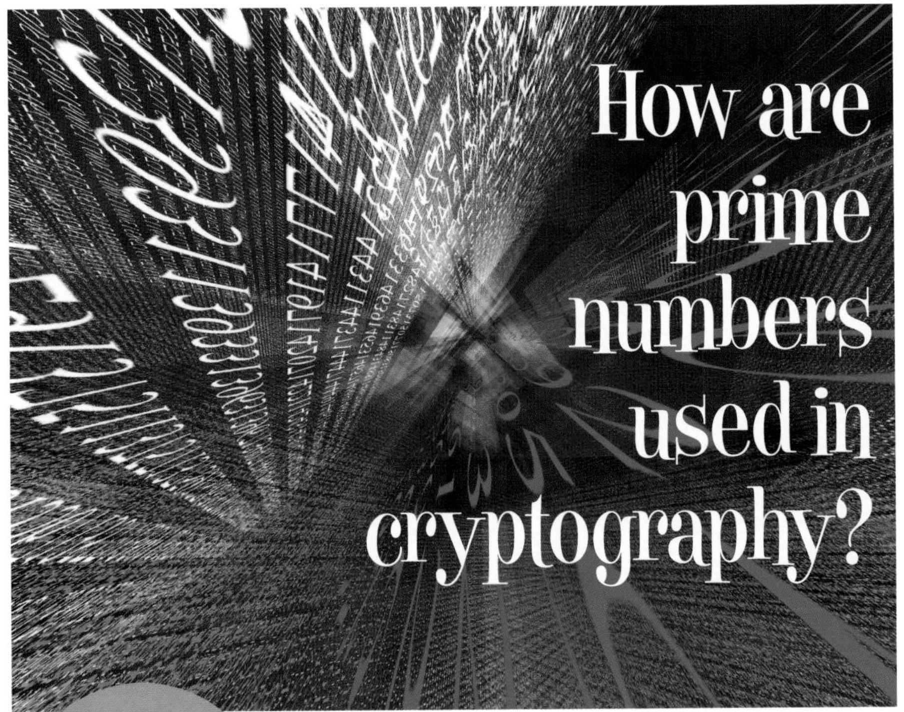

How are prime numbers used in cryptography?

As you may remember from math class, a prime number is any number that has no divisors other than itself and the number 1 (for example, the "composite" number 12 can be expressed as 2 times 2 times 3, but the prime number 17 can be expressed only as 17 times 1). While it's easy to show that numbers like 11 or 23 are prime, doing so is a much harder proposition for a number that's 100 or 200 digits long—but that hasn't stopped mathematicians from discovering bigger and bigger primes (there are an infinite number of primes, by the way).

The key to using prime numbers in cryptography is that, while it's relatively easy to multiply two huge primes together, it's nearly impossible to untangle them if you don't already know one of the divisors. (For example, unless you knew that 10,283 equals 91 times 113, you could spend an entire day trying to factor this number.) Most coding systems involve multiplying together huge, 100- or 200-number primes, resulting in an even bigger number that can be factored easily only by someone who already knows one of the primes used.

Why were they called "code talkers?"

During World War II, U.S. forces in the Pacific employed Navajo Indians as "code talkers"—that is, soldiers who relayed top-secret orders in their native language. The reason for this was that the Japanese had no familiarity with the Navajo language, and couldn't hope to break the code unless they captured a Navajo soldier and forced him to translate the messages—something they never managed to do.

What is steganography?

Since ancient civilizations weren't very good at cryptography, they often transmitted messages by writing them in invisible ink, tattooing them on soldiers's scalps under their hair, or sewing them into clothes—a practice known as "steganography." Since these messages are uncoded, steganography is technically a different animal from cryptography, though it has the same basic purpose.

What are ballistics?

In a sense, guns have their own fingerprints, just as people do. A ballistics specialist is a person who examines bullet holes at a crime scene and determines what kind of gun was used. If an actual bullet is recovered, either from inside the victim's body or from a nearby piece of furniture, the markings on it can be traced back to a specific gun, and hopefully to the criminal who fired it.

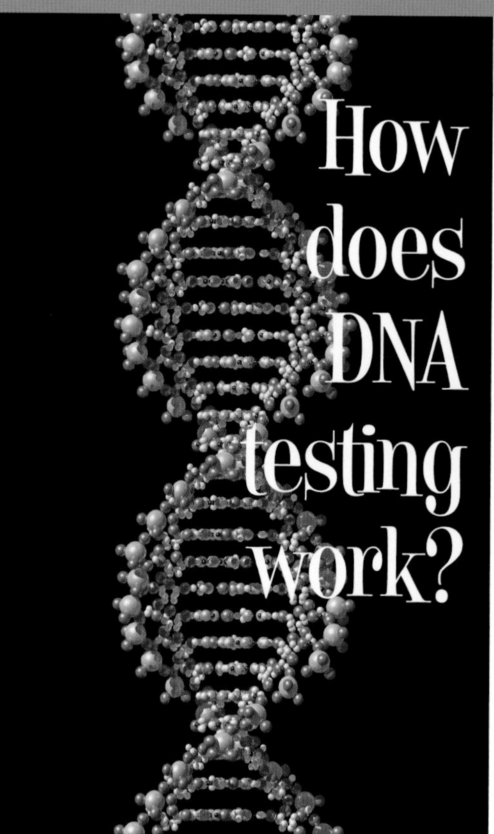

How does DNA testing work?

Every person is born with a unique genetic "fingerprint": the molecules of DNA in his or her cells. Essentially, DNA is what makes you "you," coding for everything from your hair color to your height to a good portion of your personality.

Because all our cells—and even our hair—contain DNA, detectives scour crime scenes for loose hair, flaked-off skin, or body fluids from which the perpetrator's DNA can be extracted. If the DNA is recovered intact, it can be taken to a laboratory and matched to a sample taken from the suspected criminal, to prove that he was at the crime scene. Properly used, DNA evidence can identify a suspect with an accuracy of one in a billion—making it way more reliable than fingerprinting.

Oddly enough, DNA testing usually finds its way into the news when it exonerates suspects who've been convicted of crimes they didn't commit. In many cases, a person has spent 10 or 20 years behind bars until analysis of a decades-old DNA sample from the crime scene proves he wasn't the culprit after all!

What is a statute of limitations?

After a crime has been committed, prosecutors don't have an unlimited amount of time to bring their case before a jury. For instance, many states have a 5- or 10-year "statute of limitations" for prosecuting burglars, so a criminal can get away scot-free if he avoids the authorities long enough. However, the statute of limitations doesn't apply to first-degree murder, which is why suspected killers can still be hauled into court decades after their alleged crimes!

What is forensic evidence?

When detectives examine a crime scene, they're not only looking for bloodstains or bullet holes (though they certainly won't ignore any if they stumble across them!). Often, it's the more subtle clues that wind up cracking a case—and to make the most of these, detectives are usually accompanied by "forensic specialists" trained to pick up evidence that would escape the notice of an ordinary person.

There are many different kinds of forensic evidence, some of which require different specialists to properly recognize and handle them. Not only can forensic scientists collect fingerprints, but also teeth marks (a half-eaten hamburger can reveal enough about a person's choppers to enable police to track him down), strands of hair, microscopic skin cells, and various body fluids. Other kinds of experts specialize in the equipment used to create or destroy crime-related documents, such as typewriters, computers, and paper shredders. Needless to say, with all this potential evidence, very few bad guys are able to get away with the "perfect crime"!

What is circumstantial evidence?

Very few criminals are caught red-handed, or even seen, while committing their crimes. In these cases, a prosecutor will cite "circumstantial evidence" if there's no direct evidence available (such as an eyewitness). For example, if a man says his book-store was robbed by a tall woman wearing a yellow coat, and a tall woman with a yellow coat was seen running down the sidewalk at the time of the robbery, that can be taken as circumstantial evidence that she was the same woman who committed the crime.

What is a "cold case"?

Despite recent advances in forensic evidence (such as DNA testing), some stubborn cases just refuse to be solved: either the crime scene has been investigated improperly, important witness have died or disappeared, or there are no witnesses in the first place. Detectives call these unsolved crimes "cold cases." The most famous cold case is the disappearance (and presumed murder) of labor leader Jimmy Hoffa in 1975.

Why are crime scenes closed to the public?

Next to taking care of the wounded, the most important task of police at a crime scene is not to touch anything, since this could destroy (or damage) valuable evidence. That's the reason ordinary people aren't allowed on a crime scene: a steady stream of crime tourists would contaminate the evidence so badly that the criminals responsible might never be brought to justice.

Firefighters

What is a five-alarm fire?

The exact details differ from place to place, but in general, the number of "alarms" in a fire refers to how many different fire stations respond and send trucks (though not necessarily to the number of trucks sent). So a local fire station may send two trucks to a one-alarm fire, but a huge, five-alarm fire may draw a dozen trucks from five surrounding fire stations. (It's also possible for a one-alarm fire to turn into a two-alarm fire, meaning more precincts have to send help to keep the fire under control.)

What is a false alarm?

As you probably know, a false alarm is when firemen show up at your door and there's no fire to be found. Many false alarms are understandable mistakes—say, your neighbor saw the smoke from your frying hamburger and called the fire station—but many more are called in deliberately. Because malicious false alarms keep firefighters from doing their real jobs (and endanger innocent people), phoning one in can result in some very real jail time!

Why is it called a fire engine?

Yes, a fire truck has a really big motor, but that's not where the "engine" in its name comes from. This refers to the complicated machinery on the truck that pumps water and sprays it onto the fire (for example, most of the big dials you see on a fire truck measure water pressure—if the pressure is too low, the water won't reach its intended target, with disastrous results).

In big towns and cities, fire trucks obtain their water from hydrants, which tap into the city's water supply (the reason it's illegal to park in front of a fire hydrant is that this blocks the access of the truck to water). But in rural areas without hydrants, fire trucks carry their own water reservoirs, usually one or two thousand gallons. Any more than that, and the truck would be so heavy that it could barely move!

Besides these pumps and reservoirs, fire engines contain all sorts of valuable fire-fighting equipment, including axes, protective suits, and, of course, ladders. Some trucks also carry a spray-on foam that keeps buildings from catching fire again after they've been doused with water.

How high can a fire truck's ladder reach?

Despite what you see in cartoons, fire-truck ladders can only extend six or seven stories, max—and definitely not all the way up the side of a skyscraper! This is the reason why, before the invention of elevators, most urban dwellings were only six or seven stories tall, since no one wanted to be stuck too high off the ground in case of a fire on a floor down below.

How are buildings fireproofed?

Although there's no such thing as a completely fireproof building, the technology has advanced to the point that a fire in such a building is much less likely to result in its complete destruction (which may not sound very reassuring, until you realize that an old-style wooden house can burn to the ground in hours!).

Surprisingly, even a wooden building can be relatively fireproof, if the wood used is sufficiently thick and heavy (this way, even if the beams catch on fire, enough intact wood will remain in the center of the beams to continue supporting the building). Other fireproof materials used by contractors include reinforced concrete and steel, which are designed to resist temperatures of almost 2,000 degrees Fahrenheit.

One substance that's definitely not used anymore for fireproofing purposes is asbestos, a soft, flaky mineral with amazing fire-resistant qualities. Years ago, it was discovered that breathing asbestos fibers can cause a person to develop lung cancer. Even today, asbestos is being discovered in the frames of old buildings, and has to be removed immediately.

What is a backdraft?

Fires thrive on oxygen, which they need to keep burning. Sometimes, a big fire will use up all the oxygen in the vicinity, and will temporarily stop burning even as its smoke remains extremely hot. A "backdraft" occurs when a fireman opens a door or window, allowing in a rush of air (and oxygen) that restarts the fire in explosive fashion. This is why firemen will sometimes punch holes in the ceiling of a burning building, because this keeps the fire from running out of oxygen and prevents the conditions that cause backdrafts.

Medieval Times

Why were medieval armies so undependable?

Modern armies have a rigid chain of command: the top general issues orders, and these orders are executed by the lieutenants, sergeants, and corporals below him. Medieval armies, though, were usually composed of several "private" armies under the command of local nobles. Often, these nobles couldn't agree on a single supreme leader, and each wound up fighting the battle in his own uncoordinated way—usually with disastrous results.

What is a trebuchet?

A close cousin of the medieval catapult, the trebuchet (pronounced treb-oo-shay) was a device that hurled projectiles over high walls. The average trebuchet consisted of a long, strong beam with a cloth sling attached to one end, and a falling counterweight on the other that propelled the payload high up in the air. During the Middle Ages, armies would sometimes load the bodies of plague victims onto trebuchets, then launch the corpses into an enemy city in order to spread disease!

Why were sieges once so common?

In ancient times, major cities were surrounded by thick, impenetrable walls—and invading armies didn't have the luxury of calling in an air strike to bomb a town into submission. For this reason, wars were often won (or lost) by siege: the invading army would camp out in front of the city gates, preventing food from getting in and killing or capturing anyone who tried to venture out.

Sieges weren't much fun for either side. Unless a city happened to be located next to a body of water, and could receive supplies by ship, its inhabitants might be reduced to eating their pets (or even each other). The besieging army, meanwhile, was subject to epidemics (which usually wiped out more soldiers than hand-to-hand combat) and boredom, as the siege stretched on for months or even years.

Sometimes, sieges ended from sheer exhaustion: the city's inhabitants agreed to surrender, on the condition that they be allowed to leave, and the soldiers occupied the abandoned city. On the other hand, if the besieging army managed to breach the walls, the stubborn inhabitants were likely to be massacred down to the last man, woman, and child!

What were the Crusades?

Starting in the 11th century A.D., Catholic knights and soldiers in medieval Europe—under the guidance of the Pope—launched a series of attacks to reclaim the holy city of Jerusalem (which had recently been conquered by Muslims). The Crusades, as they were called, proceeded in fits and starts over the next two hundred years, and Jerusalem was even reconquered for a short period of time—but in the end the Muslim peoples of the Middle East prevailed.

Interestingly, modern historians now believe that the Crusades didn't have much to do with religion after all. In the early Middle Ages, the nation-states of Europe were ravaged by brigands—bands of violent, underemployed knights who had no major wars to fight on Europe's borders, and who needed to sustain themselves in the meantime. Preaching crusade against the Turks and Saracens (as the Muslims were then called) was seen as a convenient way to get these bothersome knights out of Europe, so they could inflict damage somewhere else for a change!

How were medieval armies supplied?

In days of yore, it was the rare nobleman who took the trouble to provision his army—that is, equip it with a steady supply of food and drink. Instead, soldiers were accustomed to live off the land, meaning they would plunder local farms or force citizens out of their houses. What made medieval armies especially terrifying was that they didn't much care if they plundered the enemy, or people from their own country!

Why did knights have pages?

In the Middle Ages, being a knight involved a lot of work—for instance, it's very difficult to put on a 50-pound suit of armor all by yourself! That's why most knights had "pages," boys between 7 and 14 years of age who assisted the knights with their daily duties. If he performed his job well, a page could expect to become a "squire," the next step in the process of being made a full-fledged knight.

How did most medieval soldiers die?

Not, as you might expect, by being run through with swords or beaned with maces. The vast majority of soldiers in medieval armies perished from contagious diseases such as typhoid, the plague, or smallpox. This was because soldiers were often crowded together in unsanitary conditions, and if they were a long way from home, they had yet to develop resistance to the local diseases they encountered.

Why do police officers have badges?

Basically, a police officer's badge isn't all that much different from a lawyer's business card or a motorist's driving license, but it is a lot cooler! The badge serves as a means of identification, used by an officer to prove his or her identity to a citizen, or by a citizen to track down a specific police officer (most badges don't bear the officer's full name, but he or she can still be identified later by the prominently displayed badge number).

Why do police officers travel in pairs?

Policing is a dangerous activity, so it's a good idea to have someone close by who can help out in case of an emergency. When pairs of police officers travel together, one of them can get out of the car to investigate a situation, while the other can radio for help (or get out of the car herself and help her partner) in case of trouble.

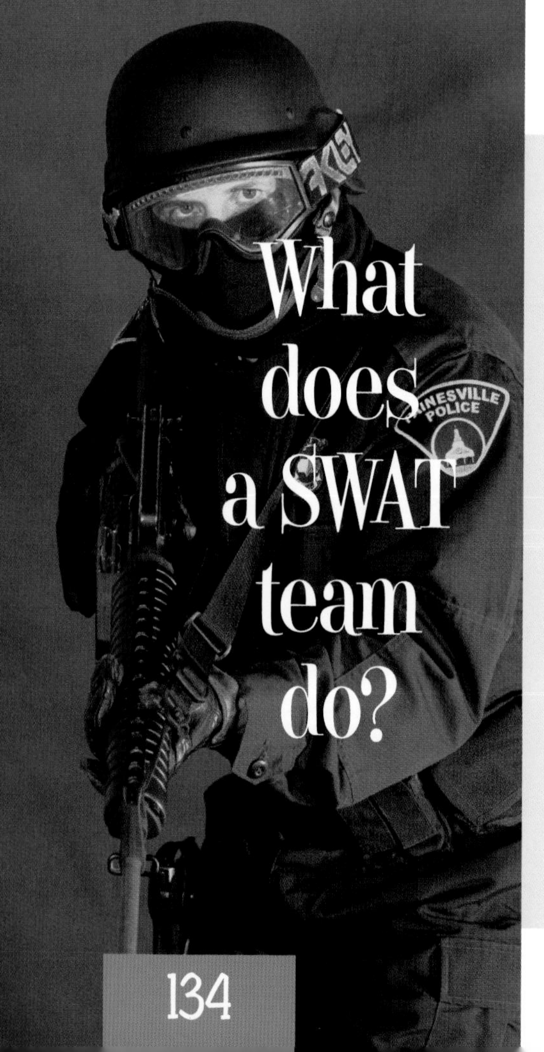

What does a SWAT team do?

The police departments of most major cities have at least one Special Weapons and Tactics (SWAT) team: a specially trained unit that can be called on to deal with high-risk operations, such as hostage rescues or assaults on heavily armed criminals. The very first SWAT teams were formed in California in the 1960s to deal with armed uprisings and riots, and were later used to combat snipers (and even bigger riots) in Los Angeles.

Today, SWAT teams have more in common with army special-ops units than with plain, everyday beat police: they're usually outfitted with various combinations of body armor, submachine guns, assault rifles, tear-gas grenades, real grenades, explosives, and battering rams. Some big cities even provide their SWAT teams with heavily armored vehicles that can withstand an assault by rocket-propelled grenades!

Because the work is so stressful, not just any policeman can join a SWAT team. As in the army or navy, candidates have to undergo thorough psychological testing, as well as months of intense training to teach them to deal with various situations.

What happens when a police officer fires a gun?

Well, the obvious answer is that someone might get hurt (unless it's a warning shot). The less obvious answer is that (in most precincts) the police officer is obliged to file a "discharge report," in which he or she explains the circumstances in which the gun was fired. Although many of these reports are filed as a result of accidental discharges (in which no one is injured), they're important to establish exactly what happened at the scene of a crime, and can be introduced as evidence at criminal trials (so a fudged or forged discharge report is likely to get an accused criminal off the hook!).

Why are police officers called "cops"?

In 19th-century England, policemen (known as "bobbies") would "cop" suspects, "cop" being an old English word meaning "seize" or "capture." That's why bobbies became known as "coppers," which criminals shortened to "cop," a word that made its way across the Atlantic to America. (By the way, you may have been taught that "cop" is really short for "constable on patrol." This sounds sensible, but there's absolutely no evidence that it's true!)

What are Miranda rights?

If you've ever watched a detective show on TV, you've probably seen a police officer reading a suspect his "Miranda rights": "You have the right to remain silent. If you give up that right, anything you say can and will be used against you in a court of law. You have the right to an attorney and to have an attorney present during questioning . . . " The reason this is called a "Miranda warning" is because it originated with a 1966 Supreme Court case called *Miranda vs. Arizona,* in which the court ruled that a criminal suspect has a right not to incriminate himself and to have a lawyer present as he's being questioned.

Despite what you see on the tube, though, police officers don't have to recite this warning to each and every suspect they arrest or take into custody—only the ones they plan to interrogate later on. And if a police officer does issue this warning, it's important for him or her to confirm that the suspect understands what he or she is saying—some convictions have been overturned because the suspect didn't speak English, and thus didn't understand his Miranda rights.

How does a tear-gas grenade work?

Tear-gas grenades don't look anything like the "pineapple" grenades you see in World War II movies. Rather, these are small canisters of compressed gas, which explode (non-lethally) when they're tossed into a rioting crowd. There are various kinds of tear gas, all of which work by irritating the eyes and respiratory system—causing uncontrollable crying and coughing and a sudden urge to run away as fast as possible!

What was the KGB?

The Russian-language abbreviation for "State Security Committee," the KGB was kind of like the CIA, FBI, and Secret Service all rolled up into one big package. From its founding in 1954 to its dissolution in 1991 (along with the rest of the Soviet Union), the KGB was widely feared, since it could target ordinary Russian citizens and sentence them to hard labor or death. Besides these domestic operations, the KGB dispatched the usual spies to various countries, especially the United States.

How are documents classified?

The U.S. government sorts documents according to their "sensitivity"—that is, how likely they would be to cause damage if the information they contained leaked out to the general public. According to the system in use today, the most sensitive documents are labeled "Top Secret," and can only be viewed by a limited number of people. Next in line are "Secret," "Confidential," and "Unclassified," the last meaning the document can be viewed by just about anybody (though you still usually have to ask the government if you want to take a peek).

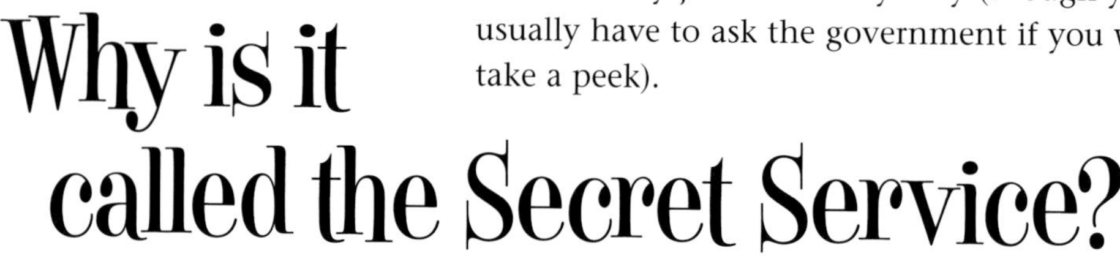

Why is it called the Secret Service?

The origin of the name "Secret Service" is so deeply buried in history that you might think it's been deliberately kept a, well, secret. The most probable explanation is that, when this organization was formed by the U.S. government in 1865, its officers didn't wear uniforms that set them apart from ordinary people, but walked around in "plain clothes." (Today, it's relatively easy to spot Secret Service agents—they're the ones in suits and dark sunglasses, with microphones in their ears!)

Oddly enough, the Secret Service wasn't founded to protect the president, but to stop the counterfeiting of paper currency, a major problem in the years after the Civil War. Even after Abraham Lincoln was assassinated in the summer of 1865, the Secret Service stuck to its appointed task, and it wasn't until the shooting of President William McKinley in 1901 that agents began accompanying presidents on public appearances. Gradually, the Secret Service's duties were expanded to include guarding the first family, the vice-president and president-elect, and all presidential candidates. And yes, as busy as it is, the Secret Service still pursues its anti-counterfeiting activities!

What is the difference between the CIA and the FBI?

Until the terrorist attacks of September 11, 2001, the Federal Bureau of Investigation (FBI) and Central Intelligence Agency (CIA) had two entirely different missions. Since its founding in 1908, the FBI has been responsible for domestic surveillance and law enforcement—that is, it only has authority over U.S. citizens (including American spies working for foreign governments). The CIA, on the other hand, is technically responsible for collecting information about foreign countries, and has been known to engage in "covert operations" (that is, spy missions) abroad.

After the 9/11 attacks, though, government officials began to reconsider the relationship between the FBI and CIA. As it turned out, these two organizations were so focused on their traditional missions that they barely communicated with each other—so clues about impending terrorist activity picked up by, say, the CIA rarely found their way into FBI files, and vice versa. Today, this situation is improving, as the FBI and CIA have put an increased focus on counter-terrorism activities—and make sure to let each other know what they're doing!

What is a spy exchange?

During the Cold War—when it was an open secret that the United States and the Soviet Union (modern-day Russia) were spying on one another—it often made more sense to exchange captured spies, rather than sentence them to prison terms or have them executed. This was because each country wanted to protect its spies, and a violent crackdown on spying would have completely shut down the flow of information.

What was SMERSH?

Many early James Bond fans probably thought SMERSH—the evil Russian organization Bond constantly battled—had been made up out of whole cloth. Oddly enough, though, the Soviet Union did have a SMERSH division during World War II (the name is a contraction of the Russian words "shpionom," meaning "death to spies!"). Perhaps because it sounded so silly, SMERSH was disbanded in 1946, many of its officers going on to serve in the KGB.

How many James Bond movies have been made?

This is a hard question to answer, since there are both "official" and "unofficial" James Bond movies, and since Agent 007 himself has been played by six different actors. That said, starting with *Dr. No* in 1962, there have been about two dozen James Bond flicks, with more on the way. (Here's another weird James Bond fact: Bond's creator, Ian Fleming, wrote the famous kids' book *Chitty Chitty Bang Bang!*)

Traffic Laws

What does "yield" mean?

You may have noticed triangular "yield" signs posted at the entrance lanes of highways. What this sign means is that the driver has to be prepared to give the right-of-way to other vehicles, and not attempt to force his way onto the highway. As you can guess, the reasons the cars on the highway have the right-of-way is that they're already going a lot faster than cars coming in from the entrance ramp!

What is an HOV lane?

During "rush hour"—that is, early in the morning, when people are heading off to work, and late in the afternoon, when they're heading back—most cities would prefer people to use mass transit, rather than their own cars. This is because subways, buses, and trains are designed to carry lots of commuters at the same time, while many folks drive to work by themselves—not an efficient use of the carrying capacity of their vehicles.

Certain cities, like New York, have attempted to solve this problem by designating high-occupancy vehicle (HOV lanes) during rush hour. HOV lanes are reserved for cars carrying at least two (and sometimes more) people, and they're designed to move faster than other lanes. Every now and then, a traffic officer peeks into cars at the lane's entrance, to keep lone drivers from "cheating."

Although it's unclear whether HOV lanes encourage people to use mass transit, they have been effective at convincing commuters to carpool—which reduces traffic and saves valuable gas.

Why do some intersections have stop signs rather than traffic lights?

As a rule of thumb, intersections have traffic lights when one or both roads are heavily traveled, and it's crucial for the cars traveling on one road to come to a complete stop to allow the cars traveling on the other road to pass. If both roads are lightly traveled, though, it can be a major inconvenience to keep drivers waiting for thirty seconds at traffic lights, so there's usually just a stop sign instead.

Why is it dangerous to pass trucks on the right?

On a busy highway—or anywhere else, for that matter—the driver of an eighteen-wheel truck has a limited range of vision. This "blind spot" is bigger on the truck's right, since the trucker (who sits in the left side of the cab) can't supplement his view in his right-hand mirror by sticking his head out the window. If you try to pass a truck on the right, and the truck driver moves to the right-hand lane while you're in his blind spot, the result can be a bad accident.

How do they figure out the load limits on bridges?

There's a funny gag in the comic strip *Calvin and Hobbes* in which Calvin asks his dad this question, and his dad replies that they build a bridge, drive heavier and heavier trucks over the bridge until it collapses, then weigh the last truck and rebuild the bridge. This isn't necessary, though: when a bridge is built, the engineers already know how heavy a vehicle can drive over it, so signs are posted warning these "high load" trucks off the road.

Why do "no parking" signs have times posted on them?

At least some of the "no parking" signs in cities allow drivers to park at certain times of the day—say, between 9AM and 9PM on weekdays. This is usually for two reasons: either to keep people from parking their cars on the street for weeks on end, or to clear the street at certain times of the day or night for municipal services like garbage collection or street cleaning.

What does it mean to have "points" on your license?

In most contexts—such as basketball games or quiz shows—accumulating points is a good thing. But the "points" you earn on a driver's license aren't good at all, and can mean the difference between driving to work and having to take the bus.

Points are assessed on a driver's license every time a policeman writes out a ticket for a moving violation. The details vary by state, but in South Dakota, for instance, a relatively minor violation like not paying attention to a road sign costs 2 points, while major violations like excessive speeding or passing a school bus cost 4 points. These points are added up over a one- or two-year period, and if they exceed a certain total, the driver can have his license suspended.

There's another reason motorists pay careful attention to the points on their licenses. All drivers have to be insured, and every time a motorist racks up points, he's liable to have his insurance rates increased—so careless driving can wind up costing him hundreds of dollars a month!

Why do juries have 12 people?

Like most of our legal institutions, we inherited our jury system from England, where it evolved gradually over the course of hundreds of years. It's not clear why English juries wound up consisting of 12 people, though the most probable explanation is that a dozen jurors is a small enough amount to be manageable, but a large enough amount to include various differences of opinion. It also helps that the number 12 was in widespread use, whether people were buying a dozen eggs at the market or hearing about the Twelve Tribes of Israel in church.

What is a grand jury?

Before the government takes someone to trial, it has to prove that enough evidence exists for a jury to produce a reasonable verdict. That's where the grand jury comes in: this is a group of about two dozen people that hears the government's case, then decides whether or not to hand down an indictment (a formal charge). At that point, a trial with a "petit jury" (that is, the usual count of 12 jurors) can proceed.

Because of their time and expense, grand juries are usually reserved for large, federal trials that involve complicated legal principles, like death penalty or racketeering cases. Once assembled, these juries may meet once or twice a week for months, or even a year.

There are two important ways in which grand juries are different from regular juries. First, grand jury proceedings are held in complete secrecy, whereas anyone can read the proceedings of an ordinary trial. And second, witnesses called before a grand jury aren't allowed to be accompanied by lawyers—which has prompted some people to criticize these juries for being unfair.

What does it mean to "take the fifth"?

The Fifth Amendment to the Constitution states that no person "shall be compelled in any criminal case to be a witness against himself." When a defendant or a witness "takes the fifth," that means he knows that anything he says can be used against him—and that he has a legal right to keep his mouth shut. As you might imagine, in the eyes of a jury, taking the fifth usually doesn't look very good!

What is a mistrial?

Kind of like the legal equivalent of a "do-over," a mistrial is when a judge suddenly decides to end a trial before the jury has had a chance to deliver its verdict—leaving it up to the prosecutor to decide if she wants to schedule a whole new trial with a whole new jury, a process that can take months (or even years).

The most common cause of mistrials is a "hung jury"—that is, a jury that has been deadlocked for days about whether to declare a defendant innocent or guilty. Usually, this happens when 10 or 11 members of the jury vote for conviction, while the remaining one or two insist on a not-guilty verdict. A judge will gently encourage a divided jury to come to a unanimous verdict, but if there's no prospect of this happening, he has no choice but to call a mistrial.

Sometimes, mistrials can be caused by the misconduct of prosecutors or defense attorneys, or by evidence that an outside party has been trying to influence a juror (which is known as "jury tampering").

What is double jeopardy?

No, it's not just part of a popular TV game show. Double jeopardy is a clause in the U.S. Constitution stating that a person can't be taken to trial twice for the same crime. The exceptions are when a trial ends prematurely because of a mistrial, and when the government retries a case under a different law—for example, prosecuting a defendant for kidnapping after his first trial (for murder) resulted in a not-guilty verdict.

Why aren't cameras allowed in some courtrooms?

Years ago, television cameras were never allowed in courtrooms—a situation that has gradually changed as more and more trials have been broadcast on TV. While most major trials can be televised, judges have the discretion to declare especially sensitive trials "off-limits" and allow only a courtroom artist to sketch the proceedings.

What is perjury?

A step beyond ordinary, everyday lying, perjury is when a trial witness (or defendant) deliberately makes a false statement, after taking an oath on the Bible to "tell the truth, the whole truth, and nothing but the truth." Perjury is a crime in itself, and can earn the perjurer a stiff fine or a term in jail.

Science &

WHAT is trigonometry? HOW do we know the universe is expanding? WHY do buildings have foundations? This section explains everything from basic science to cutting-edge research, as well as industries ranging from mining to agriculture.

Industry

What is a ribosome?

The cells of our bodies contain two different coding systems, which (properly translated) turn the information contained in our DNA into the proteins that make life possible. The first coding system is used by DNA itself: this enormous molecule consists of the four elements—A, U, G, and T—strung together in various combinations (the letters stand for specific molecules, but that's not important right now!). The second coding system is used by proteins, which are made from various combinations of 20 different "amino acids," essential molecules found in all cells.

So where does the ribosome come in? Basically, this enormously complex molecular machine translates the four-letter language of DNA into the 20-letter language of proteins. How it accomplishes this is way too detailed to go into here, but suffice it to say that a single ribosome consists of dozens of separate proteins and strands of RNA (a molecule closely related to DNA) joined together in an elaborate pattern. Each of our cells contains millions of ribosomes, which churn out proteins around the clock in microscopic "assembly lines."

What is the difference between RNA and DNA?

Technically, RNA stands for ribonucleic acid, and DNA stands for deoxyribonucleic acid (meaning DNA is similar to RNA, but lacks certain oxygen atoms). Since that explanation probably doesn't do you much good, here's another one: DNA is the huge molecule that determines your heredity (that is, what you look like, and what your biological kids will look like, if you have any). RNA, though equally important, isn't quite as stable as DNA, and is produced (and broken down) by cells as they synthesize proteins.

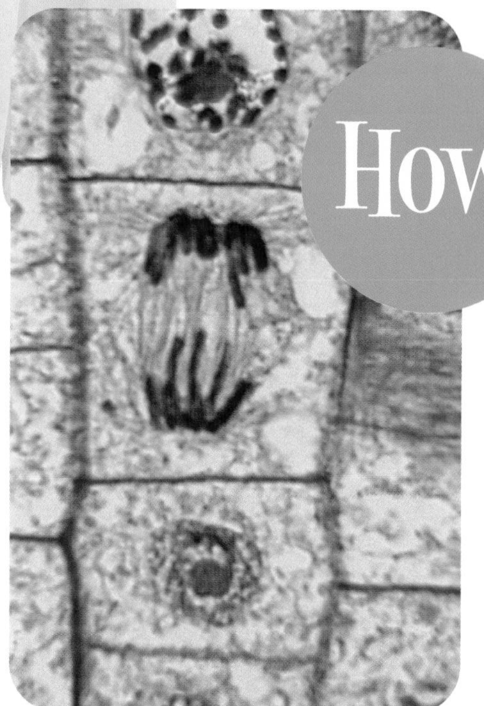

How do cells divide?

If any single thing encapsulates the miracle of life, it's "mitosis," the process by which a cell duplicates its DNA and splits into two new cells. It looks simple enough when you see it in a movie (speeded up, of course), but mitosis is a complex process, requiring faultless timing and the close cooperation of dozens of different, highly specialized proteins (not to mention microscopic cell components like "centrosomes" and "microtubules").

How do cells die?

There are two basic ways the cells of your body can bite the dust: common, everyday injuries (such as scraping your arm on the sidewalk, which wipes out thousands of skin cells simultaneously), or by a natural process known as "apoptosis," which is what happens when a cell decides to die (or is prompted by neighboring cells to die).

When a cell is damaged or infected by a virus, and is no longer working properly, the malfunction triggers the creation of various proteins, which themselves trigger apoptosis. The cell becomes unusually round; its chromatin (the material its DNA is wrapped in) starts to degrade; the DNA itself falls apart; and the cell quietly explodes into smaller bodies called "vesicles," which are promptly mopped up by the body's immune system.

As gross as this sounds, the programmed death of certain cells is necessary for the continuing health of others—and apoptosis is also crucial in fetal development. For example, the reason you have spaces between your fingers is because the cells that used to be there died while you were still in the womb!

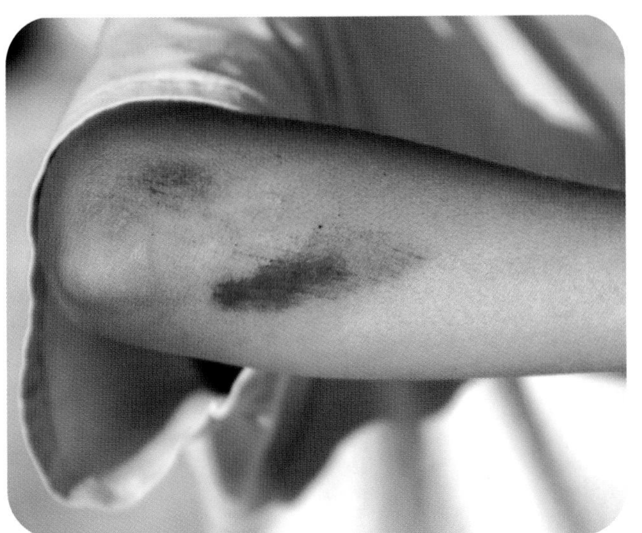

What are stem cells?

You may have read about an ongoing controversy concerning stem-cell research. Stem cells are primitive cells obtained from human embryos; the reason they're a subject of research is that they're "undifferentiated," meaning they can potentially be grown into specific cell types (say, liver cells or brain cells) that can be used to treat diseases or to repair human organs.

What are mitochondria?

What batteries are to your Game Boy, mitochondria are to cells. These microscopic "organelles" synthesize a chemical called ATP, which powers all of the cell's functions. Because mitochondria have their own DNA, scientists believe they were originally separate cells that were slowly absorbed (and incorporated) by primitive bacteria a few billion years ago.

What was the first cell?

Since life evolved on earth more than four billion years ago—and since primitive cells didn't leave fossils—it's impossible to know exactly when the first cell arose, or what it looked like. However, it's probable that the ancestor of all modern cells contained short, primitive strands of RNA (not DNA) and an equally primitive cell wall. It's also possible that there were many different kinds of proto-cells, and only one was durable enough to replicate itself and spread around the globe.

Colors

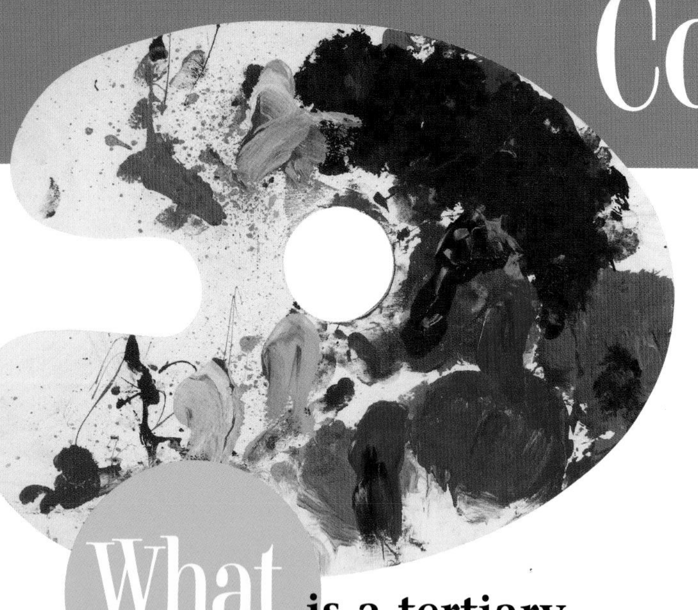

What is an afterimage?

Because of the way the human retina (the part of the eye that perceives light) works, if you stare at a certain color for a long time, and then close your eyes, you'll see a ghostly "afterimage" of the complementary color. For example, if you stare too long at a green traffic light, when you close your eyes you'll "see" a reddish image of the same apparent shape and size.

What is a tertiary color?

In painting, primary colors are combined to create secondary colors—for instance, blue paint mixed with yellow paint produces green paint. A tertiary color is a color that's formed by mixing a primary color with a secondary color. For example, green and yellow produce a bright tertiary color called chartreuse, while blue and green can be combined to form aquamarine.

How many colors are there?

Technically, colors exist on a continuum—that is, there's no way to distinguish the "next closest color" from any other color, since all colors gradually blend into each other. The average computer monitor can reproduce millions of distinct colors, though most of these just register as "red" or "blue" to the average person.

That said, there are still plenty of named colors beyond your everyday green and yellow, as you can see whenever you open a box of 64 or 128 crayons. Just a partial list of these "official" colors includes such unusual specimens as brass, carrot, khaki, and olive drab. There are also "international" colors like safety orange, which is used for warning signs.

By the way, they may number in the millions, but any color on a computer screen can be reproduced by mixing together various proportions of red, green, and blue light and varying the light's vibrancy and brightness.

Why can't we see ultraviolet light?

The colors we see correspond to various wavelengths of light, and humans (like other creatures) evolved to see those wavelengths of light that help us survive the best. For this reason, we can see the range of colors roughly corresponding to the colors of the rainbow, but not ultraviolet light (which has a shorter wavelength than violet) or infrared light (which has a longer wavelength than red). If it had been crucial to our survival, you and I would see ultraviolet light as well as we see the color green!

What are primary colors?

You may have been taught in school that red, blue, and yellow are the three primary colors—that is, the three colors that can't be created by mixing together other colors—but that's only half the story (or, since we're talking about colors, only half the picture!).

Red, blue, and yellow are actually what are called "subtractive" primaries—that is, the colors of reflected light (such as the light you see reflected off red, blue, or yellow paint). In this system, you can mix blue and yellow together to get green (which is called a secondary color), or red and blue to get purple (which is also secondary).

Of course, when you're finger painting, the subtractive primaries are all that matter. But TVs and computer screens, which emit rather than reflect light, make use of the "additive" primaries: red, green, and blue. Just as red, blue, and yellow can be combined to produce any other color in the subtractive system, red, green, and blue can be combined to produce any other color in the additive system.

Why do you have a favorite color?

When asked, most kids will name a favorite color—or at least a color they happen to like a bit more than all the others. Scientists have shown that different colors affect people in different ways—for instance, blue and green are calming and reassuring, while red is exciting and passionate. So if you have a strong preference for the color green and your brother likes the color red, that may explain why you fight all the time!

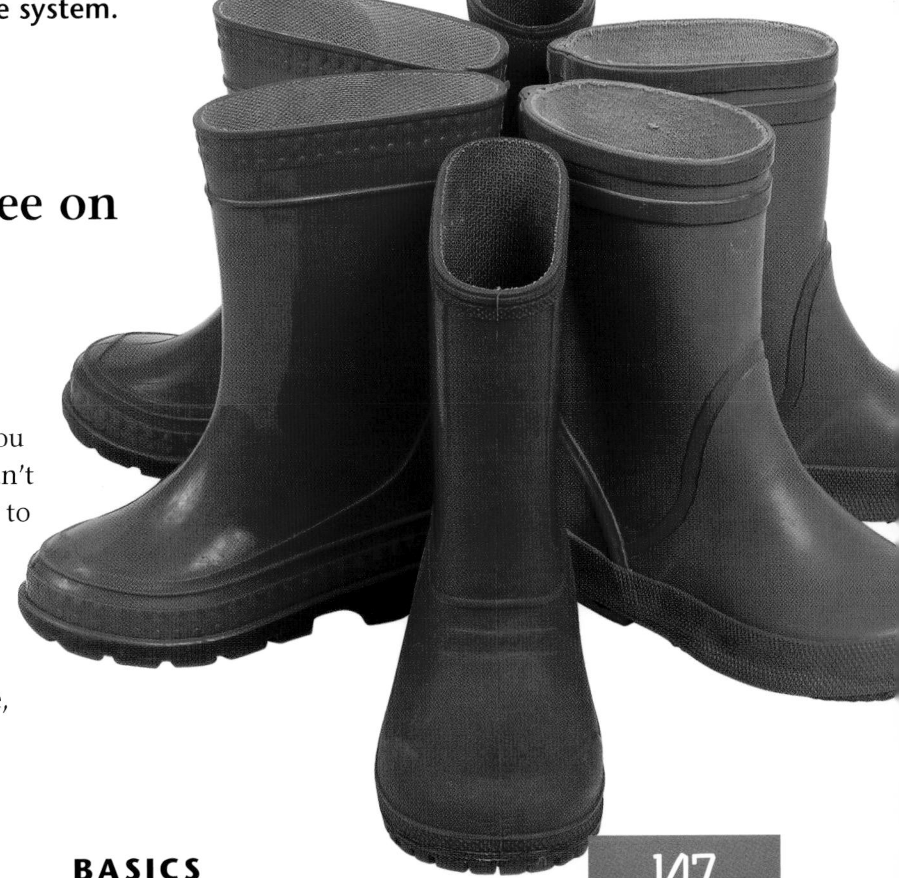

How do people agree on the color "red"?

This is a question that has tormented philosophers for hundreds of years. Since color is a subjective experience—that is, you can recognize the color red, even if you can't explain it to other people—there's no way to know if someone else's "red" is the same as your "red." Still, because most humans function pretty much the same way, it's relatively easy to agree (or at least not to argue) about common colors like red, blue, and green.

What does it mean to "blow a fuse"?

You mean, besides yelling at your brother for using your Game Boy without permission? A fuse is a small device that monitors the amount of electricity flowing through a wire. If this current reaches a dangerous level (say, because all the appliances in your kitchen are on at the same time), a metal strip in the fuse melts, causing it to "blow" and shut the current down. As inconvenient as it is, a blown fuse is much easier to deal with than an electrical fire!

Why do most blackouts occur during the summer?

It takes a lot more electricity to run an air conditioner during the summer than to run an oil heater during the winter (that's because an air conditioner relies completely on electricity, while a burner requires only a small amount of AC power to start combusting fuel). During a heat wave, millions of people are likely to be using their air conditioners simultaneously, which can cause a blackout if the electric utility isn't able to meet the surging demand.

Why does electricity need to travel through wires?

Although electrons—the zillions of subatomic particles that make up an electric current—can travel through pretty much any medium (including a complete vacuum), a wire is the only practical way to transmit electricity for energy purposes: otherwise, the electrons would quickly disperse and wouldn't be of much use to your toaster.

Still, if you're determined to transmit energy without wires, there are other means at your disposal. Scientists have spent years trying to perfect "wireless energy transfer," which involves beaming high-powered electromagnetic waves from one location to another. The problem with wireless energy transfer is that, even more so than electrons, electromagnetic waves have a tendency to dissipate with distance: it's easy enough to beam them out, but difficult to focus them tightly enough to be "caught" by a receiver.

This pretty much rules out beaming energy to meet the needs of an entire city, but over small distances, wireless energy transfer works just fine. For example, it's possible (though perhaps not very efficient) to recharge batteries wirelessly.

Why do electrons have a negative charge?

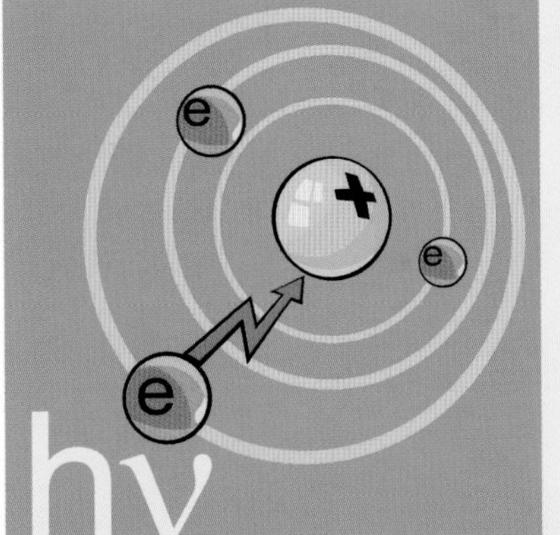

One of the funny things about physics is that, as you drill further and further down into the most fundamental concepts, you often encounter an element of chance. That's the case with the so-called "negative" charge on electrons (as opposed to the "positive" charge on protons, which reside in an atom's nucleus). In physical terms, it's not meaningful to say that an electron's charge is "negative" in any real sense; it's only called that to distinguish it from the "positive" proton. In fact, if electrons had been dubbed "positive" and protons "negative," it wouldn't have made any difference!

Now that we've gotten that out of the way, one of the most enduring mysteries of physics is why electrons and protons should have equal and opposite charges (and, if you want to get technical about it, why the even smaller "quarks" that make up protons and neutrons have charges of negative 1/3 or positive 2/3, compared to the electron's negative 1). This principle of equality of charge is so deeply rooted in physics that a basic law dictates its conservation: the total amount of positive and negative charge in the universe can never be changed.

What does a transformer do?

One of the simplest—and also one of the most dangerous—of all electrical devices, a transformer is a coil of wires that "steps up" (increases) or "steps down" (decreases) a current's voltage. Transformers are an important component of high-voltage power lines, because they step up the current that goes into the line from the utility and step down the current that comes out of the line into your house—otherwise, all your appliances would probably explode!

How does an electric meter work?

You might think a substance as nebulous and free flowing as electricity would be difficult to track. Well, think again: an electric utility assigns each of its customers an electric meter, which measures the amount of electricity flowing into a residence. It used to be that an electric company employee had to read these meters in person every month, but today, many meters transmit their readings automatically to the utility's headquarters.

Why is it called electromagnetism?

Until the 19th century, scientists thought electricity and magnetism were two entirely separate phenomena. The details of electromagnetism are too difficult to go into here, but essentially, an electric current produces a small magnetic field, and a magnetic field can be used to stimulate a small electric current.

Elements

How was the Periodic Table discovered?

As scientists explored (and discovered) an increasing number of elements in the 18th and 19th centuries, they began to notice that these substances' atomic weights, chemical properties, and even appearance were all related in subtle ways: for example, sodium and potassium form salts easily, fluorine and chlorine are highly reactive, and carbon and silicon have a talent for forming large numbers of chemical bonds with other elements.

Although these were all tantalizing hints to some larger structure, it wasn't until the mid-19th century that a Russian chemist named Dmitri Mendeleev arranged the existing elements in rows and columns based on their atomic weights (that is, the number of protons in their nuclei) and chemical properties.

Although some other chemists were skeptical, Mendeleev was so convinced of the truth of his Periodic Table that he predicted the existence of yet-to-be-discovered elements that would fill certain gaps. For instance, in 1871, Mendeleev postulated an element called "eka-aluminum," which would inhabit the space directly below aluminum on his table. Four years later, scientists discovered the element gallium, which had all of eka-aluminum's predicted properties!

Why are they called "noble" gases?

As you look down the columns of the periodic table, you'll see six elements piled up on the far-right edge: helium, neon, argon, krypton, xenon, and radon. These gases aren't called "noble" because they're somehow better than the other elements; rather, they received this name because they rarely ever combine with other elements to form chemical compounds (so they're "noble" in terms of being standoffish and never mixing with the common folk!).

What is the lightest metal?

Most people are familiar with lithium only as a medication (it's used, in small doses, to treat manic depression). But not only is lithium the lightest of all metals, it's the third lightest element in the universe, after hydrogen and helium. In many ways, though, lithium is very un-metal-like, at least compared to iron and copper: for example, if you drop a solid piece of lithium in water, it will vaporize instantly!

What does iodine look like?

One of the strange things about many elements is that they look very different in their "pure" state than in the compounds most people are familiar with. The element iodine, for example, imparts a purple tint to "tincture of iodine" (a medicinal solution consisting of alcohol and iodine), but in its pure state it's a dull black solid.

What is beryllium used for?

The second-lightest metal (after lithium), beryllium is useful for two things: imparting a green tint to emeralds, and reflecting (rather than absorbing) the neutrons produced by nuclear reactions. As you can guess, it's this second function that makes beryllium so sought after on the world market: if a nation places a big order for this relatively rare element, that's a sure sign that it's probably developing nuclear weapons.

What are the transuranic elements?

Technically, a transuranic element is simply any atom whose nucleus contains more protons than a uranium atom (a uranium atom has 92 protons, while a plutonium atom has 94 and a curium atom 96). Scientists are constantly creating new transuranic elements in high-speed collisions, but most of these last for only a tiny fraction of a second before they decay. It's believed that some super-heavy elements may actually be stable, but the equipment doesn't exist yet to create them!

How can you turn one element into another?

In ancient times, scientists and philosophers searched for ways to turn iron and lead into gold, by means of incantations, magic potions, and a mystical substance called the "philosopher's stone." But if these "alchemists" had known modern chemistry and physics, they would have abandoned the spooky stuff and built themselves a high-powered particle accelerator!

The fact is, elements transmute themselves into each other all the time, either by natural processes like radioactivity (for instance, when an atom of uranium emits two protons, it becomes an atom of thorium) or lab-engineered collisions in which one or more protons are knocked out of an atom's nucleus, causing it to turn into an atom of another element.

As you can guess from the above paragraph, what distinguishes one element from another isn't its appearance, weight, or chemical properties—it's simply the number of protons in its nucleus (which correspond, roughly, to the number of electrons circling its nucleus). In principle, there's nothing to prevent scientists from one day figuring out how to knock three protons out of a lead atom and turn it into an atom of gold, though that's still a very long way away!

Agriculture

How did humans learn to plant crops?

We'll never know for sure, of course, but "archaeobotanists" (scientists who study primitive crops) have come up with a reasonable explanation for how our primitive ancestors discovered farming about 12,000 years ago.

In prehistoric times, humans had long since figured out, by trial and error, which wild plants could be eaten (as it turned out, many of these edible plants grew in the "Fertile Crescent" area of the modern-day Middle East). By further observation and experimentation, these early settlers learned that edible plants popped up seasonally, and produced seeds that, when planted in similar types of soil, produced yet more plants.

From there, it was only a short step to collecting these seeds in bulk and deliberately planting them in patches of soil, a technique that, historians now believe, was invented independently by about a half-dozen different civilizations. Further along in the domestication process, people learned how to select and breed food crops for edibility, better nutrition, and ease of harvesting methods.

What was the "Columbian Exchange"?

No, it wasn't a stock market for coffee beans. After the discovery of the New World in 1492, European settlers started transplanting American crops into their home countries, and the crops of their home countries into America. Not all of these plants prospered in alien soil, but the ones that did (like tomatoes and potatoes in Europe, and various strains of wheat in the Americas) changed the face of agriculture the world over.

Why are crops rotated?

Even ancient farmers recognized that planting the same crop in the same soil, year after year, produces diminishing returns, as the soil's nutrients get depleted (and as pests and parasites flock to their accustomed meal). That's why most farmers "rotate" their crops by planting, say, wheat one year, and oats or barley the next. It's also common to occasionally allow a field to lie fallow (that is, to not plant any crops at all), in order to freshen the soil.

What was the worst crop failure?

The history of civilization is littered with crop failures—that is, the unexpected obliteration of an entire harvest, whether by drought, disease, or mismanagement.

Although it wasn't the worst crop failure in history, the Irish Potato Famine is one of the best known. In the mid-19th century, potato crops in Ireland were attacked by a fungal disease known as "the blight," which rendered them inedible. Ordinarily, this might not have been such a disaster, except that in the previous 200 years, the people of Ireland had grown completely dependent on the potato as their main source of food. The result was widespread starvation, and the deaths of anywhere from 500,000 to 1.5 million Irish citizens.

The Irish Potato Famine is widely known for another reason: as you may have learned in history class, "the blight" prompted the emigration of millions of Irish families, many of them to the United States. Historians haven't settled on an exact number, but it's probable that by the time it ended, the Potato Famine reduced the population of Ireland by a full one-third!

What is the most versatile crop?

Although soybeans are edible by themselves, these wonder beans are mostly grown for their oil, which is used as an ingredient in processed food (unlike other vegetable oils, soybean oil can withstand the high temperatures used in cooking). Soybeans that don't have their oil extracted usually wind up in animal feed, or in healthy foods like tofu. By the way, the U.S. is the biggest grower of soybeans, accounting for half the world's annual crop.

What caused the Dust Bowl?

In the 1930s, the Midwestern U.S. experienced a horrendous series of "dust storms" that prompted many farmers to emigrate to other states (where they became known as "Okies," whether or not they came from Oklahoma). The "dust" in these storms was composed of loose topsoil that, because of ill-advised farming techniques, had been left exposed to the scorching heat of the summer sun— and then blew away in the unusually strong winds.

Why is rice grown in paddies?

Unlike wheat, rice is what is known as a "semi-aquatic" crop, meaning it can be grown either on land or in shallow pools of water, known as rice paddies. The reason most farmers prefer to grow their rice in paddies is that weeds aren't as adaptable to an aquatic environment, so the rice can grow in peace—and the farmers can harvest bigger yields than if they grew the crop on dry land.

Computer Security

What are computer viruses?

Just like real viruses—which insert bits of genetic code into living cells, prompting them to manufacture yet more viruses—a computer virus is a tiny program that worms its way onto the hard drive of your computer (where all your information is stored). Once it has settled in, the computer virus sets to work making copies of itself, which causes your computer either to slow down or to begin acting strangely (you might have trouble opening a certain file, for example, or your entire computer may suddenly shut itself down).

So how does a computer virus spread itself? Unlike living viruses—which evolved naturally and are spread mostly by air or hand-to-hand contact—computer viruses are programmed by people, and require people to spread them to other computers. Usually, this is done by computer users who unwittingly send friends e-mails with innocuous-looking attachments, or by more malicious people who deliberately post virus-riddled files on Web sites.

Why is it called a Trojan Horse?

A variant on the standard computer virus, a Trojan Horse is a virus that pretends to be a legitimate program—for instance, the virus may present itself on a Web site as a computer game, but when the user installs it, it unveils its true nature and takes over his computer. The reason it's called a Trojan Horse is after the tale from Homer's *Aeneid* in which Greek warriors build and hide inside a giant wooden horse, present it as a gift to the people of Troy, and then sneak out in the middle of the night and conquer the city!

What is a firewall?

Mostly used by companies trying to protect the information on their employees' computers, a firewall is a program that monitors the boundary between different "zones of trust"—the employees within the company belong to one (trustworthy) zone, and the rest of the Internet-using world belongs to the other (untrustworthy) zone. A firewall allows communication within the company to go on unhindered, but rebuffs anyone from outside who tries to hack into the company's network.

Why is it called Spam?

We may never know for sure, but it's likely that the use of the word "spam" to refer to unwanted e-mail harks back to a famous sketch by the British comedy troupe Monty Python's Flying Circus. In this routine, a waitress recites her diner's specials, most of which include lots of Spam (a canned meat sold by Hormel): "We have eggs and Spam; eggs, cheese, and Spam; Spam, Spam, Spam, and Spam . . . "). You have to admit, this annoying, repetitious use of the word "Spam" suits junk mail perfectly!

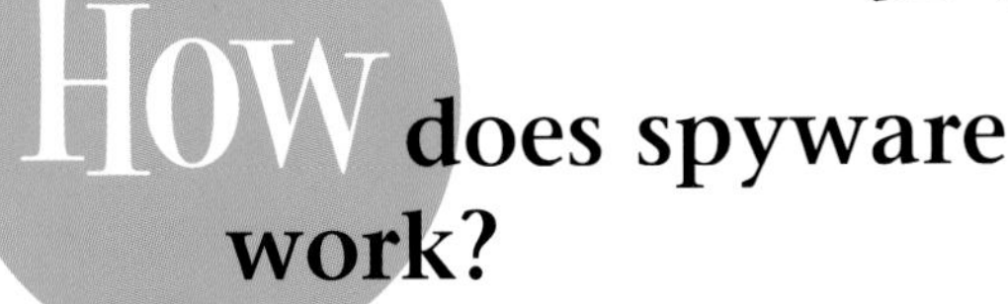

How does spyware work?

Although it's every bit as annoying as a computer virus—and often winds up doing more damage—spyware technically doesn't replicate itself. Most often, a spyware program takes control of your web browser, causing annoying pop-up ads to constantly appear, or redirecting your results on search engines. Spyware (and its close relative, "adware") has become such a problem that a huge market has sprung up for anti-spyware programs!

What is a hacker?

Most of the time, the Internet is a good thing—a quick, easy means to share information with hundreds of millions of people around the world. But some of the time, the Internet can be a bad thing—because having your computer connected to a worldwide network means that you're vulnerable to individuals who have mastered the technology involved, and know how to use a "back door" to access information on your hard drive (or, more commonly, the hard drives of a prominent company). These people are known as "hackers," though no one is quite sure why!

Surprisingly, very few hackers use their abilities to try to get rich (though, of course, banks closely guard their account information from online attacks). Rather, most hackers serve a useful social function, probing the online defenses of major corporations and pointing out (in Internet forums or in e-mails to the company itself) the vulnerabilities in its system, so the firm can take the appropriate safeguards against a truly malicious attack. In fact, many software companies release early versions of their programs to these "ethical hackers," who torture-test the product and point out any flaws.

What was the worst computer virus?

To date, the "I Love You" virus of Valentine's Day 2000 stands as the most damaging computer virus ever released: this cyber-critter could actually forward itself from the e-mail programs of infected computers, in e-mails with the header "I Love You." Since people love to be loved, a huge number of users opened the "I Love You" attachment, infecting their own computers and helping spread the virus even further.

Construction

How are skyscrapers built?

You might think the main challenge of building a hundred-story skyscraper is finding enough construction workers who aren't afraid of heights. As it turns out, though, that's the easy part: the big problem is making the lower floors of the skyscraper strong enough to support the enormous weight of its upper floors.

Skyscrapers really took off, so to speak, when advances in the steel industry (in the early 20th century) allowed for the mass production of the long, seamless beams that comprise the "skeleton" of any tall building. As strong as they are, steel girders are also fairly thin and compact, allowing the lower floors of a skyscraper to be both strong and functional (that is, the supporting beams leave enough room for people to actually work on the lower stories!).

The biggest skyscrapers are composed of dozens of vertical steel beams, which stretch, unbroken, all the way up the structure's height and are joined together at every floor by a network of smaller girders. This "tinker-toy" technique theoretically allows a skyscraper to be built to any height, though for practical reasons, most architects are content with the scale of the Empire State Building.

How big is a wrecking ball?

A wrecking ball has to be pretty heavy to smash through the wood and bricks of your average house. Most wrecking balls weigh about two or three tons, though some heavy-duty models can weigh in at as much as six tons. By the way, modern wrecking balls aren't perfectly round; demolition experts have discovered that pear-shaped balls (which are weighted more toward the bottom) get the job done more efficiently.

Why do buildings have foundations?

Well, to begin with, a skyscraper without a foundation would tip over whenever the wind blew! A building's foundation (the part of its structure that extends underground) conveys its enormous weight to the ground beneath, anchoring it firmly in place. If a building has an insecure foundation—or if the ground it's built on isn't suitable for bearing heavy loads—disaster can result.

Why are buildings condemned?

Buildings can be condemned (that is, slated for demolition) for a variety of reasons. Unsafe buildings are often condemned, as are some buildings that have been bought by real-estate developers (who would rather tear down the entire structure and start a new building from scratch). Occasionally, a city may invoke its right of "eminent domain" and condemn structures to make way for a new highway or stadium (after paying the buildings' owners a fair price, of course).

While it's possible to demolish a condemned house with a wrecking ball, that's not a practical option for larger structures, such as factories and apartment buildings. In these cases, professionals are called in to bring down the buildings with controlled implosions: explosives are placed at key points throughout the structure, then, when everybody has been safely evacuated, someone outside flips a switch and the entire building comes crashing down in a huge puff of smoke. As you can guess, controlled detonations draw huge crowds, and the spectacular implosions often make it onto the evening news!

Why do construction workers wear hard hats?

Construction sites are littered with loose bricks, bolts, and other small, dense building materials, so it makes sense that construction workers wear hard hats to protect them from falling objects (a hard hat is enough to prevent injury from a falling brick, but a falling wheelbarrow is another story!). Hard hats used to be made out of metal, like military helmets, but these days they're mostly manufactured from hard plastic.

What is the difference between cement and concrete?

What we call "cement" is a carefully formulated mixture of limestone, calcium, silicon, and various other ingredients that has been hardened by baking; "concrete," on the other hand, is cement that has been mixed with sand and gravel. Because it's much stronger, concrete is the preferred material for construction purposes, along with hardened steel (about 6 billion tons of concrete are produced every year, roughly one ton for every person on the planet!).

How loud is a jackhammer?

There's a reason jack-hammerers wear earplugs: these machines produce noise in the 100-decibel range, enough to damage a construction worker's hearing if he doesn't use protection for extended periods of time. What makes jackhammers so loud is that they're powered by compressed air, which is why these devices are sometimes called "pneumatic drills."

How did the first labor unions arise?

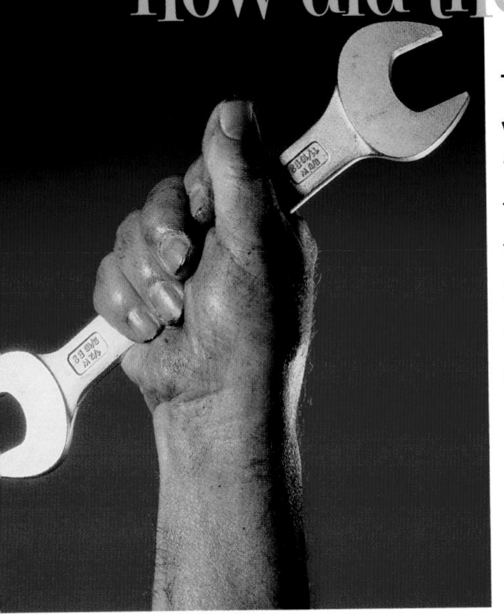

The idea of laborers banding together to negotiate better pay and working conditions has very old roots. In medieval Europe, "guilds" of artisans would set prices for their wares, take in and train selected newcomers (called "apprentices"), and band together to oppose harmful legislation. The labor unions that sprung up in the 18th and 19th centuries shared many of these attributes, with one major difference: most of these unions represented unskilled workers who toiled in the dangerous, overcrowded factories of the Industrial Revolution.

Although it's impossible to pin down the very first union in the modern sense, a major turning point in labor history was the passage of the "Masters and Servants Act" in England in 1867. This law legally recognized the right of trade unions to bargain with management over hourly wages and factory conditions (though there would still be criminal penalties for illegal strikes). Before this act was passed, labor unions in England had an uncertain legal status—and in other countries (including the U.S.) it took an equally long time for union membership to be recognized as a legal right of workers.

What is a scab?

Yes, it's that ugly thing that forms after you scrape your knee, but "scab" also has another meaning. When a union goes on strike, "scab" is the name given to anyone who crosses the picket line and reports for work. Some companies will actively recruit scabs during a strike, though (because of the bad feelings they cause) very few of these people choose to stay employed after the strike has ended.

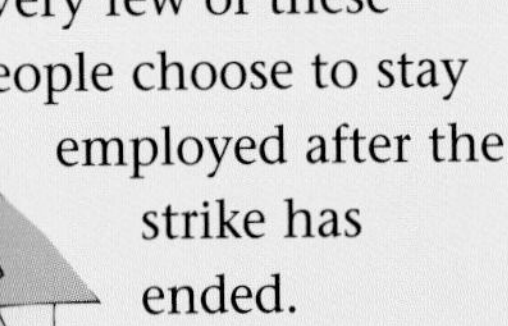

What is the biggest union in the U.S.?

The Service Employees International Union (SEIU)—which represents janitors, government employees, and health-care workers (other than doctors)—has about 1.8 million members in the U.S. and Canada (which is where the "international" in its name comes from). The SEIU used to be part of a larger affiliation of labor unions called the AFL-CIO, but went its own way in 2005 because of policy differences.

Why are they called "Teamsters"?

The labor union known as the "Teamsters" is so old that it was founded before the automobile age. Its name is derived from workers who drove teams of horses through the streets, a common way to transport goods before the advent of trucks. Today, the Teamsters continues to represent most of the nation's truck drivers, but it also has members from hundreds of other professions, ranging from paralegals to dental technicians.

What is a slowdown?

Sometimes, unions don't have to go on strike to get their point across. In order to put pressure on management, union members may choose to slow down the work process, usually by performing all their tasks "by the book" (and that book can sometimes be very thick!). Slowdowns are especially effective in transportation-related industries like airports and railroads, since they cause irate customers to blame management for delays.

What is a strike?

When a labor union is unable to reach agreement with management about pay increases or working conditions, the result is usually a strike—the employees walk off the job en masse and march in front of the factory with picket signs until management agrees to their terms (or at least sweetens its initial offer).

In the U.S., large strikes are relatively rare—and when they do happen, they usually only last for a few days. In 2005, for instance, the New York Transit Workers' Union walked off the job for three days, bringing the city's mass-transit system to a complete halt until a compromise was struck with management. Other strikers aren't so lucky: when the nation's air-traffic controllers went on strike in 1981, then-President Ronald Reagan fired all 13,000 of them, saying they had acted illegally.

Sometimes, as a preemptive move during labor negotiations, a company will refuse to allow its employees to work, a strategy called a "lockout." Lockouts are most effective when only some of the company's employees belong to a union, since non-union members will put pressure on the union to come to terms so everyone can go back to work!

Why are some unions so hard to join?

In some professions, union membership can mean the difference between making a comfortable living and just getting by from day to day. That's why certain unions will only accept new members who have been vouched for by existing members, and not just anyone who comes in off the street. Usually, these are the unions that have the strongest contracts with management, meaning that once you've joined, you can expect to have a well-paying job for the foreseeable future!

Mining

What is the deepest mine?

Wherever there's the chance of finding gold, you can be sure people will dig as deep into the ground as is humanly possible. The East Rand mine in South Africa extends to a depth of about three miles, and is only a few feet deeper than the next deepest mine, the Western Deep mine, in the same country. (To give you a sense of just how deep that is, the Empire State Building is 1,472 feet tall, from the bottom of its base to the top of its spire—so the East Rand mine extends down for a distance equal to the height of eight Empire State Buildings!)

As you can guess, working in a mine that deep poses some unique dangers. That far underground, the pressure of earth pushing down from above is almost 10,000 tons per square meter, or close to 1,000 times normal atmospheric pressure—so the roof of the mine has to be unusually strong to protect the workers. There's also the small matter of the temperature, which is well over 100 degrees Fahrenheit—so miners are kept cool by the world's deepest air conditioners (and good luck finding a repairman if one of those happens to break down).

Why is it called the "mother lode"?

In mining, a "lode" is the technical term for a vein of ore (that is, a lengthy deposit of minerals that can snake underground for miles). The term "mother lode" was originally used to refer to a 70-mile-long vein of quartz deposits, flecked with gold, found in northern California during the Gold Rush. Since then, though, the term has been widely used as a figure of speech that translates roughly as "hitting the jackpot!"

What was the world's first mine?

As long as you accept a narrow definition of mining as the extraction of minerals from the earth—and not necessarily digging a miles-deep hole to reach them!—then human beings have been engaging in this practice for tens of thousands of years. There's evidence that primitive peoples mined the iron-containing ore hematite from the "Lion Cave" in Swaziland, Africa, about 43,000 years ago, not to forge metal tools (which was a much later development) but to create pigments for cave painting.

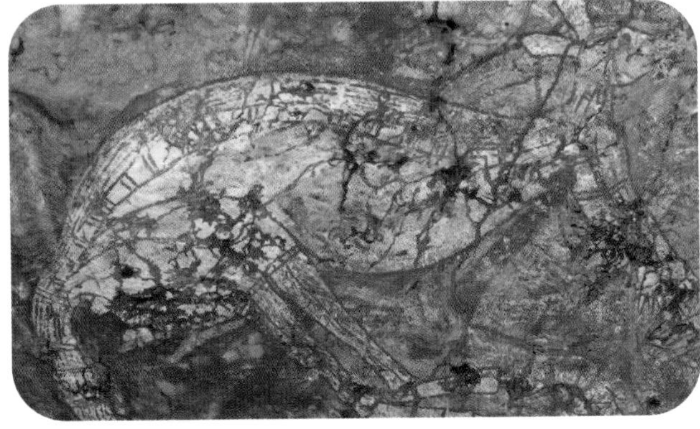

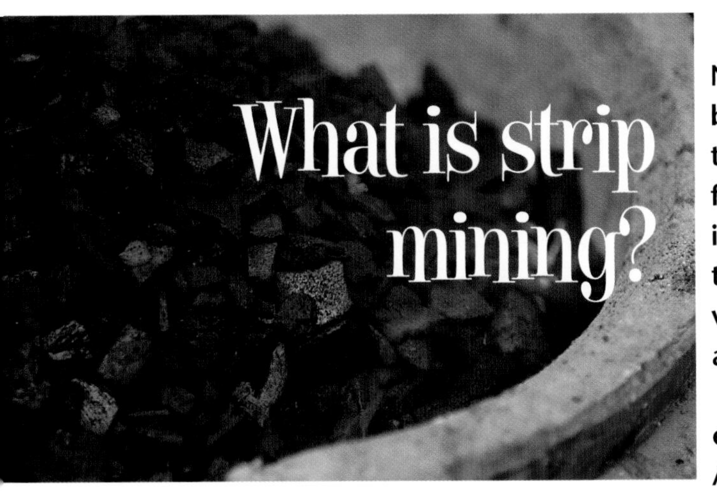

What is strip mining?

Not all of the earth's ores and minerals are buried miles (or even hundreds of feet) under the ground. Coal, in particular, can often be found only a few dozen feet below the surface, in wide seams extending for acres in all directions. Deposits like these are most easily reached via strip mining, which involves overturning vast areas of rock and soil with enormous machines.

However, many people believe the negative effects of strip mining outweigh its benefits. After an area has been strip-mined, it can look, literally, like a deserted moonscape—since all the soil has been overturned, the land can't be reclaimed with crops, and people in nearby towns have often left to escape the noise and devastation. (It's possible to "recover" a strip-mined area for other purposes, but this is an enormously expensive process that few companies are willing to undertake.)

By the way, the underwater counterpart of strip mining is called "dredging." Since people don't live underwater, dredging for minerals has much less of an environmental impact—unless, of course, you happen to be a fish!

What causes mine explosions?

Extracting minerals from deep inside a mine can release dangerous gases trapped in the earth. For example, coal miners often encounter accumulations of the flammable gas methane, which is normally removed by ventilation equipment. If too much methane is allowed to build up, and there's a sudden spark from a lamp, the result can be a huge explosion that collapses the mine and traps or kills the miners.

What is a quarry?

A quarry is a bit like the mining equivalent of a well—a big open hole in the ground where people can go to collect rocks and minerals (such as quartz). Some quarries yield big, square rocks known as "dimension stones," which were used to build the pyramids in Egypt!

What does a prospector do?

In a way, prospecting is the most important part of the mining process—after all, if you dig a diamond mine in a place without any diamonds, you've just wasted a ton of money. A prospector's job is to study the geologic features of a prospective mining area and figure out if there are any valuable minerals to be found. While good prospectors are worth their weight in gold, incompetent ones can bankrupt a mining company!

Airlines & Airports

How many people work at airports?

It takes a lot of manpower (and womanpower) to keep a major airport running. To take just one example, Kennedy Airport in New York employs about 35,000 people, ranging from airplane mechanics to booking agents to the people who run its numerous shops and restaurants. Like other international airports, Kennedy (which occupies almost 5,000 acres of land) can be considered a small city!

Why do so many airlines lose money?

Way back in the 1950s and 1960s, running an airline was like having a license to print money. Today, though, many major airlines operate on the brink of bankruptcy and occasionally are forced to go out of business.

There are a number of reasons why it's so expensive (and unprofitable) to run an airline these days. First, there's the increasing cost of fuel: a large passenger jet consumes about 1,000 gallons of gasoline every hour, meaning even short flights can cost thousands of dollars more than they used to. Second, even before the terrorist attacks of 9/11, airlines had begun to spend an increasing amount of money on security, which is even more crucial today—and the drop-off in casual air travel after 9/11 wasn't good for business, either.

However, in the opinion of most experts, the main thing that has dented the profits of the big airlines is increased competition. Today, travelers are accustomed to scouring the Internet for the cheapest possible fares, and they have more low-cost options to choose from (these "no-frill" airlines don't serve food, for instance, but most people are willing to endure a little bit of hunger for a less expensive ticket!).

Why do short flights tend to cost more than long ones?

One of the enduring mysteries of air travel is why a 3,000-mile flight from New York to Los Angeles often costs less than a 700-mile flight from Atlanta to Chicago. The reason for this is that airlines calculate fares based at least partially on demand, and because many more people travel from New York to L.A. (and vice-versa) than from Atlanta to Chicago, the airlines can afford to offer lower fares for this popular route.

What is a "hub"?

If you've ever traveled with your parents, you may have noticed that the flights of certain airlines tend to "change over" at certain cities (for instance, many Delta Airlines flights originate or change over at Atlanta International Airport). A "hub" airport is where an airline concentrates most of its business, and as you can guess, the bigger the airline, the more hubs it has: American Airlines, for example, has hubs in Chicago, Dallas, St. Louis, and Miami, among other cities.

How does a metal detector work?

When you walk through an airport metal detector, your body is scanned by a harmless magnetic field that causes any metal objects you happen to be carrying to resonate in a characteristic way—and if you emit a "beep," you may be scanned with a handheld device that pinpoints the source of the signal. (By the way, the reason metal detectors don't use X-rays, as you see in some science-fiction movies, is that these rays can be dangerous to travelers.)

What is a duty-free shop?

In many airports, shops are allowed to sell merchandise that isn't subject to city or state sales taxes, not to mention "duties" (a kind of tax levied as you travel from country to country). The main catch is that you can only buy duty-free items from the country you're leaving—so you can't visit your local airport and stock up on cheap clothes!

What was the first airline?

Although airplanes were a crucial factor in World War I (which ended in 1918), it wasn't until the late 1920s that American businessmen explored the potential of airplane travel for regular people (as opposed to, say, mail carriers or military personnel). Foremost among these early pioneers was Juan Trippe, who founded Pan Am Airways, the first major world airline, in 1927. Pan Am's first flight was from Miami to Havana, Cuba, and it quickly established a near-monopoly on international service.

For a number of years, Pan Am was the most well-known (and most profitable) airline in the world. Unfortunately, Pan Am's fortunes started to fade in 1973, when the energy crisis (caused by an embargo on oil shipments by Middle Eastern countries) cut into its profits, and it began to face increasing competition from other international carriers. The final blow came in 1988, when a Pan Am flight from London to New York was blown up by terrorists, killing everyone aboard. The airline was sued by the victims' survivors and finally went out of business in 1991.

Clocks

What is the world's most accurate clock?

This is a hard question to answer, since scientists are constantly inventing newer and more accurate ways of keeping time; the current record-holder is a clock in England that's accurate to one second in about 100 million years. This isn't the kind of clock you can hang on the wall, though; it's based on the atomic vibrations of a single atom of mercury (which, for the record, vibrates about a million billion times per second).

How fast does time go?

That's easy: one second per second! Seriously, though, this is the kind of question that has driven scientists (and philosophers) nuts since the beginning of history. Since there's nothing we can measure time against, there's no way to tell how fast it goes, except in a psychological sense. So one answer to this question might be: time goes faster when you're having fun!

How does a water clock work?

Some ancient civilizations kept time by the observation of stars and planets, but others hit on a more earthbound idea: letting water drip out of the bottom or side of a large bowl at a regular rate, then measuring time according to the level of water inside the bowl. Although these clocks were accurate enough for most purposes, their main flaw was that it's extremely difficult to control the flow of water—as you can see for yourself whenever your toilet acts up!

How did time start?

This is another question that scientists are a long way from being able to answer. According to the most widely accepted theory, time started when the universe did, at the Big Bang about 15 billion years ago. (Since time didn't exist until then, it wouldn't make sense to ask what happened "before" the Big Bang.) But some scientists believe time did in fact exist before the massive explosion that created our universe—in which case it's possible that time doesn't have an origin, but has existed forever.

How long have people worn watches?

Although wristwatches are a fairly recent invention (only becoming widespread in the 20th century), pocket watches have been around for a surprisingly long time. The first recognizable watch was invented way back in 1524, but it had one major flaw: since batteries hadn't been invented yet, timepieces had to be driven by weights, like the pendulum of a grandfather clock. Imagine fishing a miniature grandfather clock out of your pocket, and you can guess why this watch's time hadn't quite come!

The real breakthrough in watch technology happened 150 years later, in 1675. That's when a tiny gizmo called the spiral balance spring allowed for the creation of smaller, more accurate watches that could tell time within a margin of error of 10 or 20 seconds, compared to 10 or 20 minutes for earlier models. The next big innovation was the incorporation of a tiny piece of quartz, the regular vibrations of which made watches even more accurate.

Whatever mechanism they used, until modern times, all watches had to be wound by hand. Today, of course, most folks wear battery-powered watches, which makes winding them a thing of the distant past.

Why does time go faster when you're higher off the ground?

According to Albert Einstein's theory of relativity, time passes more slowly in a gravitational field (the explanation is too complicated to go into here, but it involves the acceleration of moving objects). Because the earth's gravitational field is slightly stronger at ground level than, say, a thousand feet in the air, a clock ticks slightly faster at high altitudes. (The effect is way too tiny for an ordinary person to notice: if a super-accurate clock were to orbit the earth for 10,000 years, it would only pick up about one second compared to a clock on the ground!)

Oddly enough, the same effect that makes time go faster at high altitudes also causes it to go faster when you're traveling at high speeds. In everyday life, this effect is incredibly small: for example, you'll age about 10 billionths of a second more slowly during a flight from New York to Los Angeles than will your cousin standing still on the ground. But the effect becomes more noticeable at high percentages of the speed of light (about 286,000 miles per second). If you were somehow to travel to a nearby star and back at 60 percent of light speed, you'd age one-fifth more slowly than a person staying put back on earth.

Why is it called denim?

For a long time, historians assumed that the name of this popular cotton weave derived from the French town of Nîmes—"serge de Nîmes" meaning "fabric from Nîmes." While this is probably true, it's also possible that the word denim comes from "serge de nim" ("nim" being another kind of fabric popular at this time), or that "serge de Nîmes" actually described a fabric manufactured in England in the 17th century, which was named after the French town of Nîmes to make it seem more exotic.

Whatever the case, there's no denying the impact denim has had on American clothing. Because it's so durable (one clothing magazine described it as "substantial, forthright, and unpretentious"), denim was the natural choice when Levi Strauss created his first pair of blue jeans in the late 19th century. For decades, jeans were sold to laboring men as work pants; it was only after World War II that they became popular for everyday use. (By the way, the reason denim pants are also known as "jeans" is probably because "jean" was another fabric once used for work pants.)

Why do men's and women's shirts button on the opposite sides?

You may have noticed that men's (or boys') shirts button left side over right, while women's (or girls') shirts button right side over left. No one is quite sure why this is, but the most likely theory is that men have always dressed themselves, and the left-over-right system is easier for right-handers (which most people are). Wealthy women, on the other hand, were more likely to be dressed by their servants, who, being right-handed (and facing the opposite way), were more comfortable with a right-over-left arrangement.

How was the zipper invented?

Technically, the zipper was conceived by Elias Howe, the inventor of the sewing machine. In 1851, Howe received a patent for what he called an "automatic, continuous clothing closure," but he never got around to marketing his nifty little device. It wasn't until 50 years later that an inventor named Whitcomb Judson unveiled his zipper-like "clasp locker" at the Chicago World's Fair, and a couple of decades later, this idea was improved on by Gideon Sundback (yes, people had much cooler names back then!). By the way, the word "zipper" was coined in the 1930s by the B.F. Goodrich Company.

How does a lint roller work?

Lint is composed of loose fabrics that cling to articles of clothing (either picked up from the surrounding air or shed from the garment itself). A lint roller is a low-tech device that scoops up these fabrics on a round surface coated with adhesive. You can get the same job done with a piece of scotch tape, but it'll take you much more time!

How are clothes dry-cleaned?

Some clothes—like sports jackets or evening gowns—can't be thrown into a washing machine and dryer, because they're likely to shrink and wrinkle. Instead, these items are dry-cleaned, meaning they're cleaned with chemicals rather than with detergent and water. Because dry-cleaning is so involved (not to mention dangerous, if you don't know what you're doing), your mom and dad give their dry-clean–only clothes to a neighborhood cleaner.

Why do clothes need to be ironed?

Some clothes (like shirts and underwear) are prone to wrinkling, which happens because the fibers they're woven from get kinked out of shape. An iron deals with the kinks by softening them with steam, then straightening them out with its broad, flat underside. (Because most clothes sold nowadays are designed not to wrinkle, ironing has become something of a lost skill!)

Why do you put on a "pair" of pants?

Think about it for a second—you don't wear a "pair of shirts," so why do you wear a pair of pants? The answer has to do with the history of pants, which is more complicated than you might think, since what we know today as pants used to be (or still are) called slacks, trousers, breeches, or pantaloons (okay, maybe your mom doesn't call them pantaloons, but you get the general idea).

People in western Europe started wearing pants-like garments in the 16th century, a habit they probably picked up from the Ottoman Turks (who themselves learned about pants from the Persians and Scythians, a nomadic tribe of northern Europe). The most likely reason that "pants" were pluralized is that one separate "pant" was put on each leg, then joined together around the hips by a cord or belt.

As pants became more popular, seamstresses learned to create a single garment with both "pants" joined to a strip of cloth encircling the hip. Old habits die hard, however, and "pants" have remained plural to the present day.

Locks & Keys

How does a combination lock work?

A simple, three-number combination lock has a simple mechanism. Inside the lock are three "cams," circular gizmos with a small notch cut out on one side. The cams are laid on top of each other so that the lock will open only when the notches all line up, and the way you line the notches up is by turning each cam individually, with the lock's dial. The combination of the lock is the recipe for how far each cam has to be turned to line up with the others.

What is a skeleton key?

From the way they're used in movies, you might think those long, spindly, sinister-looking skeleton keys are somehow more advanced than ordinary keys. Actually, though, skeleton keys are extremely primitive, and are rarely used nowadays because it's so easy to pick their locks.

What is a "latchkey kid"?

Only a few years ago, it was unusual for parents in the U.S. to allow their grade-school kids to come home from school while they were still at work. The media called these tykes "latchkey kids," derived from the British word for "house key." You don't hear much about latchkey kids anymore, probably because so many kids nowadays are trusted to look after themselves!

Why do hotels use key cards?

Believe it or not, years ago hotels handed their guests plain, ordinary, metal keys, just like the kind you use to open your front door. Today, though, most hotels rely on computer-generated "key cards," which activate an electronic lock when they're slid into a special slot on or by the door.

When you think about it, the attraction of the key card is easy to see. Unlike an ordinary key, it can't be duplicated by a customer (so he can't, say, sneak back into his room after he's checked out of the hotel). It's also much cheaper to replace than a metal key, and allows the hotel staff greater flexibility in assigning rooms.

Today, key cards are so common that some people believe (falsely, as it turns out) that they contain more information than just your room number—for years, rumors have circulated that a thief who swipes a hotel guest's key card can access his credit-card number and go on a buying spree. Even though this has been disproved, certain guests have become so distrustful of key cards that some hotels are switching to newer, even more advanced systems.

What does it mean to get the "key to the city"?

It'd be nice if it were a key that actually worked, but the "key to the city" that's sometimes bestowed on visiting dignitaries is strictly ceremonial, symbolizing the goodwill of the mayor and other important people. This tradition comes from medieval England, where honored guests received the "freedom of the city," meaning they were allowed to own land or start their own businesses.

What is a retinal scanner?

Just as all people have different fingerprints, they also have different patterns of blood vessels in their retinas—the part of the eye that absorbs light. A retinal scanner works by scanning a person's eye with a low-intensity beam of light, matching the results to its database, and letting the person in if he's a proper match. The technology is effective, but because many people object to having their eyes scanned, it has yet to catch on outside high-security workplaces.

How do thieves crack safes?

If all a safe had to do was hold valuables inside, forever, it would be impossible to "crack." The reason even the most advanced safes are vulnerable to thieves is that there always has to be a legitimate way to get inside, whether by the safe's owner or by a professional locksmith (in case the lock malfunctions). A successful safecracker can recognize the safe's "weak spot" and get to work accordingly.

It's not easy, though, so too bad if you were planning on this as a career. The most secure safes have advanced combination locks, which make the one on your school locker seem about as effective as a wad of gum. It's possible for a thief with advanced equipment and excellent hearing to "pick" the lock, though this can take so long that he's likely to be caught in the process. If the lock is too tough, a thief may attempt to drill through the side of the safe, or even blow it up with explosives.

Because modern safes are so hard to crack, the most popular Plan A among thieves is to steal the entire safe, take it to a remote location, and work on it at their leisure. This makes sense if the safe is small, but it's hard to sneak a two-ton bank vault out the back door without being noticed!

Robots

Why are so many people afraid of robots?

Science-fiction writers have long speculated about what would happen if human beings created genuinely intelligent, thinking robots. Unfortunately, many of them have come to the conclusion that the robots would see themselves as superior, and either eliminate or enslave the human race. This distant prospect (not to mention the alien-looking appearance of movie robots) probably has a lot to do with the average person's "robotophobia."

What is the "Turing Test"?

Proposed way back in 1950 by the pioneering scientist Alan Turing, the Turing Test is a simple way to determine whether a machine has reached a human level of intelligence. One robot and one human are hidden out of sight in separate rooms, and a human investigator asks them a series of questions via e-mail. If the answers of the robot are indistinguishable from the answers of the human, then the robot is, for all practical purposes, just as smart as the human is!

What is the difference between an android and a robot?

That's simple: androids haven't been invented yet! Conceived by science-fiction writers, androids are robots that have a human appearance (and behave in such convincingly human fashion that most people don't know they're artificial). It's often thought that a true android would need to possess human skin and hair in order to pass itself off as a real person, but we'll have to let future generations decide that issue.

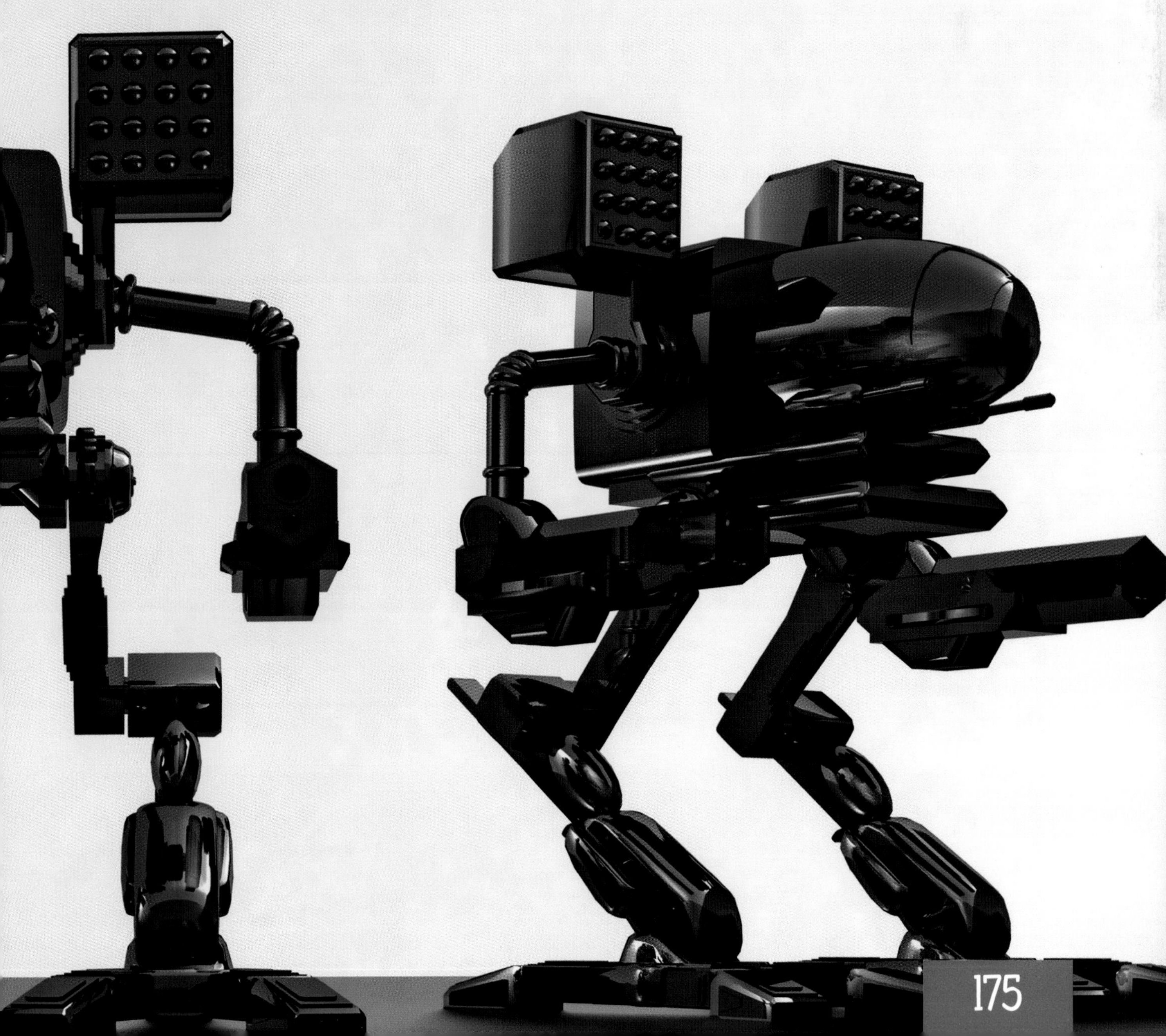

Why is it called a robot?

Although the concept of a mechanical man has existed for centuries, the word "robot" is a relatively recent invention: it was coined by the Czechoslovakian playwright Karel Capek in his 1920 play *R.U.R.* (which stands for "Rossum's Universal Robots.") Capek probably derived this word from the Czech verb "robotovat," which means "to work."

Capek's robot was made of metal, which is the way most people envision robots. But if you're not overly preoccupied with what your mechanical man is made of, references to primitive robots are scattered throughout early literature. For example, the ancient Jewish legend of the "Golem" tells of a monster made out of clay, and the Greek god Hephaestus supposedly had a pair of artificial servants forged, more appropriately, out of pure gold.

Amazingly, the Renaissance inventor and painter Leonardo da Vinci sketched plans for a primitive robot in his notebooks—though it's unclear whether he actually contemplated building this robot or was just playing around with the idea as a way to understand human anatomy.

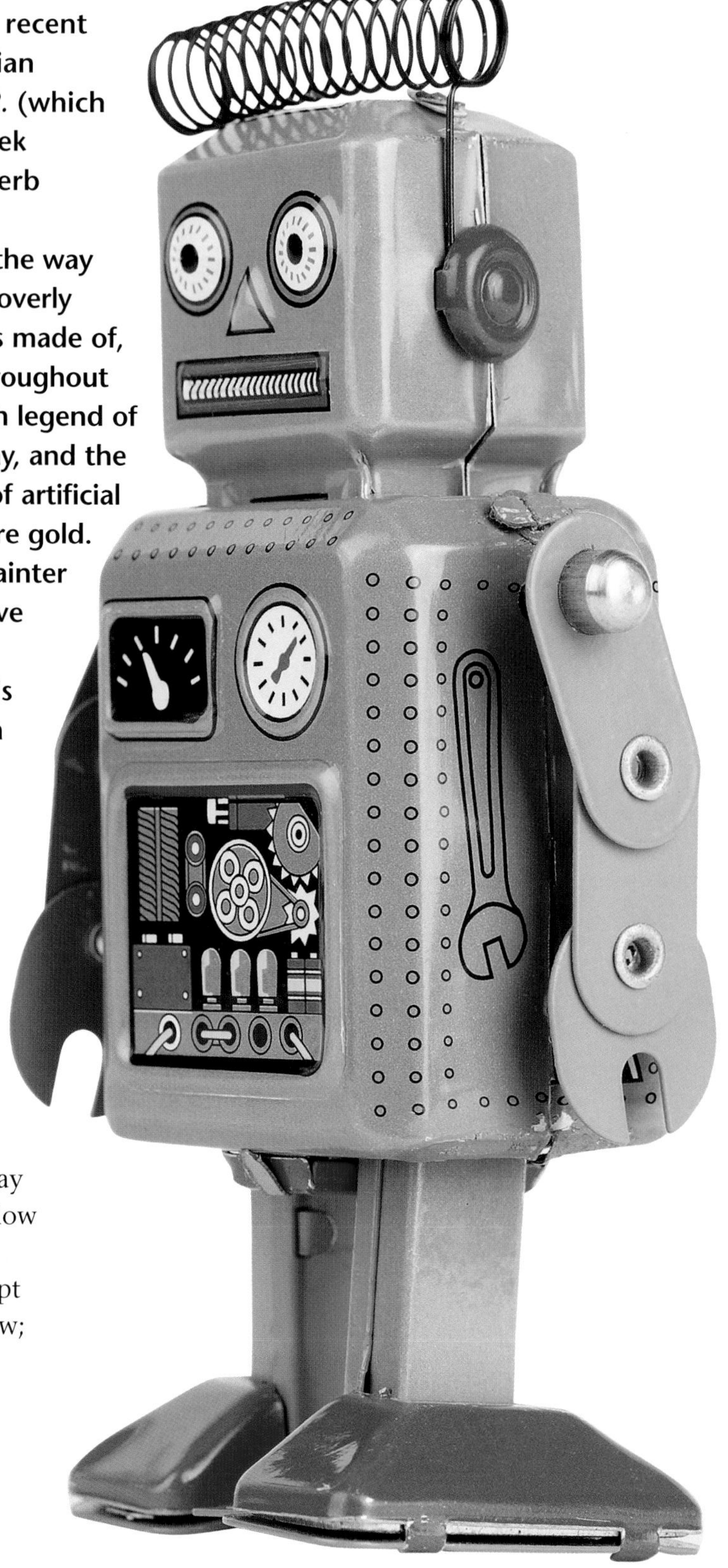

What are the Three Laws of Robotics?

The science-fiction writer Isaac Asimov conceived a future in which intelligent robots served mankind, subject to three basic laws: 1) a robot may not harm a human being, or, through inaction, allow a human being to come to harm; 2) a robot must obey the orders given to it by human beings, except where such orders would conflict with the First Law; and 3) a robot must protect its own existence, as long as this does not conflict with the First or Second Laws.

How are robots used in the home?

Fifty years ago, it was widely expected that the households of the 21st century would be equipped with robotic butlers that tutored the kids and spoke in perfect English. Unfortunately, though, most of the robots employed in homes today are either toys (such as robot dogs) or squat, self-propelled vacuum cleaners. Yes, some people do own robotic butlers, but the most these gizmos can usually do is mix a single drink and (maybe) bring it to the dinner table without spilling it!

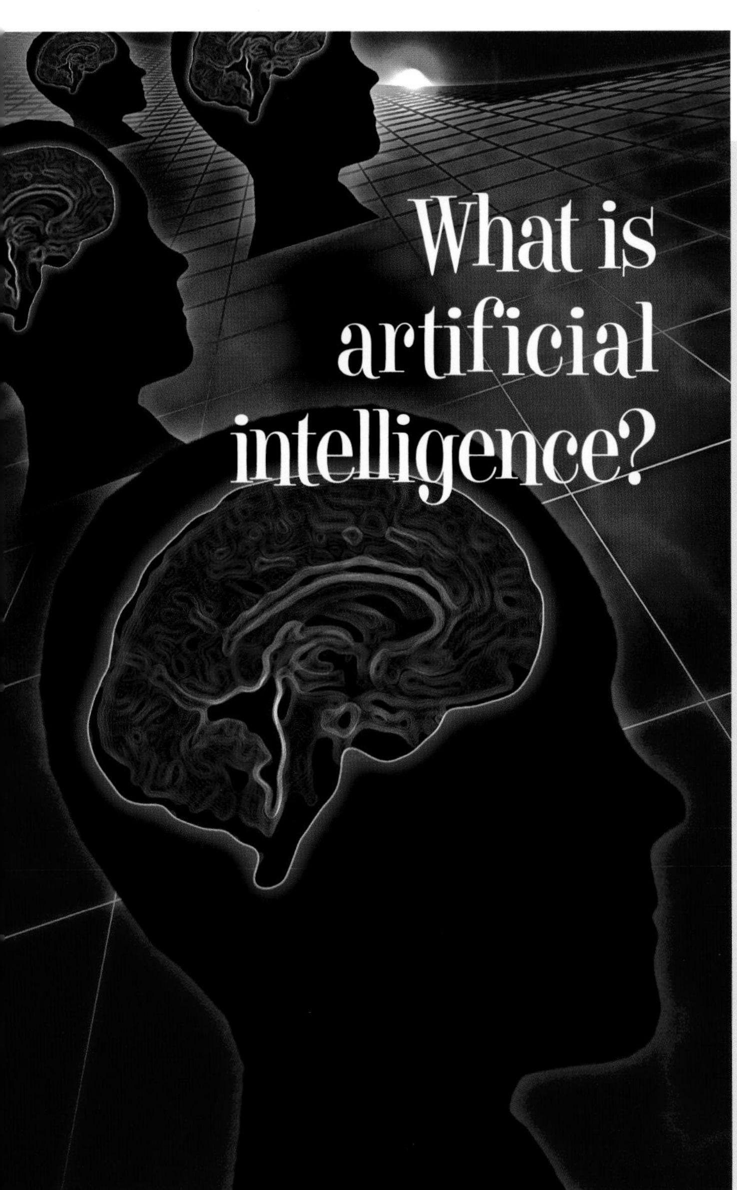

What is artificial intelligence?

As the technology goes, building a human-sized robot with movable arms and legs (and fingers and toes) is a relatively easy proposition. The much harder part is creating an artificial "brain" that allows the robot to perform complicated tasks (and, perhaps, even be aware of itself and what it's doing). You might think scientists have been making steady progress in artificial intelligence (or "AI," as it's usually called), but you'd be wrong: even the most advanced robots barely reach the intellectual level of a two-year-old child!

Part of the reason artificial intelligence is such an elusive goal is that scientists don't really understand how the human brain works, so there's no single, reliable model for a robot brain. Some researchers take a "top-down" approach, programming their robots with detailed instructions (kind of like writing a sophisticated computer program). Today, though, most experts prefer the "bottom-up" approach: they equip their robot with simple, intuitive rules (such as the difference between left and right), and then sit back as it "learns" from experience.

Telephones

How big were the first cell phones?

As is the case with most gadgets, the very first cell phones (which came on the market in the 1980s) were unbelievably big and clunky compared to the sleek models of today. Even still, these early cell phones were considered status symbols, since only rich people and wheeler-dealers could afford to buy them (and to use them, since making a cell-phone call used to be much more expensive!).

Why did the first area codes have low numbers?

Before the age of touch-tone phones, callers had to use old-fashioned dial phones—and dialing "8" or "9" took a lot more time than dialing "1" or "2." For this reason, area codes were designed to reduce the amount of work a person had to do when calling long-distance. For example, New York was assigned the easy-to-dial area code 212, while Washington, D.C., had 201 and Los Angeles had 213. Today, of course, practically no one uses dial phones, so there's no longer any real need for this system.

How do cell phones work?

As you've probably realized, the main difference between cell phones and "ordinary" phones is that old-fashioned phones require old-fashioned phone lines—thin wires that snake into your home from outside lines. (Yes, a portable phone doesn't have wires, but that's because it transmits a signal to a receiver in your home that is itself connected to the phone line).

Rather than wires, a cell phone transmits its signal using radio waves. However, this isn't as simple as one phone transmitting a signal directly to another phone, like a walkie-talkie. The "cell" in cell phones stands for "cellular," which refers to the fact that a cell-phone area is divided into cell-like grids, each of which has its own transmission tower. This grid collects, sorts, and routes the various phone calls, so that thousands of people in a big city can all talk on their cell phones at once.

Because there are so many different kinds of cell phones—many of which use different kinds of grids—buying the right phone is one of the most complicated decisions a person can make!

What is IP telephony?

Over the past few years, companies have figured out how to transmit phone calls over the Internet—which means, with the proper equipment, you can call someone on your computer and have a normal conversation. The big advantage of IP (Internet protocol) telephony is that long-distance calls don't cost any more than local calls, for the same reason that it's just as cheap to send an e-mail to the other side of the world as to your neighbor next door.

How can phones still work when the power is off?

The phone lines that come into your home carry a small amount of electricity—just enough to provide a dial tone during blackouts. That's why, during the big East Coast blackout of 2003, many cell-phone customers were left without service (since the local transmission towers had stopped working), but people with "land lines" were able to talk on their phones just fine.

How was the telephone invented?

Every school kid is taught that Alexander Graham Bell invented the telephone in 1875. The story isn't quite that simple, though, for two main reasons: first, it's difficult to define exactly what a "telephone" is (a way for two people to talk over large distances? a wire that carries sound in electrical form?), and second, the idea of the telephone evolved so gradually, over so many years, that it makes no sense to assign credit to just one person.

That said, many people believe that the Italian Antoni Meucci should be credited with inventing the telephone, since he demonstrated his "teletrophone" (a transmitter and a receiver joined by an electrical wire) as far back as 1860. About a dozen years later, Elisha Gray of Chicago unveiled his "harmonic telegraph," which included many features of the early telephone.

There's no evidence that Alexander Graham Bell stole his idea for the telephone from Gray or Meucci, but he did take one very important step: he had his invention patented, thus forever associating his name with the device (which is also why so many phone companies have the name "Bell" in them).

How long does it take to trace a call?

You've probably seen movies in which the hero tries to keep the bad guy on the phone for a few minutes so the police can trace the call and figure out where he's dialing from. Well, this is nonsense—the fact is, if the authorities are alerted in advance, a phone call can be traced the instant the call is made, in the same way that "Caller ID" tells you the number of the person on the other end as soon as the phone rings.

Asteroids & Comets

How can we defend the earth against asteroids?

It's not likely to happen tomorrow, or the day after, but scientists believe the earth is due to be hit by a massive comet or asteroid sometime soon—"soon" being, in astronomical terms, sometime in the next few thousand years. Since the dinosaurs were wiped out by a giant asteroid that smashed into the earth 65 million years ago, a comparable impact could conceivably wipe out the human race, as well as most other species.

But don't lie awake nights worrying about this: some very talented scientists are busy thinking up ways to prevent an asteroid collision from ever happening. As matters stand now, there are two possible ways to destroy an approaching asteroid and save the day. If a three-mile-wide rock is spotted millions of miles away, there may be enough time to launch a space probe to "nudge" it slightly and deflect its orbit, so it misses the earth by a few hundred (or few hundred thousand) miles. And if the asteroid isn't detected until it's right on top of us, experts are studying ways to destroy it with ultra-powerful nuclear weapons (hopefully before it has entered the atmosphere, in which case this technique may cause more problems than it solves!).

What comet has the strangest orbit?

Unlike planets, which revolve around the sun in roughly circular orbits, comets are notorious for their "elliptical" trajectories. The strangest comet in this regard is 2000CR105, which veers as far away as 50 billion kilometers from the sun and as close as 6 billion kilometers (for the sake of comparison, the earth is about 150 million kilometers from the sun). This comet is so strange that it has led some astronomers to speculate about a massive planet, way beyond Pluto, that has influenced its orbit.

How can we detect approaching asteroids?

The National Aeronautics and Space Administration (NASA) is pretty good at keeping tabs on the asteroids we know about—the agency catalogs the biggest objects in the asteroid belt and assesses how likely they are to stray into earth's orbit. What worries the experts, though, are the asteroids we don't know about yet. It's possible for ground-based telescopes, working in tandem, to detect approaching asteroids, but a space telescope orbiting far beyond the earth would be much more efficient!

Why is there an asteroid belt?

Astronomers have long been puzzled by the asteroid belt, a collection of millions of asteroids (of diameters ranging from a fraction of an inch to a few hundred miles) orbiting around the sun between the planets Mars and Jupiter. For a long time, it was believed that these asteroids were the remains of an ancient planet that was destroyed hundreds of millions or billions of years ago, possibly by an impact from an enormous comet.

Today, though, most scientists subscribe to a more plausible (though much less dramatic) theory. It has long been believed that terrestrial planets like Mars and Earth formed from the gradual "accretion" (that is, the merging together over hundreds of millions of years) of bands of rocks and debris orbiting the sun. In this view, the asteroid belt isn't composed of the remains of a destroyed planet; rather, it's a collection of loose rocks that never managed to accrete together into a planet in the first place—probably because the huge gravitational field of Jupiter interfered with the process.

Why don't more asteroids hit the earth?

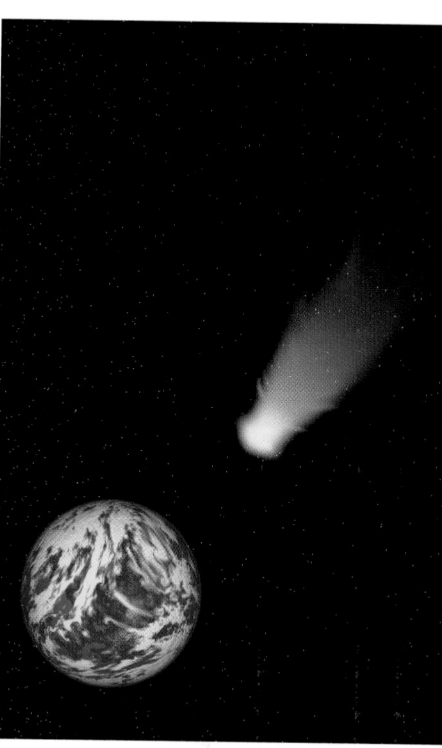

As big as it seems to us, in astronomical terms, the Earth is relatively tiny—and asteroids are even tinier. The vast majority of asteroids in our solar system come nowhere near to hitting the earth, to the extent that a rock passing within 100,000 miles of our planet is considered a "near miss" by astronomers! Also, scientists believe the massive gravitational fields of Jupiter and Saturn help to "sweep up" objects approaching from beyond the solar system, so they don't even come near to approaching (much less menacing) the Earth.

What is the Kuiper Belt?

As the Asteroid Belt is to, well, asteroids, the Kuiper Belt is to comets. This belt—which is actually shaped more like a thick donut—is a collection of millions of icy fragments beyond the orbit of Neptune, and is the source of many of the small comets that approach Earth. As distant as it is, though, the Kuiper Belt is our next-door neighbor compared to the Oort Cloud, another collection of comets about 1,000 times as far away as Pluto!

Space Exploration

How many flying saucers have visited earth?

Anything is possible, so there's no way to state with 100 percent certainty that no flying saucer has ever landed on earth. But most scientists are comfortable putting the odds at about one in a million: despite what you may have seen on TV shows or read in magazines, there's absolutely no proof that UFOs have visited our planet. Most sightings can easily be explained as optical illusions, or as unpublicized flights of top-secret military aircraft.

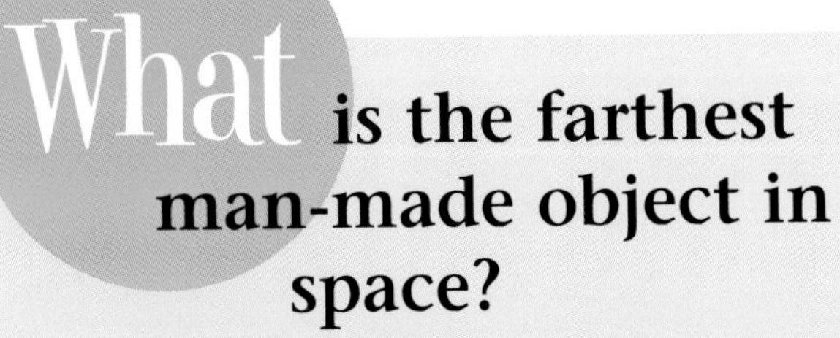

What is the farthest man-made object in space?

As of April 2002, *Voyager I*—a probe launched from Earth in 1977—officially passed beyond the orbit of Pluto, making it the most distant man-made object in the universe. (As tempting as it is to say that *Voyager* has journeyed completely outside the solar system, scientists can't say this for certain, since there may be other, as yet undetected planets circling around the sun beyond Pluto's orbit!)

What is the SETI project?

For quite some time now, scientists have realized that we're unlikely to be visited by real, flesh-and-blood aliens—and, conversely, that we're unlikely to be able to visit them anytime soon. The reason is that the distance between stars is so incredibly vast (trillions upon trillions of miles) that even a fast round trip would take thousands of years.

That's where the SETI (Search for Extraterrestrial Intelligence) Project comes in: it's an organized effort to detect radio signals from outer space. SETI involves huge arrays of radio antennae pointed at various areas of the sky, in the hopes of one day being able to receive an "intelligent" broadcast (in the same way an alien civilization could conceivably intercept our TV transmissions!). This is a much more promising (and cheaper) proposition than developing a rocket technology to carry us to the nearby stars.

With so many stars out there, SETI seems like a sure bet, right? Well, that's part of the problem—nobody knows how many other intelligent civilizations there are in our galaxy (that is, if there are any at all), and we certainly don't know at which stars, out of billions, to aim our receivers. So SETI is a slow, steady process that may (or may not) pay off decades, or centuries, down the road.

What is panspermia?

Ever since ancient times, scientists and philosophers have speculated about the origins of life. Today, it's widely accepted that the single-celled organisms that populated the earth 3 billion years ago gradually evolved into the plants and animals we see today. But where did those original organisms come from in the first place?

Most scientists believe (and with good reason) that the very first bacteria evolved gradually, over hundreds of millions of years, in the primitive earth's oceans. But others have put forward the theory that life on earth may have been "seeded" from outer space, since it's possible for a microbe, buried deep within a meteorite, to survive a million-year-long journey in the frozen depths of space, and then reproduce itself when it reaches a more welcoming environment. This theory is known as "panspermia."

Keep in mind that panspermia doesn't magically "explain away" the very first cells. Rather, the theory says that these cells evolved naturally somewhere else—in a gas cloud, say, or on another planet—and slowly made their way to Earth via completely natural processes.

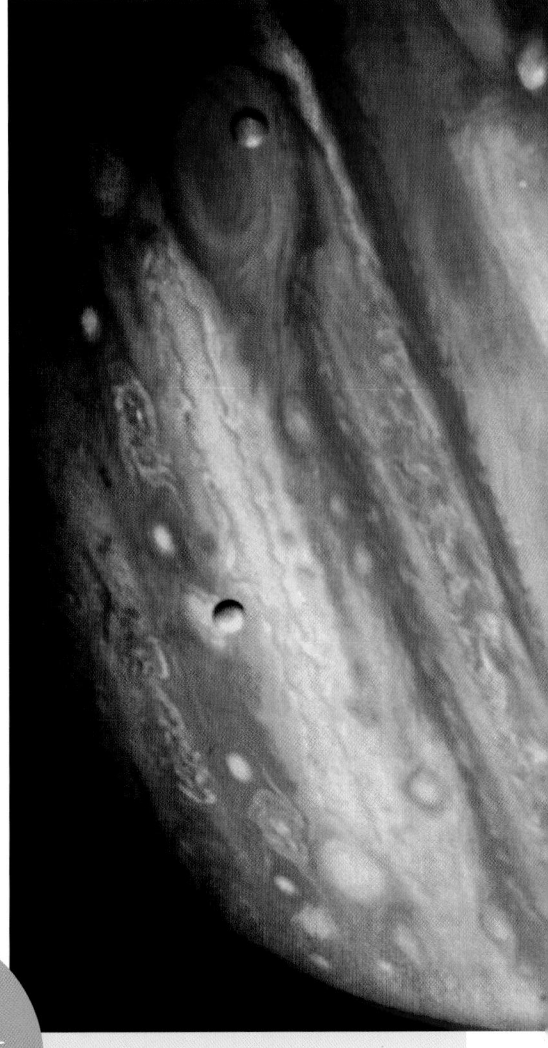

Why are aliens called "little green men"?

No one knows the exact origin of this phrase, but the most likely explanation goes back to Edgar Rice Burroughs (the creator of Tarzan), who referred to the "green men of Mars" in his 1917 novel *A Princess on Mars*. The "little" part is more mysterious: it may have originated as a sarcastic remark by an astronomer or a government official, despairing that folks raised on comic books expected to find "little green men" on other planets.

Why are scientists interested in Jupiter's moons?

You might think experts in search of extraterrestrial life would focus their efforts on Mars, but practically nobody believes Mars harbors any microscopic life (it may once have, a billion years ago, but almost certainly not now). What really perks up scientists' interest are Jupiter's moons Europa and Callisto, since there's evidence that these satellites may have liquid water, which is essential for life. A manned mission to Jupiter is out of the question, but experts are hoping future space probes will be able to land on these moons and search for microscopic organisms.

Why do rockets have stages?

Before a rocket is launched, most of its weight comes from the enormous amount of fuel it needs in order to climb out of earth's atmosphere. Once that fuel is spent, though, there's no longer any need for the rocket to carry the massive containers the fuel was stored in, which are jettisoned into space. Because the biggest rockets have multiple stages, by the time they reach orbit they pretty much have been reduced to a tiny passenger cabin!

What was Project Apollo?

In 1961, the U.S. embarked on an expensive, ambitious program with one seemingly impossible goal: to land a man on the moon no later than 1970. Project Apollo, as it was called, was fueled partly by scientific curiosity, but partly by a desire to restore the national prestige of the U.S. and get to the moon before the Russians did.

Project Apollo wasn't just a matter of building an enormous rocket and shooting it into space. Many, many problems had to be solved before that, such as designing advanced computer circuitry to run the spacecraft's vital functions, teaching astronauts to deal with weightlessness, and perfecting the design of the massive boosters needed to lift a ship out of earth's orbit. For the first few years, the National Aeronautics and Space Administration (NASA) perfected its technique on smaller, unmanned ships, and then built the enormous *Apollo* spacecraft that took men to the moon in July 1969.

By the time it ended in 1972, Project Apollo had cost about $25 billion, money well spent for the technological advances (like modern computers) it helped usher in. Ironically, though, the Russians never even came close to reaching the moon—so the Space Race turned out hardly to be a "race" at all!

How do astronauts go the bathroom?

As you can imagine, doing a one's business in the weightless environment of outer space poses some sticky hygiene issues. Rather than water—which would float out of the bowl, along with everything else—a space toilet relies on air suction to draw the astronaut's waste into a special compartment. Since this is a more involved process, astronauts have to be especially careful—they can't just zip in and out of the bathroom like you do at home!

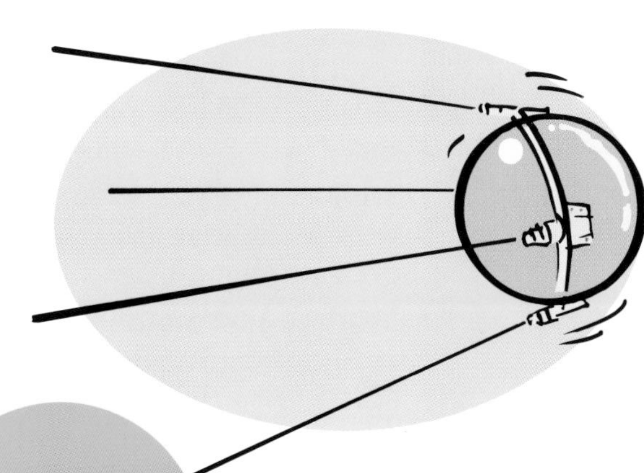

What was Sputnik?

In 1957, the Soviet Union launched the very first satellite into space, called *Sputnik I* (*Sputniks II, III, IV*, and *V* followed over the next few years). The result in the U.S. was instant panic: there was a feeling that the scientists in the Soviet Union had embarrassed their American counterparts, and that the U.S. needed to surpass the Russians' efforts lest the entire globe be circled by Communist satellites. In effect, *Sputnik I* was the opening gun of what became known as the Space Race.

Why are animals launched into space?

In the early days of the Space Race, scientists in the U.S. and Soviet Union knew a lot less about outer space than they would have liked. Specifically, they had no idea if a human being could function over long periods of time in a weightless environment, or if astronauts would be injured by the acceleration required to launch a rocket out of the atmosphere.

Although there may have been earlier, unpublicized examples, the first animal known to be launched into space was a rhesus monkey named Albert I, on a V-2 rocket in New Mexico in 1948. Albert I survived the trip, but his successor, Albert II, wasn't as lucky: he crash-landed after reaching a height of 83 miles. One of the most famous animal-nauts was a Russian dog named Laika, who spent 10 lonely days in orbit on a Sputnik satellite and died when the craft burned up in earth's atmosphere. (Laika was known in the U.S. as "Muttnik.")

Today, animal testing in outer space is conducted in much more humane conditions. Since humans have pretty much mastered acceleration and short-term weightlessness, most animal experiments today concern the long-term effects of a zero-gravity environment.

What is quantum cosmology?

Physicists use two theories to explain the world. General relativity concerns the relationship of space, time, and matter on large, universe-sized scales, while quantum physics does the same for the microscopic regions within and between atoms. The problem is, there's evidence that these two theories are incompatible in extreme conditions—namely, the infinitely hot, infinitely dense "singularity" of the Big Bang. Quantum cosmologists try to devise new theories that incorporate both relativity and quantum physics, not an easy task!

Why is it called "quantum foam"?

In the past few years, physicists have come to the conclusion that empty space isn't infinitely divisible—that is, space is composed of "atoms" of space in the same way that a basketball is composed of "atoms" of various elements. If these scientists are right, at unbelievably small scales—about a trillionth of a trillionth the size of an atomic nucleus—space looks like a chaotic "quantum foam" rather than a smooth expanse of nothingness.

How do we know the universe is expanding?

When an object recedes, the wavelength of the light it emits becomes slightly shortened (for the same reason the whistle of a train lowers in pitch as it rumbles past you). Astronomers have measured the light emitted by distant galaxies, and have demonstrated that this light is "blue-shifted"—meaning these galaxies are speeding away from us at a high velocity. Since every galaxy in the universe appears to be speeding away from every other galaxy in the universe, this is conclusive proof that the universe is expanding.

What is "quintessence"?

Scientists have long assumed that there are only four forces in the universe. The first, gravity, causes objects to fall and matter to lump together into stars and galaxies; the second, electromagnetism, regulates the behavior of atoms (and lurks behind such familiar phenomena as light and electricity); the third, the strong force, holds the tightly bound nuclei of atoms together; and the fourth, the weak force, is responsible for radioactive decay.

What is inflation?

For some physicists, the Big Bang doesn't explain all the properties of the universe—such as the fact that the night sky appears the same no matter what direction we look in. These scientists have proposed a theory called "inflation," in which a microscopic region of space suddenly began doubling in size every trillionth of a trillionth of a second, expanding the universe to billions (and possibly trillions and quadrillions) of light years in diameter and "smoothing out" any initial differences.

What is the Big Crunch?

Although the universe is expanding now, there's no physical law that says this expansion has to continue forever. At some point, it's possible (though unlikely) that the force of gravity will put a "brake" on the expansion, and the trillion or so galaxies in the universe will start collapsing in on each other. If this happens, the fate of the universe will be a "Big Crunch," a kind of reverse Big Bang in which all the galaxies squeeze together into an infinitely small, infinitely dense point (or "singularity," as physicists call it).

Recently, astronomers have discovered evidence that the expansion of the universe is speeding up, not slowing down as most theories predict. One possible cause of this expansion is a fifth force called "quintessence" (literally, "the fifth essence"), which acts as a kind of anti-gravity, causing galaxies to repel rather than attract each other. If quintessence is proven to exist, it could have dire implications for the distant future of the universe, trillions of years from now.

How was the Big Bang discovered?

One of the most important scientific discoveries of all time was made in 1964, when two scientists named Arno Penzias and Robert Wilson tried to figure out why their radio dish was picking up an unusual amount of "noise" (that is, stray radio transmissions that couldn't be traced to a particular source). After ruling out all the other possibilities, Penzias and Wilson concluded that the transmissions were originating randomly, in every direction, from the deepest regions of outer space.

By itself, this may not seem all that remarkable. However, Penzias and Wilson had unwittingly settled an age-old question: how did the universe begin? In the 1940s and 1950s, scientists had proposed a "Big Bang" theory, which held that the universe began about 15 billion years ago in an unbelievably violent explosion. According to this theory, the intense radiation released by the Big Bang should have cooled down by the present day to exactly the kind of low-energy radio waves detected by Penzias and Wilson. (By the way, these remnants of the Big Bang also cause those eerie flickers of light when your TV set is between channels!)

Chemistry

What is a chemical compound?

It may not sound like much of an explanation, but a chemical compound is any chemical that can be written down with a formula: water, for example, is technically known to chemists as H_2O, while salt is NaCl. However, the elements themselves don't determine the compound; you also have to know precisely how these elements are joined together, since different configurations result in compounds with different chemical properties.

Why do chemicals sometimes blow up?

We all know from cartoons that adding a tiny drop of one chemical to a beakerful of another chemical can result in a powerful explosion. This isn't far from the truth: if a careless chemist mixes, say, concentrated hydrochloric acid with plain tap water, the result can be a deadly blast (not to mention the release of toxic chlorine gas). For this reason, science teachers are very careful about which chemicals they allow their students to handle!

What is organic chemistry?

Scientists have long known that the element carbon has special chemical properties: it can form multiple, complex bonds with virtually any other element, including itself. Because molecules containing carbon are essential to life (at least, life as we know it here on earth), the study of these molecules is known as organic chemistry.

Besides carbon, organic chemicals usually (but don't necessarily have to) contain hydrogen, oxygen, and nitrogen, and are divided into broad categories according to how they react with other chemicals. The substances called alcohols, for instance, always contain a "tail" of oxygen and hydrogen, and sugars feature either a characteristic carbon-hydrogen-oxygen or carbon-oxygen unit. (By the way, most ordinary folks use the words "alcohol" and "sugar" to refer to one thing, but there are dozens of different alcohols and sugars from the perspective of an organic chemist.)

Not all organic substances are necessarily found in living organisms. For example, crude oil contains huge amounts of carbon, because it has formed from the slowly cooked remains of dead organic matter.

Why is it called a "mole"?

The chemical quantity known as a "mole" has nothing to do with the ground-digging critter; rather, this word is derived from "molecule." A "mole" is defined as the number of a chemical's molecules equal to the number of atoms in 12 grams of carbon, and it's a huge number: a mole of sodium chloride (that is, salt) contains approximately 6 times 10 to the power of 23 molecules, or a bit under a trillion trillion!

How many chemicals are there?

Well, you can do the math: there are 92 naturally occurring elements, and a variety of ways they can join together (see the question about chemical bonds elsewhere on this page). The fact is, there are trillions upon trillions of possible chemicals, only a small percentage of which have been investigated by scientists (who are constantly cooking up new chemicals and examining their properties).

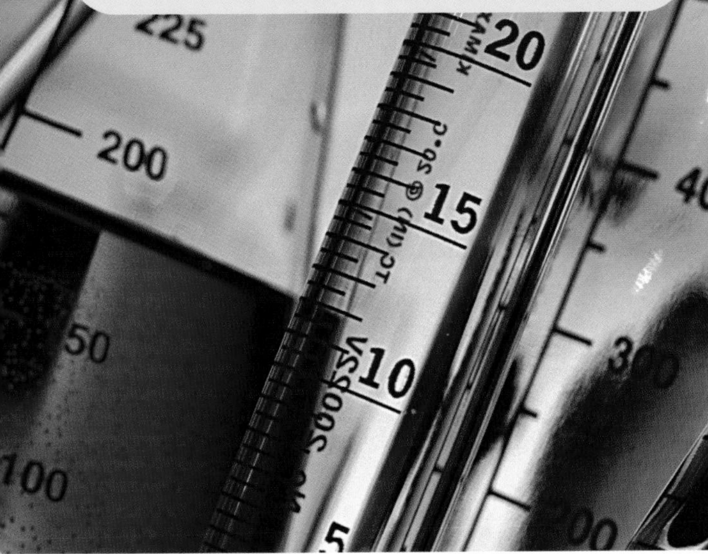

How do atoms stick together?

One of the things that makes chemistry possible is the fact that atoms can join together in various ways, making some molecules easier to "pry apart" than others. Covalent bonds, in which two or more atoms share the electrons that circle their nuclei, are by far the strongest. As you can guess, "single" bonds in which two atoms share a single electron are weaker than "double" bonds, and "triple" bonds (in which three electrons are shared) are the strongest of all—meaning it takes more energy to break a triple bond than a single or double bond.

However, atoms needn't bond only by sharing electrons. Equally important in everyday chemistry are so-called "ionic" bonds, in which a negatively charged ion (that is, an atom with a surplus of electrons) attracts a positively charged ion (an atom with a deficit of electrons). One of the important properties of molecules formed from ionic bonds is that they're relatively easy to dissolve in water: a good example is common table salt, NaCl, which is made up of a single sodium atom joined ionically to a single chlorine atom.

What is the most stable element?

In the hot interiors of stars, light elements like hydrogen and carbon are constantly being fused into heavier elements, a process that releases energy. Iron represents the end stage of this process: when a star has fused all its lighter ingredients into iron, fusion comes to a halt, because there's no more energy to be extracted from an iron nucleus. But even though iron is the most stable element, it's not the last: when a star explodes, the result can be the creation of even heavier elements like uranium or thorium.

Entropy

What is the Second Law of Thermodynamics?

It may sound complicated, but the Second Law of Thermodynamics is actually pretty straightforward: it states that you can't turn energy into work with 100 percent efficiency. For example, when a car engine burns gasoline, not all of the energy that's released goes to turn the car's wheels: a lot of it is dissipated as "useless" heat that can't be recovered. (By the way, "thermodynamics" means "science of heat.")

The Second Law of Thermodynamics—which was discovered in the 19th century—has some profound implications. Essentially, it means that the universe is constantly "winding down" into a more chaotic and disordered state. Some scientists believe that, billions or trillions of years from now, our universe is doomed to a "heat death" in which all its matter and energy have been turned into useless radiation.

You don't hear much about the three other laws of thermodynamics, so here they are. The First Law says that energy is conserved during any process (that is, you can't have more or less energy after doing something than when you started), and the Third Law says it's impossible to reach absolute zero, the lowest possible temperature (though you can come to within a few billionths of a degree). There's also a so-called "Zeroth Law," which defines what it means for two systems to have the same temperature.

Why can't there be a perpetual motion machine?

If there's one rock-solid rule of the universe, it's that there's no such thing as a free lunch, meaning it's impossible to build a machine that does an unlimited amount of work using a limited supply of energy. Even still, people throughout history have claimed to invent "perpetual motion machines" that will solve all of the world's energy problems. Needless to say, none of these gizmos actually work, though that hasn't stopped folks from continuing to try!

How hot is a black hole?

You might not think this question has anything to do with the other topics on this page. But the fact is, thanks to entropy and the Second Law of Thermodynamics, black holes actually have a tiny temperature, about a few millionths of a degree. This is surprising, because for a long time physicists believed that a black hole (literally a "hole" in space where matter is so dense that not even light can escape its gravitational pull) had no temperature at all!

What is Maxwell's Demon?

What is entropy?

For such an important concept in physics, entropy is surprisingly difficult to pin down. Basically, it's the tendency of any system to become more disordered with time (so you may notice that it's closely related to the Second Law of Thermodynamics, defined on the facing page. A good everyday example of entropy would be the tendency of your room to get messier and messier, until your mom yells at you to clean it up.

In the 19th century, physicists trying to disprove the Second Law of Thermodynamics came up with a clever thought experiment. Imagine two containers of air, one hot and one cold, connected by a tiny door. A microscopic "demon" stationed at the door measures the speed of the zillions of air molecules as they approach. Because even cold air has a sprinkling of fast-moving ("hot") molecules, the demon allows these molecules to pass through the door into the hot container, but doesn't allow any of the molecules from the hot container to pass into the cold container.

So what's the joke? Well, if the demon does his job right, the air in the hot container gets hotter (because it's receiving "hot" molecules from the cold container), while the air in the cold container gets colder (because it's losing all its hot molecules to the hot container). Ordinarily, you would expect the hot container to cool down and the cold container to heat up, until all the air in the two containers was at room temperature.

Maxwell's Demon gave physicists fits for almost a hundred years, but it was finally proven that it's impossible for him to exist (unfortunately, for reasons too complicated to go into here!).

How much entropy does the sun have?

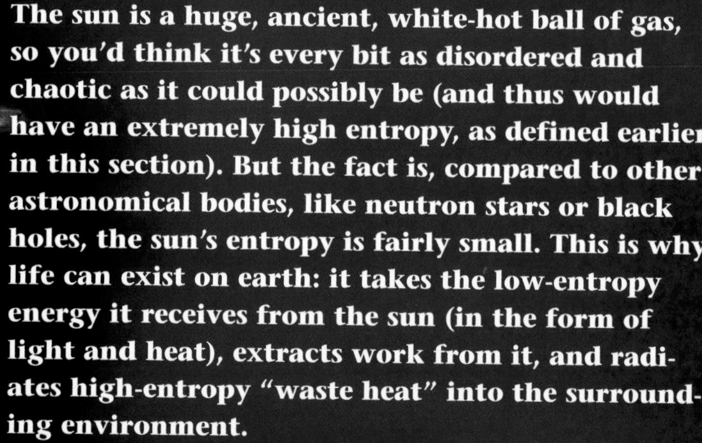

The sun is a huge, ancient, white-hot ball of gas, so you'd think it's every bit as disordered and chaotic as it could possibly be (and thus would have an extremely high entropy, as defined earlier in this section). But the fact is, compared to other astronomical bodies, like neutron stars or black holes, the sun's entropy is fairly small. This is why life can exist on earth: it takes the low-entropy energy it receives from the sun (in the form of light and heat), extracts work from it, and radiates high-entropy "waste heat" into the surrounding environment.

Why can't you "square" a circle?

In modern parlance, "squaring the circle" means trying to accomplish an impossible task. However, thousands of years ago, the ancient Greeks didn't know this was impossible—and their attempts to square the circle (that is, to construct a square with the exact same area as a given circle) led to some major advances in geometry. As Greek geometers (and many, many mathematicians afterward) gradually discovered, a circle can't be squared because it depends on the irrational quantity known as "pi"—an infinite, nonrepeating decimal that relates the circle's circumference to its diameter.

Although it was the most famous, squaring the circle wasn't the only impossible geometrical problem posed by ancient mathematicians. "Doubling the cube" (that is, constructing a cube with exactly twice the area of any given cube) is also a nonstarter, because this procedure depends on another irrational number, the square root of 2. And for reasons too complicated to go into here, it's also impossible to "trisect the angle" (that is, to divide a given angle into three equal, smaller angles, using only a ruler and a compass).

How many sides does a Möbius strip have?

One of the easiest of all geometrical figures to construct, and one of the hardest to understand, a Möbius strip is a narrow strip of paper that has been cut, given a half-twist, and glued together again. The result is an object that has only one side: you can trace the "inside" and "outside" of a Möbius strip's surface continuously, without having to lift your pencil, and if you cut it in half lengthwise with a pair of scissors the result will be two interlocking loops!

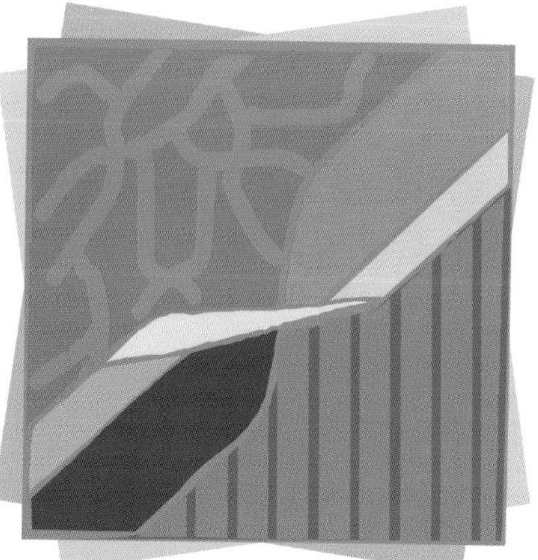

Why does geometry have "postulates"?

When he formulated his geometry, the Greek mathematician Euclid derived all his results from five basic assumptions, called "postulates." These postulates include such self-evident facts as (for instance) that all right angles are equal, and that any two points can be joined by a straight line. However, in "non-Euclidean" geometries (see the explanation elsewhere on this page), these postulates aren't necessarily true!

How did Archimedes die?

Archimedes, the most famous geometer of ancient times, is familiar to most people for two reasons: for supposedly jumping out of a bathtub and shouting "eureka!" when he discovered an especially difficult formula, and for being killed by a Roman soldier (in 212 B.C.) because he was too busy drawing geometrical figures in the sand to obey the soldier's orders!

What is topology?

Closely related to geometry, topology is the study of how one shape can be converted into another (whether those shapes are ordinary three-dimensional spheres or impossible-to-visualize four-dimensional "manifolds"). According to the rules of topology, an object with one "hole" (such as a teacup with a handle) can be turned into another object with one hole (such as a donut), but an object with two holes can never be turned into an object with zero, one, or more than two holes.

What is trigonometry?

Ever since the dawn of recorded history, mathematicians and geometers have puzzled over the properties of triangles: that is, the relationships between the lengths of a triangle's sides and its three interior angles, and the unique qualities of "right" triangles (which contain one right angle) and "isosceles" triangles (which have two equal sides). If the "tri" in "trigonometry" sounds familiar, that's because it stands for "three"; this word is Greek for "the study of three angles."

Although it's fairly easy to grasp on a conceptual level, what makes trigonometry such a challenging subject for kids is its confusing terminology. For example, the longest side of any right triangle is called its "hypotenuse," which is related to the other two sides of the triangle by "sine," "cosine," and "tangent" functions, among others.

The most famous equation of trigonometry is the "Pythagorean theorem," which was discovered more than 2,000 years ago: the square of the length of a right triangle's hypotenuse is equal to the squares of the lengths of its other two sides added together.

Why is it called "non-Euclidean" geometry?

The geometry you're taught in school—which involves well-behaved straight lines and right angles—was discovered thousands of years ago by the Greek mathematician Euclid. "Non-Euclidean" geometry is a more recent development, involving the behavior of lines and angles in "curved" space. For example, in flat space, the three angles of a triangle always add up to exactly 180 degrees, but if that triangle is on the surface of a sphere, the total is more than that.

Mathematics

How many colors does a map need?

Until recently, mathematicians believed—but could not prove—that any two-dimensional map needs only four colors, in order to make sure that no two countries of the same color border each other. In 1976, this theorem was finally proved, but in an unorthodox way—a computer sorted through every possible kind of map (a process that took hundreds of hours) and showed that four colors were in fact enough.

How many kinds of infinity are there?

The answer to this must seem pretty obvious: just one, right? That's what most mathematicians thought, too, until Georg Cantor proved (in the late 19th century) that there are several different "sizes" of infinity. The reasoning is too complicated to go into here, but Cantor showed that the infinity of points on a line is bigger than the infinity of counting numbers, and mathematicians later proved that there are infinitely more possible curves than there are points on a line!

What was Fermat's Last Theorem?

In 1637, the famous French mathematician Pierre de Fermat claimed to have proved a fascinating proposition: that there are no solutions of the equation $A^X + B^X = C^X$ for "X" greater than 2. To put it another way, no cube (a number multiplied by itself three times) can be equal to two other cubes added together, and so on for higher powers. Maddeningly, Fermat never explained why he believed this statement to be true; instead, he scribbled in a book: "I have found a truly marvelous proof of this proposition, which this margin is too narrow to contain."

For the next 300 years, mathematicians tried to solve what became known as Fermat's Last Theorem. Although they managed to eliminate more and more numbers (at one point, it was proved that the theorem was true for powers up to several million), a complete proof was elusive. In 1994, though, a mathematician named Andrew Wiles came up with a dense, complicated, 200-page-long proof. Since Wiles' proof used mathematics that didn't even exist in Fermat's time, many people now believe that Fermat, despite what he wrote, never really proved his theorem in the first place!

Why is it called algebra?

Many of the mathematical terms we use today are derived from Arabic, because in ancient times Arabia was home to the world's leading mathematicians. "Algebra" derives from the title of an Arabian book containing the words "al-jabr," meaning "reunion." (Oddly enough, "reunion" doesn't particularly apply to the concept of algebra, which concerns the manipulation of symbols in place of numbers.) By the way, Arabians didn't invent algebra; the concept originated in ancient Greece and Babylon.

What is a "huge" number?

The concept of "huge" numbers isn't often used by mathematicians, but it's fun to explore. Basically, a "huge" number is the inverse of an infinitely small number, that is, the number 1 divided by the smallest number you can possibly think of that isn't zero. Technically, a huge number is infinite, but it's much bigger than the kind of infinity you can reach by counting one at a time with ordinary numbers.

Why do parallel lines never meet?

Technically, they do! In some kinds of geometry, parallel lines are defined as lines that meet at a point at infinity (in the real world, there's no such thing as a single point at infinity—whatever that means!—but that's how mathematicians think). The reason you're taught that parallel lines never meet is that most kids only have to learn "Euclidean" geometry, which deals with a simple, orderly space of three dimensions.

What is a hypercube?

The world we live in consists of three dimensions: length, width, and breadth. A straight line drawn on a piece of paper has one dimension (length); a square has two dimensions (length and width), and a cube has three dimensions (length, width, and depth). A hypercube is a cube-like entity that has one extra dimension, at right angles to the other three. This is impossible to visualize, because the extra dimension, by definition, extends into a space we three-dimensional humans can't perceive.

Still, mathematicians who study extra dimensions have been able to deduce some properties of hypercubes (as well as hyperspheres, hypertriangles, and all the rest), mostly by analogy. For instance, if you pick up an ordinary cube and shine a flashlight on it, its shadow on the wall will be a two-dimensional parallelogram. But if scientists in the fourth dimension were somehow able to shine a higher-dimensional light on a hypercube, its "shadow" would be a three-dimensional cube that appeared magically in the middle of your living room!

How does a scanning tunneling microscope work?

A favorite tool of nanotechnologists, scanning tunneling microscopes (STMs) use the strange laws of quantum physics to manipulate molecules on the atomic level. Unlike a regular electron microscope, an STM doesn't actually shoot a beam of electrons at its target; rather it registers weak electric currents that "tunnel" mysteriously between the tip of the probe and the material being studied.

What is a nanotube?

A close relative of the buckminsterfullerene (see the question elsewhere on this page), a nanotube is an artificially constructed, molecule-sized tube measuring a few dozen carbon atoms in circumference. Because they can potentially be built to any length—and are extremely strong—nanotubes are being investigated for their ability to conduct (and to channel) light and electricity on a submicroscopic scale.

What is nanotechnology?

Over the past few decades, scientists have learned how to manipulate matter at the atomic scale, arranging atoms one at a time in various structures as if they were tiny Lego bricks. Because atoms and molecules are separated by lengths of the order of a nanometer (about one millionth of a millimeter), this science of the very small is known as "nanotechnology." However, this term is also often applied to science on much bigger distance scales (like a whopping one-thousandth of a millimeter).

Although nanotechnology has zillions of potential applications, scientists are most excited about its use in medicine. There may come a day when tiny, microscopic "nanobots" programmed to destroy cancerous cells can be injected into a patient's bloodstream, or when livers and kidneys are grown in laboratories with the aid of nano-machines, then transplanted into needy patients. Already, scientists are figuring out ways to encapsulate medications in submicroscopic, nano-engineered molecules, which convey them to different parts of the body!

What is a buckminsterfullerene?

It sounds like a mouthful, but this complicated, nano-engineered molecule (which consists of 60 carbon atoms arranged in the shape of a soccer ball) was actually named after the architect R. Buckminster Fuller. Long before scientists had even conceived of nanotechnology, Fuller had designed a structure called the "geodesic dome," which resembles the top half of the molecule that now bears his name.

What is a quantum dot?

Even the tiniest transistors (in, say, a computer) routinely handle electric currents that consist of trillions of electrons. This gives you some idea how small "quantum dots" are: these nanoparticles are submicroscopic traps that each contain a few hundred electrons. Because quantum dots can be assembled into larger structures, they're sometimes called "artificial atoms."

Why is it called "smart dust"?

One potential application of nanotechnology is microscopic, dust-sized sensors that can detect everything from light to temperature changes to tiny vibrations. These nanobots would be able to communicate with each other, and even to join together if the need arose. Needless to say, nanotechnicians are a long way from creating smart dust, and even if they did, they'd have to think hard about the "gray goo" problem (see the question below).

How do you make "gray goo"?

Not all scientists are optimistic that developments in nanotechnology will wipe out the world's problems. In fact, some experts are worried that nanotechnology may wind up wiping out the world instead—especially if submicroscopic, nano-engineered robots somehow evolve out of the control of the scientists who invented them.

Imagine this situation: a scientist creates a molecule-sized machine that, say, converts rotting vegetables into oil. Since there would have to be trillions upon trillions of these nano-machines to produce any usable results, they would have to be given the ability to "self-replicate": that is, to reproduce themselves like bacteria. If something went wrong with the nano-machine's programming, this reproduction process might spin out of control, resulting in vast hordes of nanobots digesting everything on earth and leaving behind a planet covered with "gray goo."

This is only speculation, of course, but it has some observers worried enough to call for stricter regulation of nanotechnology research—just in case some well-meaning scientist brings the world to the brink of destruction!

Particle Physics

What makes the kaon such a weird particle?

Although it only appears briefly in high-energy particle collisions, the kaon (which is also known as a "K-meson") is one of the strangest particles yet discovered. Most elementary particles don't distinguish between "left" and "right" directions, but somehow the kaon does. This "parity violation," as it's called by physicists, may have profound implications for such enduring mysteries as why time moves forward and not backward!

Why do particles come in three different families?

One of the enduring mysteries of particle physics is why the basic constituents of matter are repeated on three different levels, or families. Everyday matter is made of protons, neutrons, electrons, and neutrinos, but there are also higher-energy analogs of these particles (for example, the "muon" is a higher-energy version of the electron, and the "tau" is a higher-energy version of the muon). Physicists have their theories, of course, but they haven't yet conclusively figured out why nature duplicates itself this way.

What is the difference between bosons and fermions?

Physicists find it convenient to classify particles according to their "spin"—that is, the way they rotate. Roughly speaking, fermions are particles that have "one-half" spin, and include protons, neutrons, and electrons, while bosons are particles with "zero" or "one" spin, and include photons and gluons. The reason this distinction is important is that fermions obey the "exclusion principle": two fermions in exactly the same state can't occupy the same place at the same time, but two bosons can.

What is the Higgs boson?

The details are way too complicated to go into here (in fact, you'd have to be a particle physicist yourself to understand them!), but the Higgs boson is a hypothetical particle that allows other particles (like protons and electrons) to have mass. Today, physicists are planning bigger and bigger particle colliders to detect the Higgs boson, which some observers have dubbed (not too seriously) "the god particle."

What is a graviton?

In the language of particle physics, the forces of nature are mediated by particles: for example, a beam of electromagnetic energy is composed of zillions of photons. By this reasoning, the force of gravity should be transmitted by particles called "gravitons." Because individual gravitons would be so tiny and weak, they're unlikely ever to be directly detected, but one of the primary goals of physics is to at least develop a theory that confirms their existence.

What is the Standard Model?

In elementary school, an atom seems simple enough, consisting of a nucleus of protons and neutrons circled by a bunch of electrons (you may also have learned that protons and neutrons are made out of smaller particles called "quarks"). On an everyday level, in fact, protons, neutrons, electrons, and "neutrinos" (ghostly particles that carry away energy from nuclear processes) are all anyone needs to worry about.

If you're a particle physicist, though, things aren't quite so straightforward: you also have to consider all those exotic, short-lived particles that appear in high-speed particle collisions. The "Standard Model" is the way in which physicists classify the dozens of elementary particles that have so far been discovered, ranging from ordinary protons and neutrons to bizarre "K-mesons" and "Tau antineutrinos." What makes the Standard Model especially appealing to physicists is that it predicted the existence of certain massive particles—such as W and Z bosons—before they were actually discovered in particle colliders, an excellent sign that a theory is on the right track.

Why do physicists use particle colliders?

In a way, a scientist investigating the ultimate building blocks of matter has a lot in common with a little kid smashing two toys together in his bedroom. One of the most important tools employed by particle physicists is the particle collider: a huge, football-field–sized device that accelerates particles close to the speed of light and smashes them together.

The reason colliders are necessary is that many of the elementary particles of interest to physicists exist only at extremely high energies: that is, they appear briefly in the billion-degree temperatures of a high-energy collision, then decay into lower-energy particles a tiny fraction of a second later. Bigger (and more expensive) colliders produce yet more exotic (and even shorter-lived) particles.

Of course, these high-speed collisions would be useless if there weren't some way to "photograph" them. That's why particle colliders include very sophisticated detection equipment, which can identify and track a rare particle that exists for (say) only a millionth of a millionth of a millionth of a second!

Probability

How old are the earliest dice?

Ever since the dawn of history, human beings have been playing games of chance—and since there weren't any slot machines 10,000 years ago, dice are one of mankind's earliest inventions. Archeologists have found primitive knucklebones (which have four irregular sides) that were likely used for gambling in prehistoric times, and have also unearthed a wide variety of dice of all shapes and sizes that were rolled in ancient Rome, China, and other civilizations.

Since the purpose of dice is to generate random numbers, dishonest gamblers looking for an edge have found numerous ways to "load" dice—that is, to tamper with them so that some faces (and therefore some numbers) are more likely to come up than others. This can be done by shaving one of the die's corners, say, or by loading its inside with unequal weights. Needless to say, this resulted in lots of heated arguments (and gunfights) in the Old West—and even today, casinos won't allow gamblers to use their own dice.

What does an actuary do?

When a person buys life insurance, the insurance company carefully considers how likely that person is to die within a certain period of time (at which point the family receives a cash payment). An actuary is a person who calculates the "life expectancy" of the insurance company's customers. A good actuary can save an insurer money, but a bad one can cause the insurer to go out of business!

What is the "law of averages"?

If you flip a coin 100 times in a row, it's entirely possible that it will come up "heads" the first five or six times—but by the time you're done, you'll have a fairly even number of heads and tails (perhaps not 50 heads and 50 tails, exactly, but 52 heads and 48 tails or 44 heads and 56 tails). This is the "law of averages" at work: it states that the more times you do something the outcome of which has a specific probability, the more likely it is that that probability will be reflected in the results.

How do scientists create random numbers?

Although everyone "knows" what a random number is, this concept can be surprisingly hard to explain on a mathematical level. Basically, it has to do with how the number is generated, or created. Throwing a single die produces a random number between 1 and 6, but asking your friend to "think of a number between 1 and 10" isn't quite random because you may already know that she's more likely to choose the number 7 than the numbers 2 or 9.

Because random numbers are used for security purposes, scientists are constantly trying to devise new, more foolproof ways to generate genuinely random numbers, and not "pseudo-random" numbers that look random but really aren't (an example of a pseudo-random number would be the decimals of the number pi, 3.1415929 . . . , which look random but can be reproduced by a second-grader with a calculator!). Some techniques derive numbers from unpredictable processes in the natural world—for example, since no one knows when a single radioactive atom will decay, this process can be used to generate a truly random number that can't be duplicated by anyone else.

How is it possible to have a "winning streak"?

Although many people believe otherwise, there's nothing mystical about throwing a "seven" five times in a row with a pair of dice. According to the laws of probability, the occasional winning streak is inevitable, and luck has nothing to do with it. The situation is pretty much the same in sports, although some skill is involved. For instance, when a player has a "hot hand" in a basketball game—say, sinking ten baskets in a row—that's also (mostly) the law of probability at work!

What is the "birthday paradox"?

Imagine that you ask 23 kids in your class what their birthdays are. What do you think the odds are that two of them will have the same birthday? It seems unlikely, because there are only 23 kids and 365 days in a year. In fact, though, the odds are better than one in two that two kids will have the same birthday (and if you ask 60 other kids in your class, the odds shoot up to 99 in 100). This is called the birthday paradox, and it's a well-known result of probability theory—though the proof is way too detailed to go into here!

What is Schrödinger's Cat?

One of the strange things about quantum physics is that it's possible for an elementary particle (such as a photon or an electron) to exist in two "states" simultaneously until it's measured by a human observer.

In 1935, a physicist named Erwin Schrödinger made use of this strange property in a thought experiment (that is, he only described the experiment; he didn't actually perform it!). A cat is placed in a sealed box, and attached to the box is a radioactive nucleus that has a 50 percent chance of decaying in the next hour. If the nucleus decays, it activates a mechanism that kills the cat; if the nucleus doesn't decay, the cat stays alive.

The point of this thought experiment is that, until it's registered by a human observer, the radioactive nucleus exists in a "superposition" of decayed and undecayed states—so, does the cat exist in a superposition of "dead" and "alive" states? Over the years, Schrödinger's Cat has driven physicists nuts, as they attempt to explain (not always convincingly) how the weird rules of quantum physics give way to the straightforward rules of classical physics on a large scale.

How is quantum physics different from classical physics?

Entire textbooks have been devoted to this question, but it all boils down to this. Classical physics (that is, the physics of macroscopic objects like cars, basketballs, and people) is "deterministic," meaning it's possible to predict how a classical object will behave. Quantum physics, though, is "probabilistic"; for example, physicists can calculate the odds that a given electron will emit a photon, but there's no way to predict in advance exactly when (or if) this will happen.

What is the Uncertainty Principle?

According to the rules of quantum physics, it's impossible to measure a particle's exact location in space—as you try to pin down the particle's position with greater and greater accuracy, its momentum (that is, the product of its mass times its velocity) increases proportionately. In practical terms, though, the Uncertainty Principle only applies to electrons or protons, and not to airplanes or baseballs!

What is the measurement problem?

In quantum physics, a system isn't in a definite state until it has been measured—and since all measuring is ultimately done by human beings, it's hard to avoid the conclusion that people are somehow necessary to bring the universe into existence! Needless to say, many scientists are uncomfortable with this prospect, and have advanced theories about how measurements (with or without humans) cause quantum systems to settle into one state or another.

What is Planck's Constant?

Quantum physics obtained its name because it depends on "quanta" (that is, finite increments) of energy: a system doesn't gain energy continuously, but accumulates it in unimaginably tiny bits. Planck's Constant (discovered by the German physicist Max Planck) determines the size of these jumps, and as you can imagine, it's an incredibly tiny number.

How was quantum physics discovered?

The story is way too detailed to go into here, but at the start of the 20th century, scientists were convinced that there had to be more to the world than the "classical" physics of Isaac Newton. This was because the structure of the atom didn't make sense in classical terms: its negatively charged electrons and positively charged nucleus should instantly have annihilated one another, making stable matter impossible. As scientists attempted to solve this conundrum, they slowly discovered the principles of quantum physics.

What is the EPR Paradox?

Next to Schrödinger's Cat (see the facing page), the EPR Paradox has given physicists fits for decades. Named after three scientists (including Albert Einstein) who were uncomfortable with the weirdness of particle physics, this paradox was first posed as a thought experiment.

Two electrons exist together in a quantum superposition of a "spin up" and a "spin down" state (this refers to the way the electrons rotate about their axes). One electron is zapped to one location, and the other to another location billions of miles away. Because (according to the rules of quantum physics) an electron doesn't have a definite "spin" until it's measured, all the experimenters can know is that one electron has to be "spin up" and the other one "spin down." But here's the catch: the instant one electron is measured, and is shown to be "spin up" or "spin down," its companion billions of miles away instantaneously (faster than the speed of light!) becomes "spin down" or "spin up."

Amazingly, a few years ago, the EPR Paradox graduated from a thought experiment to an actual experiment—and all the weird predictions of quantum physics were verified!

Arts &
Enter

WHAT was the first science-fiction movie? HOW were fireworks invented? WHY does Western music have seven basic notes? Here's the section where you'll find questions and answers about all the things people read, watch, listen to, and just generally enjoy.

tainment

Decorative Arts

Why is it called "Plaster of Paris"?

That's a good question, since the art of making plaster (a building material created by heating gypsum, a common mineral, and combining it with water) has existed for almost 10,000 years, long before the city of Paris was even founded. The reason this material is sometimes called "Plaster of Paris" is that, by royal decree, all the wooden houses in 18th-century Paris were coated with plaster to protect them from fire.

What is origami?

It makes sense that origami, the art of paper folding, arose shortly after the invention of paper. Paper thin enough to be folded (as opposed to thick, unfoldable parchment or papyrus) was invented in China about 2,000 years ago, and spread a few hundred years after that to Japan, where "origami" soon became a popular hobby.

Origami most likely originated as an elaborate way to wrap presents: a gift of a fish, for instance, would be more memorable if it was bestowed in an elaborate, butterfly-shaped wrapper. As the art of papermaking improved, and paper itself became less expensive, even common Japanese people could afford to fold paper as a form of artistic expression, and not just when they needed to give a present.

For most of Japanese history, the art of origami was passed down verbally or by instruction. The very first origami book in Japan, *How to Fold 1,000 Cranes,* was only published in 1797! (And no, those aren't construction cranes: the crane is a sacred bird in Japan, and there's a belief that anyone who folds 1,000 origami cranes will be granted one wish.)

What is trompe l'oiel?

A French phrase meaning "trick the eye," trompe l'oeil is an ultra-realistic style of painting that reached its peak in Renaissance Europe (though the form had been pioneered by the Greeks and Romans a couple thousand years earlier). In the hands of a master, a trompe l'oiel portrait can be so convincing that you'd swear there was another person in the room!

What is macramé?

Knitting involves weaving together individual strands of yarn, but the basic elements of macramé are much lumpier: thick, colorful knots of fabric. Because it's so bulky, macramé is rarely used for clothing, but its patterns make for great wall hangings and decorative jewelry.

How do you make egg tempera?

No, it's not a recipe for breakfast. Egg tempera is a kind of paint that uses ground-up egg yolks as a binder (that is, the medium that retains color). Egg tempera was most popular before the 16th century, when it was largely replaced by oil-based paints—which are cheaper (not every struggling artist in the Renaissance could afford to buy eggs) and dry more slowly, allowing a painter to change his mind or correct his mistakes.

Why is it called a "mosaic"?

The capital-M "Mosaic" means all things related to Moses, but the small-m "mosaic" has a more prosaic origin: it derives from the Latin word "musaicum," which means "work of the Muses." (The Muses were the Greek goddesses who were supposed to inspire artists.) With that in mind, it may not surprise you to learn that mosaics—pictures created by assembling small bits of stone, tile, or glass—were invented by the ancient Greeks.

How can glass be "stained"?

As you probably know, stained glass is a very different thing from a stained shirt. Stained glass is created by mixing small amounts of metal compounds (containing, say, lead or copper) into a vat of molten glass. The blown glass takes on a distinctive tint, depending on the type of compound added, and in what amounts. Cobalt, for example, creates a deep blue color, while silver (oddly enough) produces a yellow hue.

In medieval times, stained glass was used almost exclusively in churches. Artists assembled shards of differently colored glass into portraits of saints and biblical figures, which the congregation found especially awe-inspiring on sunny days (when the portraits were lit up from outside). The cathedral of Chartres, in France, contains some of the most elaborate and beautiful stained-glass portraits ever made.

Although it had a brief revival in the 19th century, stained-glass art is rarely produced nowadays, though some people pursue it as a (fairly expensive) hobby.

What is batik?

In this Indonesian art form, an elaborate pattern of melted wax is applied to a piece of fabric, and the fabric is then dyed with various colors. Since wax repels water, the dye isn't absorbed by the waxed portions of the fabric, resulting in a colorful design. Depending where in Indonesia a batik is made, it may portray animals, people, or abstract, mystical patterns.

Jazz

How was jazz invented?

Today, the music we call "jazz" encompasses so many different genres—Dixieland, big band, bebop, etc.—that the word has become practically meaningless. But when "jass" first started to become popular in 1920s New Orleans, audiences heard something fairly easy to pin down: African-American musicians playing bright, brassy melodies in march, blues, and ragtime rhythms, using trumpets, clarinets, and other instruments that up to then had been devoted to classical music.

Once it escaped the confines of New Orleans, jazz quickly evolved into the kinds of music we're familiar with today. The most noteworthy person in this regard was Louis Armstrong (1901–1971), who was probably the most popular musician in America (and possibly the world) until Elvis Presley burst onto the scene in the 1950s. By exporting jazz to a white audience, Armstrong laid the groundwork for the Big Band era and lived long enough to see the advent of bepop and free jazz, which put more emphasis on improvisation and musical dexterity than old-style New Orleans jazz.

What is free jazz?

Most forms of jazz—like big band or bebop—employ at least a few hard-and-fast rules, usually involving rhythm, melody, or harmony. In free jazz, though, players play pretty much whatever they feel like playing, and sometimes don't even pay any attention to what the person next to them is doing! This sounds worse than it actually is: in the right hands, free jazz can be just as much fun to listen to as "tuneful" jazz, though needless to say it's not to everyone's taste.

What was ragtime?

Often regarded as a bridge between classical music (in which musicians follow a printed score) and jazz (in which musicians improvise as they play), ragtime was a popular type of piano music during the first two decades of the 20th century, mostly played and composed by African Americans. The most famous ragtime composer was Scott Joplin (1867–1917), whose music was rediscovered in the 1970s when his compositions were used in the hit movie *The Sting*.

What is a piano trio?

One of the great things about jazz is that there's no such thing as a "standard" ensemble—players are free to use as many instruments as they like, in any combination. That said, one of the more popular jazz configurations over the last fifty years has been the piano trio, which consists of piano, drums, and bass. The reason piano trios have endured for so long is because they're surprisingly versatile, equally suited to soft, romantic music or hard-driven bebop.

Why is it called bebop?

If ever a word was suited to the music it describes, it's bebop. This blisteringly fast form of jazz was invented in the 1940s by such musicians as Dizzy Gillespie and Charlie Parker; it's possible that "bebop" refers to the quick one-two drum combo with which many songs began and ended. The main thing you're likely to notice about bebop (or "bop," as it's also called) is that it's much harder to follow, since musicians improvise not on a song's melody, but on its underlying chords—which only other jazz musicians are likely to recognize.

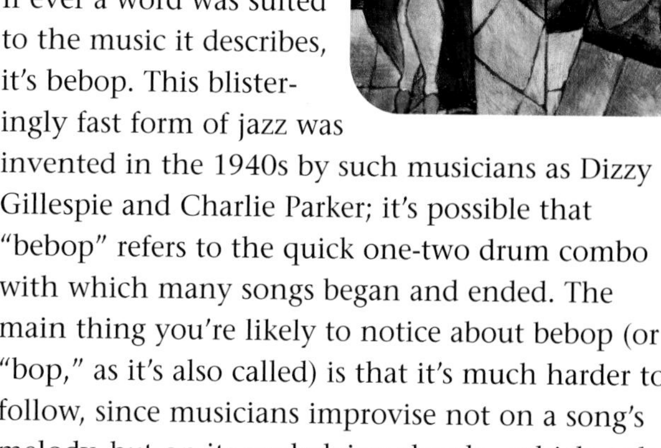

Why do so many jazz musicians play the saxophone?

The saxophone is one of those odd musical instruments that was invented way ahead of its time. It was introduced in Europe in the 1840s by the German Adolphe Sax, who hoped to see it used by orchestras for symphonic music. Unfortunately, the saxophone was pretty much ignored by classical musicians and composers, and it wasn't until the advent of jazz in the 1920s and 1930s—across the Atlantic Ocean, in the U. S.—that it found a home.

The reason jazz musicians take so well to the sax is its "bluesy" tone, which talented players can use to express joy, sadness, or even anger. Also, depending on its size, a saxophone can produce pleasing sounds across the entire range of the musical scale. The very first jazz saxophonists, like Coleman Hawkins and Lester Young, played the gruff, meaty tenor saxophone, while bebop pioneer Charlie Parker (in the 1940s) preferred the lighter-toned and nimbler alto sax and John Coltrane (in the 1960s) pioneered the high-pitched, Eastern-sounding soprano sax. Some players even specialize in the huge baritone sax, which produces notes so far down in the register you'd think you were hearing a whale song!

Music

How many scales are there?

Although most classical music is written in the diatonic scale (see the explanation elsewhere on this page), that's far from the only way to order musical notes. Some Western music is written in pentatonic, octatonic, or "Phrygian" scales (these names refer to the way the notes are "divided up" from octave to octave). Most Eastern music is written in scales employing semitones or microtones, which make it sound especially alien to Western listeners raised on "whole" notes like do, re, mi, etc.

What is a chord?

There are some technicalities involved, but essentially, a chord is a musical note that's produced by sounding three, four, or more separate notes simultaneously (for example, you can produce a chord by pressing three keys on a piano at the same time). However, not just any group of notes will produce a nice-sounding chord; they have to be carefully selected according to the intervals between them, in order to produce a pleasant result.

What is an octave?

As mentioned elsewhere on this page, the notes of the Western seven-tone scale correspond to specific frequencies—and the human ear is built in such a way that it interprets a doubling of these frequencies as the same note in a higher register, or "octave." For example, a standard "A" note vibrates at 440 Hertz, while an "A" note in the next highest octave vibrates at 880 Hertz. Theoretically, there is a huge number of octaves, though people can hear only those in the middle ranges (the low ones are way too low to hear, and the high ones are way too high, except for dog's ears!).

Why are songs written in a particular key?

The details are way too complicated to go into here, but the "key" a song is written in basically refers to the relationship between its chords. Some musicians refer to the key as the piece's "center of gravity," that is, the basic note toward which all the music tends (though this is a major simplification!). Western music has 15 different standard keys, ranging from "G major" to "D minor."

Don't worry if this all sounds too complicated: the fact is, the key in which a composition is written is much less important to the listener than it is to the musicians playing it. (You may not be able to identify the key of Beethoven's *Fifth Symphony*, for instance, but even a beginner would notice the resulting dissonance if the string section played it in F sharp and the horn section played it in B minor!) In classical music, especially, keys are often assigned by composers for the effect they're intended to have on the listener: "minor" keys can be especially sad, while symphonies written in the uncomplicated key of C major are usually bright and cheerful.

What does it mean to have "perfect pitch"?

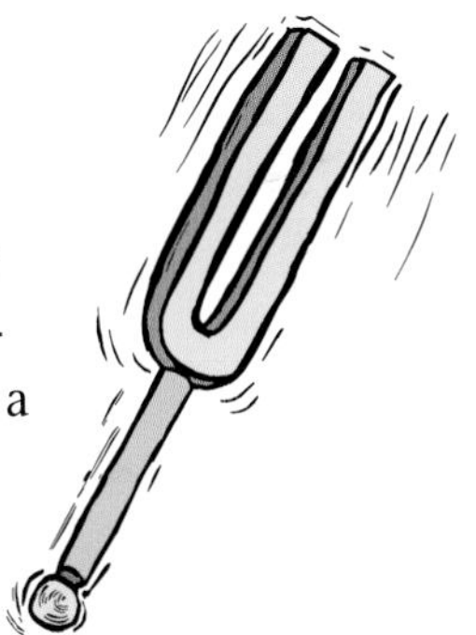

The "do, re, mi, fa, so la, ti, do" notes of Western music are all associated with the specific vibrations of corresponding tuning forks—for example, the note "A" is produced by a tuning fork vibrating at 440 Hertz. A person with "perfect pitch" can either instantly identify a note being played, or can sing perfect notes that vibrate at exactly the right frequency. Surprisingly, very few musicians (or even composers) have the gift of perfect pitch!

Why does Western music have seven basic notes?

Western music—that is, the music of the Western Hemisphere, which includes everything from classical to jazz to pop music—has a long and complex history, most of which can be traced back to the countries of ancient Europe. One of the defining features of western music is that it mostly uses a "diatonic" scale, that is, a repeating sequence of seven notes that gradually ascends from octave to octave. (If all this sounds dry and technical, think of the "do, re, mi, fa, so, la, ti, do" you've been taught in school. The starting and ending "do"s are the same note, but an octave apart.)

The origin of the diatonic scale is a matter of some dispute. Some musicologists (scholars who study music) believe that there's something inherently "natural" about this scale, because the seven notes are separated by intervals that are especially pleasing to the human ear. It's also possible that the diatonic scale arose because ancient flutes had the appropriate number of holes, or because it was the scale most suited to the lyres (stringed instruments) played by the ancient Greeks.

Poetry

What is the longest poem?

This isn't an easy question to answer, because poetry can be rhymed, unrhymed, metrical, nonmetrical, or even written in paragraphs rather than separate lines! That said, one of the longest poems in the English language is *The Faerie Queene*, written in the 16th century by Edmund Spenser. *The Faerie Queene* consists of six long books of rhyming sonnets, and it's one of the most impressive accomplishments in the history of poetry.

What is free verse?

When kids are taught to write poetry, they're usually encouraged to rhyme—but the fact is, very few serious poets (at least in the past hundred or so years) have written rhyming verse. Today, most poets write in free verse, which has no rhythmic or rhyming structure (you might think this makes it easier to write, but that's not necessarily the case). More ambitious poets might write in blank verse, which still doesn't rhyme but has a regular metrical pattern.

What is haiku?

It's odd that the traditional Japanese verse form known as haiku—a short, three-line poem, the first line of which has five syllables, the second seven syllables, and the third five syllables—has become so popular in America. When it originated in Japan, the point of haiku was to convey grand, important themes—like religion, or nature, or love—with the fewest words possible. But soon after haiku was imported to the U.S. in the late 19th century, teachers saw its short length and simple rules as the ideal way to introduce children to writing poetry.

The dignified, tradition-bound haiku pioneers of long-ago Japan might be horrified to see what's become of it in the modern age. On the Internet, thousands of people write haiku on themes ranging from cartoons to lunchmeat to popular movies, some of which are very funny. But because it's become such a popular verse form, most professional poets have learned to stay away from haiku, lest one of their creations be posted on the Web for other people to laugh at!

Why is it called "doggerel"?

About as far from serious poetry as you can get, "doggerel" is a derogatory term for a simple, rhymed, easy-to-compose poem that says nothing of value (a familiar example would be anything that starts "roses are red, violets are blue . . . "). As you might have guessed, the word comes from the Old English "dogge," meaning a worthless mutt.

What is the poet laureate?

In 1617, the English king James I appointed Ben Jonson "poet laureate" to his court, meaning it was Jonson's duty to write verses for ceremonial occasions such as marriages, funerals, and the celebration of military victories. (By the way, the word "laureate" means "crowned with laurel," a mark of honor in ancient Rome.) Although court poets had existed in earlier times, Jonson was the first "official" poet laureate—and even then, it wasn't until John Dryden was appointed to the post in 1670 that the laureate received a written statement of his responsibilities.

Today, most countries have poet laureates of one form or another, even if that's not always what they're called. The U.S. didn't have an official poet laureate until 1985, though for about 50 years before that there was a similar position, "Consultant in Poetry to the Library of Congress," which must have been much harder to fit on a business card!

The most famous poet laureate (or consultant) in the U.S. was Robert Frost, who read a specially written poem, "Dedication," at the inauguration of President John F. Kennedy in 1961.

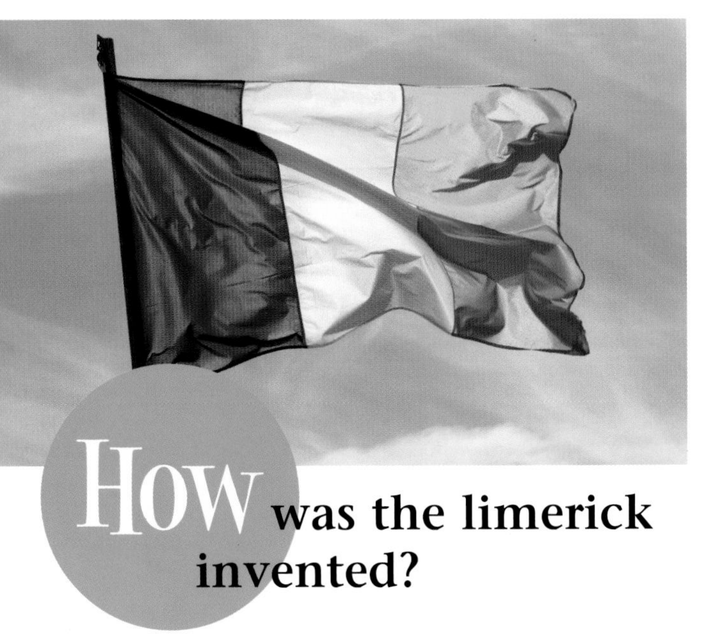

How was the limerick invented?

One of the most popular—but usually one of the most poorly executed—verse forms, a limerick has a rhythmical, five-line structure and a humorous theme (most start with some variant of "There once was a man from Nantucket . . ."). The limerick has nothing to do with the city in Ireland; scholars think its name was invented in the late 19th century (though the verse form existed before that), probably because an early limerick actually referenced the city of Limerick!

Why are some words so hard to rhyme?

When you start to write doggerel (see the definition on the previous page), you learn pretty early on that some words are easy to rhyme, and some aren't. "Moon" is easy—this simple, one-syllable word rhymes with everything from "June" to "swoon" to "buffoon." The reason words like "angry" or "orange" are difficult (or impossible) to rhyme is usually because they have a unique origin that isn't shared by many other English words.

Rock 'n' Roll

What was payola?

When rock music first became popular in the 1950s, record labels would pay radio DJs to hype certain bands. This drew the attention of the U.S. Congress, which convened public hearings and outlawed the practice, known as payola, in 1960. In retrospect, though, it's hard to understand what the big deal was—some people believe the congressmen overreacted simply because they hated rock music!

Why is it called doo wop?

This style of rock music, which was especially popular in the late 1950s and early 1960s, is instantly recognizable—as the lead vocalist sings, the backup singers harmonize nonsense syllables like, well, "doo wop doo wop." Doo-wop music was pretty much rendered extinct by the British Invasion, but even today you can hear it in TV shows and movies set in the 1950s.

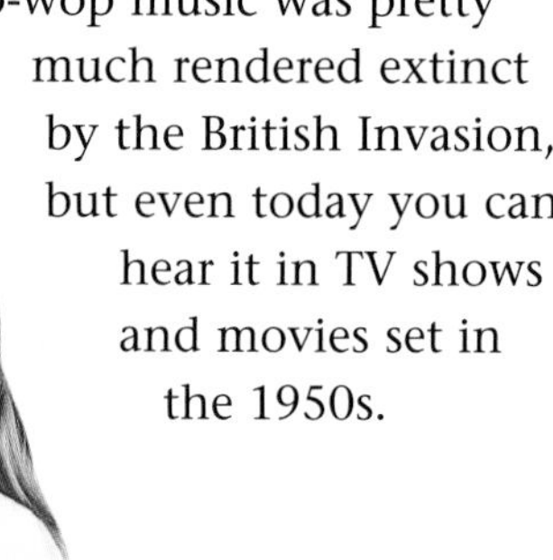

What was the British Invasion?

In the early 1960s, rock music in the U.S. wasn't as much fun as it used to be. The birth of rock 'n roll in the 1950s saw such charismatic singers as Elvis Presley and Buddy Holly, but only a few years later, the sales charts were dominated by much blander groups that all sounded pretty much alike.

Oddly enough, while American rock 'n roll was at a low point, British bands that had been exposed to the music of the 1950s were developing their own unique style. Many folks consider the official start of the British Invasion to be the day in February 1964 when The Beatles appeared on the popular U.S. TV series, *The Ed Sullivan Show*. The result was instant Beatlemania: the British supergroup dominated the U.S. charts, and other bands like The Rolling Stones and The Kinks followed in their wake.

The British Invasion pretty much petered out by 1966, when American rock groups took a cue from their overseas cousins and began playing more adventurous music. But ever since then, many of the biggest innovations in rock music—such as "punk rock" and "glam rock"—have originated in England.

Why is it called punk rock?

The very first punk rockers, who appeared in England in the mid-1970s, combined loud, primitive music with extreme disregard for authority (some early punk rockers made fun of Queen Elizabeth, which didn't exactly endear them to the government). Like the first British Invasion of the early 1960s, punk rock landed on American shores in the late 1970s, spawning such popular bands as The Ramones. (By the way, "punk" means a kid who has way too much attitude!)

How was rock music invented?

The origins of rock music have been a source of heated argument for decades, but nowadays, most people believe that rock had its roots in a few key African-American performing artists of the early 1950s, who themselves drew on the black blues tradition. The three biggest innovators were Chuck Berry, Bo Diddley, and Little Richard, flamboyant performers who combined up-tempo guitar playing with a driving beat.

As popular as they were with black audiences, though, these performers didn't get the chance to break into the mainstream. In the 1950s, because of racial prejudice, record labels were much less willing to give African-American musicians wide exposure. That's why black performers were less than thrilled when, in the late 1950s, Elvis Presley became the biggest rock star on the planet by adapting their style for a white audience (to be fair, though, Presley always acknowledged the debt he owed to his African-American forebears). Even still, for years afterward rock 'n' roll was known as "black" music, and some white parents wouldn't allow their kids to listen to it!

What was the most popular rock band of all time?

That's an easy one—until they broke up in 1970, The Beatles were the 800-pound gorilla o the rock world, selling millions upon millions of albums and dominating singles charts worl wide. But based on sheer longevity, you can also make a case for The Rolling Stones, who have played together since the early 1960s an are still touring today!

Why do so many rock musicians play the guitar?

It may not seem that way when you're taking lessons, but the guitar is one of the easiest musical instruments to learn—even if you've mastered only a few chords, you can get up on stage and do a reasonably good job. That's not the case with instruments like the violin or piano, which you have to learn much more thoroughly before you can play them in public!

How did *The War of the Worlds* cause a nationwide panic?

When it was published in 1898, *The War of the Worlds*—by the British author H.G. Wells—caused a sensation. This novel describes the destruction of London by a fleet of Martian spacecraft, the people of England (and the world) being saved in the end when the Martians are infected, and wiped out, by common germs.

Forty years after this novel appeared, in 1938, a radio troupe led by the actor Orson Welles broadcast an adaptation of *The War of the Worlds* as part of a Halloween special. The trouble was, most of the people tuning in to this broadcast had no idea that they were listening to a staged radio play, and thought that the Earth was actually being invaded by Martians!

The result was panic all over America. Hundreds (and possibly thousands) of people fled New York, imagining that they were hearing explosions or seeing the distant flashes of Martian ray-guns (in the radio play, the first wave of invaders appeared in nearby New Jersey). Eventually, the hysteria died down, and the CBS Radio Network had to promise never again to scare listeners unnecessarily!

What was the first science-fiction movie?

Today, its special effects wouldn't impress a three-year-old, but way back in 1902, Georges Melies' film A Trip to the Moon wowed audiences the world over. In this 14-minute short, a cannon shoots a giant bullet into outer space, which winds up hitting the Man in the Moon in the eye! Afterward, the astronautsinside the bullet get out to explore, encountering giant moon mushrooms and strange creatures called "Selenites" who chase them back to their ship.

What was the first sci-fi TV show?

Many TV shows in the late 1950s and early 1960s—such as *The Twilight Zone* and *The Outer Limits*—had sci-fi elements, but it wasn't until *Lost in Space* debuted in 1965 that the tube had its first space-faring hit. Unfortunately, over the next three years, *Lost in Space* became increasingly silly, incorporating fantasy elements that diluted its sci-fi appeal. In the opinion of most fans, it wasn't until 1966, with the debut of the original *Star Trek*, that hard-core sci-fi truly made its way onto TV.

Why was *Star Wars* such a huge hit?

It may seem hard to believe, at a time when big-budget sci-fi movies are as common as TV cartoons, but when the first installment of *Star Wars* hit American theaters in 1977 there hadn't been a decent science-fiction movie in years. Even still, no one involved in the making of *Star Wars* (except, perhaps, for director and producer George Lucas) expected it to be a success. The film debuted in theaters with little or no publicity, because the studio wasn't confident that hard-core sci-fi would "sell" with the American public.

Boy, was that studio ever wrong! Not only was *Star Wars* a hit, but it was also a national phenomenon—on opening day, people could be seen exiting from one showing and immediately getting back in line to see the movie again. *Star Wars* went on to gross hundreds of millions of dollars (the first installment cost only $10 million or so), and permanently transformed the "rules" of cinematic sci-fi. After *Star Wars,* audiences wouldn't settle for cheesy sets and stilted dialogue; they wanted loud, fast, realistic outer-space action, and the more, the better.

What was the first sci-fi novel?

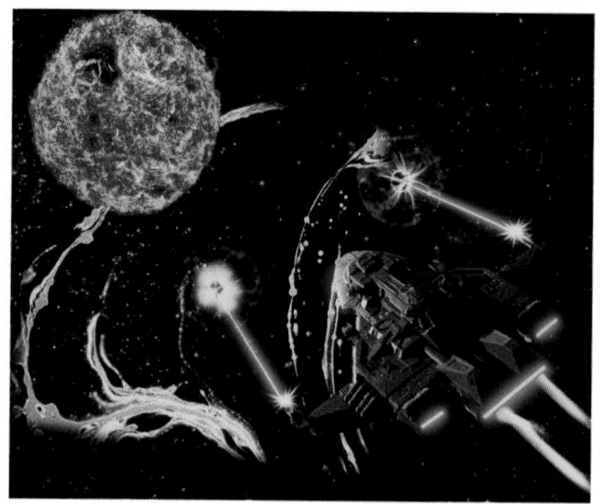

This is a difficult question to answer, since many early novels have "otherworldly" themes: for example, Mary Shelley's *Frankenstein* (published in 1818) certainly qualifies as a kind of sci-fi, as does Mark Twain's *A Connecticut Yankee in King Arthur's Court* (published in 1889), which addresses the notion of time travel. That said, most experts agree that Jules Verne—who wrote *Journey to the Center of the Earth* (1864) and *From the Earth to the Moon* (1865)—was the first modern sci-fi author.

What is the difference between fantasy and science fiction?

In the past few decades—as more and more fantasy authors include elements of science fiction, and more and more science-fiction authors include elements of fantasy—the line between these two genres has blurred. Technically, science-fiction novels are grounded in logic: if a character travels from one planet to the other, it's up to the author to provide a reasonable explanation, even if the "science" he's writing about hasn't been invented yet! A fantasy author, on the other hand, is free to invoke "magic" (or spirits, or angels) to move his plot along, whether that makes any sense or not.

What is the difference between comedy and tragedy?

For most kids, this question hardly needs to be answered: a comedy is a play that makes you laugh, while a tragedy is a play that makes you cry (or at least puts a lump in your throat). But as with so many things, the history of these two terms isn't quite so simple.

The words "comedy" and "tragedy" originated in ancient Greece, where the art of playwriting was invented. However, they had vastly different meanings 3,000 years ago than they do today. "Tragedy" derives from the Greek words for "goat song," and it used to refer to plays staged in honor of Dionysius, the goat-footed god of song and drinking. Later in Greek history, a "tragedy" meant any play that wasn't specifically a comedy; it didn't even have to be sad!

Oddly enough, ancient Greek comedies seem to have been very similar to ancient Greek tragedies: the word "comedy" means "town revel," which doesn't sound much different from the "tragedy" of a Dionysian festival. Gradually, "comedy" came to mean any play that had a happy ending. Although "tragedy" has had the same sad meaning for the past 1,000 years, the modern, ha-ha funny definition of "comedy" didn't come into vogue until the 18th century.

So now that you've read this, do you feel like laughing or crying?

Why is Broadway called "The Great White Way"?

The stretch of Broadway in Manhattan between 42nd and 53rd Streets contains more closely packed theaters than any other city in the world (this was even truer about 50 years ago). It's thought that the phrase "Great White Way" originated with a portion of Broadway that was lit up in the 1880s, one of the first New York streets to be illuminated at night, and then took hold as Broadway became increasingly packed with flashing neon signs, billboards, and theater marquees.

What was commedia dell'arte?

Kind of like the Renaissance equivalent of a TV situation comedy, commedia dell'arte was a highly stylized form of theater popular in 17th-century Italy. Most commedia dell'arte plays focused on farcical situations like illicit affairs and mistaken identities, and they sometimes made references to current scandals in the church or government. One commedia dell'arte character is still familiar today: Arlecchino, or Harlequin, a descendant of modern-day mimes.

What is the longest-running musical?

The Fantasticks, a gentle musical loosely based on William Shakespeare's *Romeo and Juliet*, debuted in 1960 at the Sullivan Street Playhouse in New York and finally closed in 2002, after 42 years and more than 17,000 performances. Because of its long history, *The Fantasticks* has long been a favorite of regional theaters, and it has been staged by many high schools and middle schools as well.

What does "off-Broadway" mean?

In New York, the biggest, most expensive plays and musicals are usually staged in the theaters around Broadway. An "off-Broadway" production isn't necessarily cheaper or of lesser quality, but it's staged elsewhere in the city. In case you're interested, there are also "off-off-Broadway" shows, which tend to be more affordable, and some folks joke about "off-off-off Broadway" plays, which might be staged in someone's living room!

Why do actors have understudies?

The producers of a play can't afford to cancel a live performance because one of the leading actors is sick. Instead, each lead actor has an "understudy," who learns the same lines and rehearses the same stage business, and can therefore step in at the last minute if called upon. Many actors have received their "big break" by substituting for a play's lead and bringing down the house!

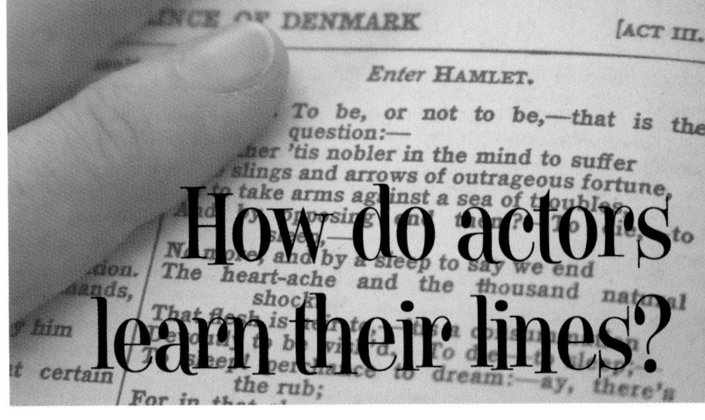

How do actors learn their lines?

For many people, the most impressive thing about being a stage actor isn't the fame or the money—it's the ability to memorize thousands of words of dialogue, and recite them flawlessly in front of a packed audience. This feat is doubly impressive in a Shakespeare play, the lines of which are written in densely packed, semi-medieval English rather than easy-to-understand American English.

According to scientists who have studied the matter, actors don't learn their lines by rote memorization, the way you might memorize a poem assigned to you by your teacher. Rather, an actor will focus not only on the words themselves, but on their meaning, rhythm, and relation to what the other actors on the stage are doing or saying, a technique that some researchers call "active experiencing." As an example of how active experiencing works, it has been shown that actors memorize lines more easily if they can be associated with some physical action—walking across the stage, say, or fiddling with a nearby prop.

Words

How big is the Oxford English Dictionary?

The OED, as it's sometimes called, is by far the biggest dictionary in the English language: it contains more than 300,000 entries, complete with definitions, derivations, and illustrations, so the entry for a single word (like "set") can go on for dozens of pages. The most current edition of the OED has more than 20,000 pages and weighs about 100 pounds!

What is the most misspelled word in the English language?

There's no way to rank this kind of thing, but one of the most widely misspelled words has already been used twice in this entry: "misspell" (which most people spell, incorrectly, "mispell"). Other widely misspelled words include "supersede" (most folks write this with a "c"), "pastime" (which, unlike "misspell," is spelled with only one "s"), and "embarrass" (many people, embarrassingly, write this with only one "r" or one "s").

Why is "colour" spelled differently in Britain?

Although American and British English are similar enough to be mutually understandable, there are some important differences. Not only are some words completely alien (the English say "lorry," we say "truck"; the English say "lift," we say "elevator"), but the spelling of many words varies as well, according to a few simple rules.

Many of the words that end in "-or" in the U.S. end in "-our" in Britain: "honour," "colour," etc. Another rule that can be confusing to American-born readers is the use of "s" instead of "z" at the end of certain words ("analyse" instead of "analyze") and the transposition of the "e" and "r" in words like "metre" (vs. the American "meter") and "theatre" (vs. the American "theater").

The differences get stranger than that. In America we write "checks," but the British use "cheques." And where do they get these cheques? Well, from their local "banque," of course, as opposed to an American "bank." There are other subtle rules, but fortunately, even though these words are spelled differently, they're all pronounced pretty much the same on both sides of the Atlantic.

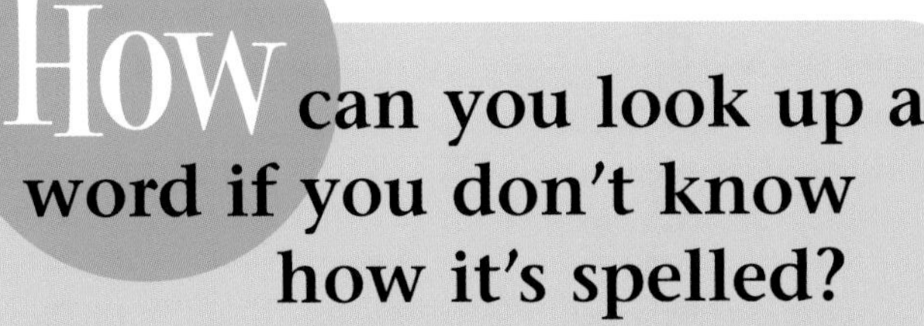

How can you look up a word if you don't know how it's spelled?

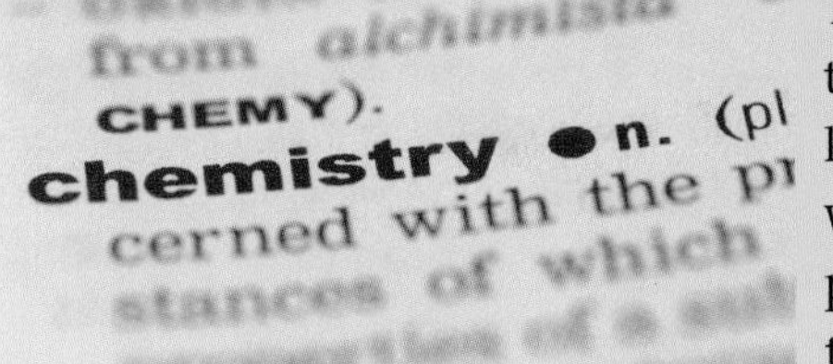

This is a question smart-alec kids always ask when their parents tell them to look a word up in the dictionary. The fact is, though, that you can nearly always tell what part of the dictionary to look in by the word's first phoneme—for example, a word with a starting "f" sound will always be listed under "f" or "ph." Then, if you sound out the second phoneme, you can figure out where in the "f"s or "ph"s the word is likely to be found. Sure, looking up a word you don't know can be hard work, but you sure learn a lot doing it!

What is a thesaurus?

No, it's not a kind of dinosaur. A thesaurus is a compendium of words that have similar meanings, and it's mainly used by speakers and writers who want to vary their vocabulary (instead of constantly repeating the word "bad," for instance, they can say "evil" or "malignant"). The most famous English thesaurus was compiled by Peter Roget and published in 1852.

How did George Bernard Shaw spell "fish"?

The famous playwright George Bernard Shaw was a firm believer in standardizing the spelling of English words. To show how silly English spelling could be, he took the "gh" sound from "laugh," the "o" sound from "women," and the "ti" sound from "nation," and put them all together to spell the word "fish" as "ghoti." Shaw made his point, but to date, tradition has prevailed and English spelling has remained the same.

What was the first dictionary?

This is a bit of a trick question, because you may notice it didn't include the word "English." One of the earliest Latin-language dictionaries, *De Significatu Verborum* (*On the Meaning of Words*), was written more than 2,000 years ago in Rome, and the first Chinese dictionary was compiled in the 2nd century A.D. (Chinese dictionaries are much different from Western-language dictionaries because the Chinese language is based on "ideograms," or symbols, rather than individual letters).

As for the English language, it's widely believed that the first recognizable dictionary was *A Table Alphabeticall*, compiled by Robert Cawdrey in 1604 and containing about 3,000 words with short definitions. (Titles used to be much longer back then: this dictionary's full name continues, "Conteyning and Teaching the True Writing and Understanding of Hard Words, Borrowed from the Hebrew, Greek, Latin or French, &c.") However, the first real, comprehensive, scholarly English dictionary was compiled by Noah Webster and published in 1806.

Why is it called world music?

Although it's used all the time on radio stations and in record stores, "world music" is a deceptive phrase. You might think it means all the music played all over the world, but it actually refers to music that doesn't fit into categories familiar to American listeners, like rock, classical, pop, or jazz. The basic rule of thumb seems to be: if it's played by native musicians on exotic instruments, using the traditional melodies of their home countries, then it's world music.

As you might imagine, even this narrower definition of world music includes a huge variety of styles and traditions. Thanks to the work of ethnomusicologists—scholars who travel to distant places to record native music—today you can hear music from virtually any region in the world, ranging from Madagascar (a large island off the coast of Africa) to the nomadic oases of the Sahara Desert. Unfortunately, though, as American pop music spreads throughout the world, it's becoming increasingly hard to find native music that's completely uncontaminated by Western influences!

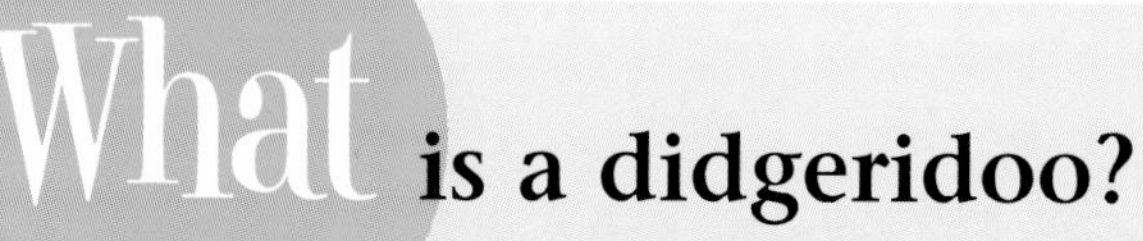

What is a didgeridoo?

Not the kind of instrument you're likely to see in your school band, a didgeridoo is a large (up to nine feet long), straight, hollow, wooden pipe played by the Aborigines of Australia. By vibrating his lips in a certain way, an experienced didgeridoo player can make his instrument produce an unearthly variety of droning sounds, usually to accompany dancing or singing. (By the way, traditional didgeridoo players use only pipes that have been naturally hollowed out by termites!)

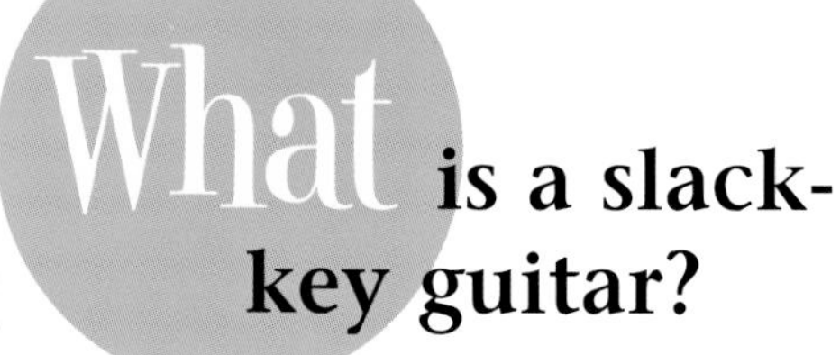

What is a slack-key guitar?

In the early 19th century, the king of Hawaii invited Mexican cowboys to visit his island, to teach the population how to handle cattle. As a parting gift, these cowboys left behind their guitars, which the native Hawaiians adapted to their traditional music by tuning the strings differently ("slacking" refers to lowering the note a string produces). Since then, slack-key guitar has become one of Hawaii's most popular kinds of music.

What is a raga?

The raga—a form of Indian classical music—may sound strange to Western ears, but it follows musical rules every bit as strict as the ones Beethoven used to compose his famous symphonies.

Without getting too technical, a raga is a musical framework in which a player can improvise endlessly over the same scale (that is, set of tones). It's this open-ended structure—as well as the use of "microtones," or notes that differ from the "do, re, mi" used by Western music—that can make ragas an acquired taste for people hearing them for the first time.

Ragas are often played on the sitar, a guitar-like instrument that has 18 or 19 strings—of which six or seven are used to play the melody, while the rest resonate in a dronelike way. The most famous sitar player is Ravi Shankar, who helped make the instrument popular in the United States way back in the 1960s.

What is gamelan?

Kind of like a percussion section run amok, gamelan is an Indonesian form of music that uses tuned drums, gongs, and xylophones, among other instruments, that musicians whack with a stick (the word "gamel" is Japanese for "hammer"). The tuning of a gamelan orchestra is very different from that used in Western music, so it can take a while to become accustomed to its odd (but, once you get used to it, harmonious) sound.

What is Qawwali?

As Klezmer is to Jews, so Qawwali—a passionate form of vocal music that's wildly popular in India and Pakistan—is to many Muslims. A Qawwali band usually consists of percussion, one or two harmoniums (a distant relative of the Western accordion), and a few singers. Qawwali songs are usually devotional in nature, but the most famous Qawwali singer of all time—Nusrat Fateh Ali Khan—was enormously popular the world over, even among non-Muslims.

Why is it called Klezmer music?

If you've ever been to a bar mitzvah or Jewish wedding, the band probably played an upbeat, jazzy kind of music with a distinct Middle Eastern tinge. This musical genre—called Klezmer—originated among Hasidic Jews in Europe way back in the 15th century. The name is derived from Yiddish, by way of ancient Hebrew, and means "vessel of song."

Why is it called "Frankenstein's Monster"?

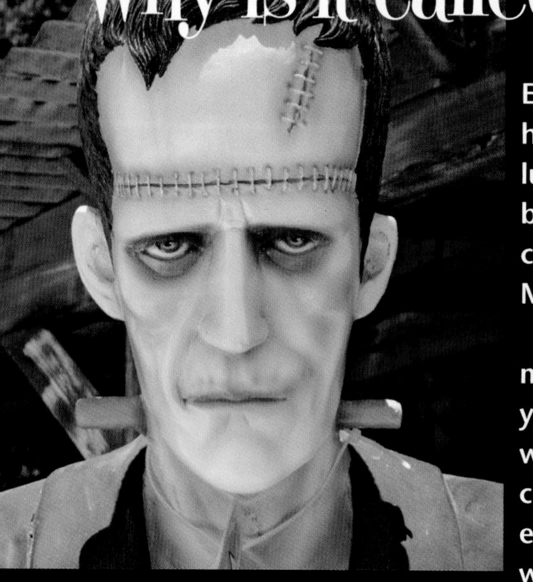

Ever since the novel *Frankenstein* was published in 1818, people have mistakenly believed that Frankenstein is the name of the lurching, murderous brute with bolts in his neck. In fact, the book's monster is never named—but since the mad scientist who created him was named Dr. Frankenstein, "Frankenstein's Monster" pretty much fits the bill.

Now that we've gotten that ugly business out of the way, you may be surprised to learn that *Frankenstein* was written by a 21-year-old woman named Mary Wollstonecraft Shelley. Because women weren't widely accepted as writers in the early 19th century—and certainly not as writers of horror stories!—the first edition of this book appeared anonymously and was a huge hit with the public. By the time the second edition was printed, in 1823, Mary Shelley felt confident enough to include her name.

Since then, "Frankenstein's Monster" has a had a busy career—he's appeared in about two dozen major movies and countless TV shows and cartoons, most of which don't have the faintest resemblance to Mary Shelley's work.

How can radioactivity turn people into superheroes?

It can't, as you may have guessed. Though it's often employed in comic books (for example, Spider-Man derives his superpowers from the bite of a radioactive spider), exposure to radioactive materials is much more likely to kill a person than to increase his strength by even a tiny percent. This plot device probably originated from the (true) fact that radioactivity can cause mutations, which might, just possibly, result in a generation of larger-than-usual creatures.

What does the "were" in "werewolf" mean?

As with the werewolf legend itself, the origin of that mysterious "were" is a matter of dispute. It may be derived from the Latin word "vir," meaning "man" (as in "man-wolf"), or it may come from the Norse term "varg-wolf," which literally means "wolf-wolf," "varg" being another word for "wolf." (A varg-wolf was an especially mean wolf that slaughtered more sheep than it ate afterward.) Aren't you glad you asked?

What are zombies?

Zombies—dead people who have been suddenly brought back to life, with an insatiable craving for human brains—don't really exist, but that hasn't stopped them from having a rich career in monster flicks. The movie that started it all was *Night of the Living Dead*, a low-budget horror film released in 1968, which set many of the zombie "rules" still in use today (such as that a zombie can only be killed by striking him in the head).

Why does King Kong climb the Empire State Building?

Filmmakers have always been eager to cash in on recognizable landmarks, and when the first version of *King Kong* was released—in 1933—the Empire State Building had only recently been completed. Bearing this in mind, it makes sense that in the remake of *King Kong* in 1976, Kong climbs one of the Twin Towers—which also had only recently been built! (In the 2005 re-remake, though, Kong once again scales the Empire State Building.)

What does "Godzilla" mean?

First things first: when this huge, fire-breathing lizard made his film debut in 1954, his name was "Gojira" ("Godzilla" is the English transliteration of this Japanese word). Well, then, what does "Gojira" mean? We may never know for sure, but it's most likely that it was created by blending together the Japanese words "gorira" (meaning "gorilla") and "kujira" (meaning "whale"). Whatever the derivation, you have to admit that "Godzilla" sounds better than "Gojira"!

Many people have speculated about why *Godzilla* (and other monster movies) are so popular in Japan. A big hint is that, in his earliest films, Godzilla attacks Japan because he's been woken up by atomic testing in the Pacific Ocean. Since the first *Godzilla* movie was made less than a decade after the end of World War II, it's possible that the concept of Godzilla was inspired by the atomic bombings of Hiroshima and Nagasaki in 1945. (Oddly enough, though, in his later movies, Godzilla is a friendly monster, protecting Japan from other, more aggressive beasts.)

What is the Mummy's Curse?

Long before the idea was popularized in monster movies, it was believed that a horrible fate awaited anyone who disturbed a mummy's tomb. Shortly after the discovery of King Tut's tomb in 1922, so many of the people involved died, supposedly in mysterious circumstances, that the legend of the Mummy's Curse took hold. (Oddly enough, no one paid any attention to the members of the expedition who went on to live long and healthy lives!)

Mythology

Why are so many mythologies alike?

Years ago, a scholar named Joseph Campbell proposed an interesting theory: that all the world's myths share some common characteristics. For instance, most mythologies feature a "hero's journey": a young man travels a long distance on a mystical quest, faces monsters and assorted perils, and returns years later in triumph. Campbell wasn't the first person to have this idea, but he's still the most famous, even though many experts now disagree with his conclusions.

What sets Norse mythology apart from others?

Although the Greek and Roman gods can get themselves into serious trouble, they're pretty much immortal and can never be killed. In Norse mythology, though, all the gods—even the all-powerful Odin—are fated to be destroyed in a cataclysm called "Ragnarok," the final battle between the forces of order and chaos.

How many gods did the Greeks have?

Not only did the ancient Greeks worship a plethora (that's an ancient Greek word meaning "a lot") of gods, but like human nobility, these gods had different ranks and relationships to each other. The founding gods were called the "Titans," and were supposed to have been deposed by the "Olympians" before Greek civilization even began to flourish. Among the Titans were Atlas, Uranus, and Rhea, while the more-familiar Olympians include Zeus (king of the gods), Hera (his wife), and Poseidon (god of the oceans).

The interesting thing about the Greek gods was that they married, had children, and squabbled among themselves, just like ordinary Greeks. When the Romans conquered the Greeks in the second century B.C., they adapted many aspects of Greek mythology into their own belief system, much to the confusion of present-day kids. That's why most Greek gods have a Roman counterpart: for instance, Zeus became Jupiter, Hera became Juno, and Poseidon turned into Neptune.

Why do so many myths feature tricksters?

The "trickster"—a god who plays tricks on mere mortals and even on his fellow gods—is a familiar figure in Native American and Norse mythology. The most famous trickster of all is Loki, from Norse mythology, who alternately embarrassed and enraged his fellow deities. One trick of Loki's wasn't too smart, though—he was the father of the great wolf Fenrir, who (at the end of time) winds up eating all the gods!

What is monotheism?

"Mono" is the Greek root meaning "one," and "poly" is the Greek root meaning "many"—so a monotheistic religion is one that posits the existence of only one god, while a polytheistic religion can have three, or ten, or hundreds. Greek, Roman, and Norse mythology are polytheistic in nature, while Christianity, Judaism, and Islam are the three main monotheistic religions.

What is Valhalla?

Most religions and mythologies have a "perfect" place where deserving people go when they die. In Greek myth, it's Elysium; in the Christian religion, it's heaven; and in Norse mythology, it's a place called Valhalla. What's interesting about Valhalla is that it reflects the value system of the Vikings who invented it: it's only open to warriors who die in battle, and pretty much all they do there is feast and fight each other!

How can we know if a myth is based on history?

The word "mythology" doesn't only refer to belief systems, like the gods worshipped by the Greeks and Romans or the creation stories of the ancient Chinese. The term also applies to national legends whose origins have disappeared in the myths of time, and which may (or may not) turn out to be based on actual historical fact.

The best example of this is the legend of King Arthur and the Knights of the Round Table. Although most of the stories about Arthur and his knights are clearly mythical (like their quest for the Holy Grail, the goblet Jesus Christ was supposed to have drunk from at the Last Supper), a few others have a ring of truth. For centuries, historians have debated whether Arthur actually existed, and if so, when. Some say he was a Roman general who lived in Britain in the second century A.D., while others think he was a Scottish lord who lived hundreds of years later.

Establishing the truths of other myths is a lot easier. The French have long mythologized Charlemagne, who was actually emperor around A.D. 800. But while the existence of Charlemagne isn't in doubt, that doesn't mean all the stories about him are true!

Strange Beliefs

What is ESP?

Some people believe that human beings have an additional sense (or senses) over and above the usual five: sight, hearing, touch, smell, and taste. This supposed sense is usually called extra-sensory perception, or ESP—but as interesting as it sounds, scientists have yet to find any evidence that it actually exists.

Practically anything can qualify as ESP, but most people use the term to refer to enhanced mental abilities: precognition (the ability to sense events before they happen), telepathy (the ability to transmit thoughts to another person or receive thoughts from them), or clairvoyance (the ability to "see" events taking place a long distance away). In the 1930s, a psychologist named J.B. Rhine claimed to prove the existence of ESP with experiments in which people guessed the order of cards. Since then, though, other scientists have found glaring flaws in Rhine's experiment, and no one has been able to replicate its results since.

That, essentially, is the problem with ESP: every time it's been tested under scientific conditions, no one has found any evidence for it. That doesn't prevent people from claiming they have special abilities, of course, but you should be very skeptical if (for instance) someone says he can tell the future!

How can ghosts exist?

Although the idea of the spirits of dead people inhabiting the world of the living makes for good campfire stories, there's no evidence of the existence of actual, real-life (or real-death) ghosts. For example, whenever a "haunted house" is investigated by professionals, it turns out that the strange things that are happening have perfectly natural explanations (such as, say, a sudden draft causing a door to slam shut).
Still, some people insist that they have had a "haunted" experience and truly believe in the existence of ghosts.

What is a séance?

A séance refers to an attempt by a group of people (usually chanting and holding hands in the dark) to contact the spirits of the dead. Some of these rituals are conducted in good faith, but many séances are run by charlatans who pound on the floor and moan when no one is looking. Believe it or not, Arthur Conan Doyle—the man who invented the super-logical Sherlock Holmes—was a firm believer in séances, which hasn't done much for his reputation!

How do scientists investigate the supernatural?

There's an old saying that "extraordinary claims require extraordinary evidence." To produce this evidence, scientists studying the supernatural test subjects under rigidly controlled conditions—for instance, not allowing a "mind reader" to insist on "do-overs" because conditions weren't exactly right or he wasn't paying attention. To date, no controlled experiment has resulted in evidence of supernatural abilities.

What is a near-death experience?

It's a fact that a person's heart can stop for a few minutes and then start beating again. Many people who have had such a "near-death experience" say they can remember going down a ghostly tunnel toward a bright, shining light, or hearing the voices of dead relatives. While there's no reason to doubt what they're saying, it's much harder to establish what actually happened—most scientists, for example, believe that the person was hallucinating because of a lack of oxygen.

Why do people believe in astrology?

Astrology—the belief that the position of the stars in the sky can affect a person's destiny—is almost as old as civilization itself. In the Western world, astrology is based on the precise arrangement of twelve major constellations (Capricorn, Leo, Sagittarius, etc.) on an individual's birth date. Depending what month you're born in, you have a different astrological "sign," which is supposed to determine your personality and prospects throughout your entire life.

In ancient times, a "horoscope" was a complicated astrological chart that gave rulers and noblemen advice about the best day to, say, wage a major battle or start bringing in the harvest. Today, though, most people know horoscopes as the page in the newspaper that offers advice and predictions based on the reader's birth sign.

As you can guess, astrology made a lot more sense back before people knew what stars really were, and how they related to the earth. Today, it's clear that there's no scientific basis for astrology, but many people still read their horoscopes as a kind of harmless fun.

Carnivals & Fairs

Why is it called a carnival?

Nowadays, traveling carnivals are completely secular (that is, non-religious) affairs, which is why it's interesting that the word "carnival" derives from the Latin words for "without meat." Before Easter Sunday, practicing Catholics observe a ten-day penance called Lent, in which they can choose to go without meat. In medieval times, the two weeks leading up to Lent were a festive period called Carnival, in which people indulged in feasts and entertainment.

What is a sideshow?

Up until the 1930s and 1940s, traveling circuses and carnivals often featured "side shows"—exhibits populated by human oddities (two common examples were the "bearded lady" and the "strong man") and dimly lit objects of dubious origin, such as pickled monsters in jars. Side shows were presided over by fast-talking showmen called "hucksters," who kept up a constant stream of patter designed to lure patrons inside, and also featured such common circus acts as sword-swallowers and fire-eaters.

Sideshows have gradually disappeared over the last few decades, for two main reasons. First, spectators today are much more sensitive about the unfair exploitation of so-called "freaks," such as conjoined twins or mentally retarded people, than they used to be. And second, most folks today are savvy enough to know that a side show in, say, New Jersey is unlikely to possess the genuine mummified corpse of Buffalo Bill!

By the way, one of the last sideshows in the U.S. is located in Coney Island, New York, and features such attractions as "Bambi the Mermaid" and "Ula, the Pain-Proof Rubber Girl."

How do knife-throwers learn their craft?

As you can imagine, the knife-throwers you see in carnivals don't learn their routines by practicing with live subjects. Usually, a beginning knife-thrower will perfect his aim over months (or years) with a department-store mannequin, and only ask for human volunteers when he's 100 percent sure of his abilities. Even still, knife-throwing accidents occasionally happen, but since throwers only miss their targets by a tiny amount (say, half an inch) the damage is usually minimal.

Why is it so hard to win some carnival games?

Despite what you may think, the majority of carnival games aren't rigged to make them impossible to win. Booth operators have a much more straightforward way of raking in cash: the expensive-looking stuffed toys they award to winners usually only cost them a few bucks each, so they still wind up taking in more money than they dole out in prizes!

That said, there are a variety of ways an unscrupulous "carnie" can lighten your pockets. For instance, a "pop-the-balloon" game can be fixed by not fully inflating the balloons (which makes them nearly impossible to pop) or by equipping players with dull darts, and a "shoot-the-basket" game can be rigged by tilting the basket at a certain angle (not to mention making the ball slightly bigger than the diameter of the basket!)

Usually, the surest signs that you're playing a rigged game are that the operator ridicules you for not succeeding (which only makes you more frustrated and determined to throw your money away), or awards you small, insignificant prizes (known as "slum prizes") every few games to keep up your interest. If either of these things happens, stop spending your money and go on a ride!

Why is it called a Ferris wheel?

At the World Exposition in Chicago in 1893, an inventor named George Washington Gale Ferris, Jr. unveiled the carnival ride that went on to bear his name. Powered by two enormous steam engines, the very first Ferris wheel was a whopping 250 feet wide and could carry more than 2,000 people at a time. It's thought that Ferris made his wheel so big in order to outdo the main attraction at the 1889 Exposition in Paris—the Eiffel Tower!

Why are some circus acts performed without a net?

Let's be honest: a high-wire or trapeze act is much more compelling if there's no net slung below to catch the performers if they accidentally fall. Because performing "without a net" can be deadly, only the very best circus artists will dare to tempt fate this way (and even then, they'll usually take other, less visible, precautions against fatal slips).

What was a flea circus?

A common carnival attraction until the 1930s, flea circuses were exactly what they sound like: collections of fleas that were coaxed to perform rudimentary stunts, such as pulling tiny carts or swinging on a miniature trapeze. Because it was so small, a flea circus was surrounded by magnifying lenses, so it could be viewed from all sides by a large crowd.

What is the world's biggest store chain?

In the U.S. alone, Wal-Mart employs about 1.3 million people—more than the U.S. Postal Service! This chain of superstores, which sell everything from groceries to guns to patio furniture, takes in about $300 billion of business every year. The reason Wal-Mart is so successful is that, because it buys its goods in enormous quantities, it can afford to sell its items at extremely low prices.

What are mall walkers?

No, it's not some newfangled security force. In many communities, the only safe, climate-controlled place where elderly people can walk for exercise is the local mall. Most "mall walkers" show up at the mall at opening time, when the aisles are less crowded, and get in two or three miles of walking before the real customers show up.

Why is it called a department store?

Until the mid-18th century, stores in America and Europe were much more specialized than they are today: for instance, a society lady would have to purchase her hats at one shop, her dresses at another, and her shoes at yet a third. This was fine for folks who could devote an entire day to shopping, but not terribly convenient for busier people with more demands on their time. As you can guess from the name, a department store consists of various "departments," devoted to items that had previously been sold in separate establishments.

The very first department store was Bon Marché (which means "Good Deal" in French) in Paris, which opened for business in 1838, adding various departments over the next dozen or so years to better serve its customers. However, Bon Marché (which is still in business) isn't the most famous department store in the world: that honor belongs to Macy's, which was founded in Massachusetts in 1851 as a dry-goods (that is, clothing and textiles) store. Macy's didn't become a true department store until it moved to New York later in the 19th century; today, the Macy's in Herald Square is billed as "The World's Largest Department Store" (though some other stores around the world dispute that title!).

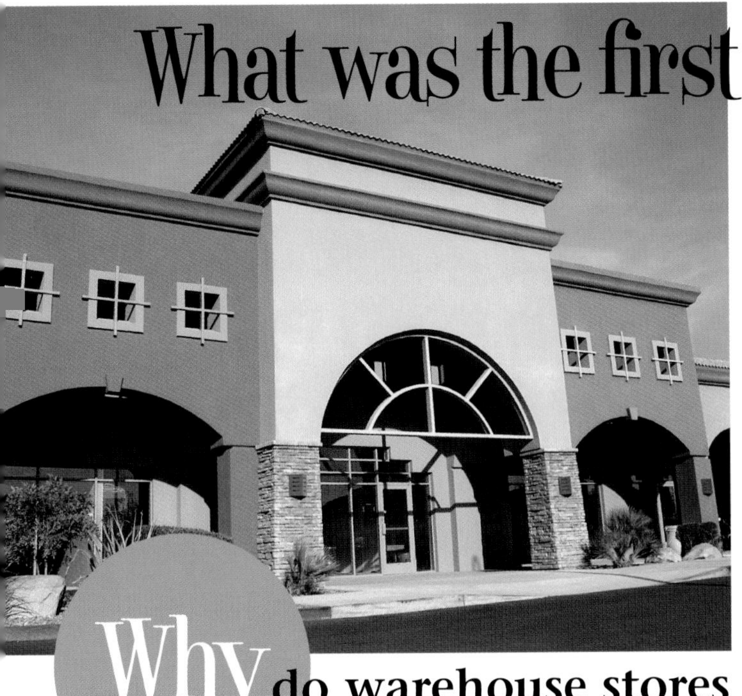

What was the first shopping mall?

If anything seems like it should be a recent innovation, it's the modern American shopping mall, with its acres upon acres of stores, restaurants, and parking spaces. But if you're not too attached to glass doors and electronic registers, shopping malls have been around much longer than you'd suspect.

In the first millennium A.D., the nation of Persia (modern-day Iran) had at least two enormous "bazaars" (that is, blocks and blocks of stores covered by protective awnings) in the cities of Tehran and Isfahan. A few centuries later, European cities featured open-air districts (usually called "agoras" or "piazzas") where citizens could buy all of their groceries and home supplies at once.

Although open-air malls had existed for decades before then, the first modern shopping mall in the U.S. was the Southdale Center in Edina, Minnesota (just outside Minneapolis), which opened for business in 1956. Southdale had most of the features that characterize today's malls: two large "anchor tenants" (that is, department stores) surrounded by a few dozen smaller shops, all enclosed under a single roof and with ample parking for shoppers.

Why do warehouse stores have such low prices?

As shoppers have long known, the secret to getting a good deal is to buy in bulk: for instance, a two-pound box of cereal costs proportionately less per serving than a one-pound box. Warehouse stores operate according to the same principle: they receive discounts from manufacturers for buying products in bulk, then sell these products to customers at a small profit margin, making up the difference with sheer volume.

What is "shrinkage"?

In store lingo, "shrinkage" refers to merchandise that mysteriously disappears before it can be sold—either because it's been hijacked off the delivery truck, stolen by employees, or shoplifted by customers. About two percent of all the goods sold in the U.S. are lost to shrinkage—which results in higher prices for everyone else!

What is a "loss leader"?

It's not necessary for a department store to earn a profit on all the merchandise it sells. A "loss leader" is a sale item (say, a cheap toaster) that a store sells to customers at a net loss, in the hopes that people who come to buy the toaster will stay and pick up other items that the store sells at a profit. This way, the profit from the customer's other purchases makes up for the loss incurred by the loss leader.

Restaurants

Why are some restaurants so expensive?

For some people, eating out isn't just a convenient way to have a meal—it's a form of entertainment, on a par with going to the movies. For this reason, cities and towns have their share of expensive restaurants, which serve lovingly prepared meals in a leisurely, quiet atmosphere. The reason you may not know about these places is that most parents take their kids to diners and fast-food joints—because having a tantrum (or throwing food) in a five-star French restaurant is a good way to get yourself thrown out onto the street!

Why do waiters receive tips?

The waiters at most restaurants aren't especially well paid, but on a busy night they can make up for this shortfall by receiving tips from customers (typically, anywhere from 15 to 20 percent of the cost of the meal). At fancy restaurants, it's also good manners to tip the maitre d' (the person who greets you at the door and guides you to your table) and the coat-check person.

Why is it called a "restaurant"?

The word "restaurant" was coined by an 18th-century French merchant named Boulanger, whose food shop in Paris allowed customers to sit down and order a meal called, literally, "restaurant"—which is French for "restorative soup." Although this was an important innovation, most historians say the first restaurant in the modern sense—that is, a place where customers could sit down and order a meal (and not just a bowl of soup)—was opened in Paris almost 20 years later, in 1782, by a man named Beauvilliers.

It didn't take long for the concept of the restaurant to spread throughout the western world. In the U.S., Delmonico's, the first restaurant to offer customers a printed menu, opened in New York in 1827. Because Delmonico's catered to businessmen on Wall Street, at first it only served lunch, but it had expanded its menu to include dinner by the time it closed nearly a hundred years later. (By the way, Delmonico's is famous for introducing many dishes—such as Lobsters Newburgh, Oysters Rockefeller, and Baked Alaska—that have become popular at other American restaurants.)

What is the difference between a restaurant and a diner?

On the eating-out food chain, a diner is midway between a fancy, full-service restaurant and a cheap fast-food joint. Historically, diners sprang up near highways and busy roads as convenient places where motorists could duck in for quick meals. At most diners, you can sit at a separate table or booth, or if you don't mind rubbing elbows with your fellow travelers, on a stool set up by the counter.

What does a maitre d' do?

No, that's not a typo—"maitre d'" is short for "maitre d'hotel," and it's the French term for the person at a restaurant who greets customers and assigns them to tables. Because they're not involved in serving or preparing food, maitre d's are mostly found at more expensive restaurants, where customers expect attentive treatment.

What do restaurants do if everyone orders the same dish?

Usually, a restaurant will keep careful track of what its customers have ordered in the past, and stock its kitchen accordingly—so if bacon cheeseburgers are an especially popular item, there'll be plenty of bacon, cheese, and hamburger meat on hand. However, it's still possible that an unusually large number of people will order the same dish on the same night—and if you're one of those people, the waiter may gently suggest (and then insist) that you order something else.

Why is it called "fast food"?

As is obvious from the name, "fast food" means, literally, restaurant or take-out food that can be eaten fast (as opposed to, say, spending two hours in a fancy French restaurant savoring a seven-course meal). It might surprise you to learn that fast food is almost as old as civilization itself. In ancient Rome, for instance, people could buy all kinds of ready-made meals at street stalls, while even the earliest Asian cities were littered with noodle shops.

In the modern sense of the term, though, "fast food" is pretty much synonymous with the world's biggest fast-food restaurant: McDonald's. The very first McDonald's opened in San Bernardino, California, in 1940, serving 15-cent hamburgers and a limited number of other items. It was more than a dozen years before the second McDonald's appeared, in Phoenix, Arizona, in 1953, but after that the pace picked up tremendously: today, McDonald's has more than 30,000 fast-food restaurants throughout the world, serving up hamburgers and fries to more than 50 million people a day!

Stadiums

What is the largest stadium in the U.S.?

Oddly enough, the largest stadiums in the U.S. are devoted to college, and not professional, football teams. The reigning champ is Michigan Stadium, also known as "The Big House," which can hold well over 100,000 screaming Michigan Wolverines fans. As big as it is, though, Michigan Stadium is dwarfed by Strahov Stadium in the Czech Republic, which can hold 250,000 people!

Why are they called multi-use stadiums?

Because the seasons for pro football and pro baseball don't overlap, some stadiums are designed to accommodate both sports (which is why, during football games in these stadiums, you can see the faint outline of a baseball diamond on the field—and during baseball games, you can see the yard lines of a football field!). Today, most new stadiums are designed for single teams, since team owners don't like to share their turf (even with a team from an entirely different sport).

How many bathrooms does a stadium need?

It varies by stadium, of course, and a typical rest room can include anywhere from 5 to 50 stalls and urinals. But to take a modern example, Citizens Bank Park in Philadelphia (the home of the Philadelphia Phillies) has about one public restroom for every 1,000 customers. As to how many of a stadium's bathrooms should be devoted to men and how many to women, that's an issue for experts in "potty parity," who study how long it takes the average person to go!

What was the first domed stadium?

When it opened for business in 1965, the Houston Astrodome (the brand-new home of the then two-year-old Houston Astros) was known as the "eighth wonder of the world." Houston was the perfect city in which to erect a domed (and air-conditioned) stadium, since temperatures during the Texas summer regularly reach 100 degrees Fahrenheit—which doesn't make for enjoyable baseball games, either for players or for fans! For the first couple of years, games at the Astrodome were played on natural grass, but lack of sunlight prompted the switch to an artificial grass that came to be known as "Astroturf."

As space-aged as it appeared in the 1960s, the Astrodome started to become a bit cramped and shabby-looking in the '80s and '90s, and even more decrepit after the Astros moved into a newer domed stadium in 2000. But the stadium did get another, unexpected turn in the spotlight: during Hurricane Katrina, which devastated the Gulf Coast in 2005, 13,000 evacuees from New Orleans were housed in the Astrodome for two crucial weeks.

Why are so many stadiums named after companies?

It used to be that stadiums were named after important people (such as Shea Stadium, named after William A. Shea, who brought the Mets to New York) or neighborhoods (such as Fenway Park in Boston). While these stadiums have so far retained their original names, they're the last of a dying breed: today, most new stadiums auction off "naming rights" to major corporations that provide funding. That's why Candlestick Park in San Francisco was known for years as "3Com Park," and why the Colorado Rockies' Denver stadium is called "Coors Field" (after a local beer manufacturer).

Naming stadiums after companies can have some unintended (and amusing) consequences. For example, the Houston Astros' new stadium was once known as Enron Park, until the Enron Corporation collapsed and wiped out the savings of thousands of employees (today, the stadium is called Minute Maid Park, after the orange-juice maker). And in Phoenix, what was once known as "Bank One Ballpark" had to change its name after Bank One was acquired by the competition—today, the home of the Arizona Diamondbacks is called "Chase Field."

Why is the food in stadiums so expensive?

Have you ever heard the expression "captive audience"? Stadium owners know that fans like to eat and drink (especially during long baseball games), which is why a hot dog that costs a buck on the street will set you back $4 or $5 in a stadium. Some arenas are so dependent on these "concession" sales that they actually search fans' belongings as they enter the stadium, to make sure they're not smuggling in any food!

What is the Coliseum?

Built by the emperor Vespasian in the 1st century A.D., the Coliseum in Rome was capable of seating 50,000 spectators, about the capacity of a modern baseball stadium. However, Roman citizens would have booed if they'd had to sit through a baseball game; they were accustomed to visiting the Coliseum to see gladiatorial combat or wild animals being set loose on convicted criminals!

Zoos

What is the difference between a zoo and a nature preserve?

Well, for one thing, most animals are a lot happier living in nature preserves! Zoos are located in or near major cities, for the convenience of visitors, and while the keepers do everything they can to keep the animals happy, the average polar bear probably wouldn't choose to live in, say, Chicago. A nature preserve, on the other hand, is a section of a creature's natural habit that has been fenced off—so rather than being kept in a cage, the animal can roam free inside its boundaries.

Why are they called "zoos"?

You have to admit, "zoo" is a funny-sounding name, especially compared to "museum" or "aquarium." "Zoo" is actually short for the not-quite-as-amusing term "zoological garden," and the word "zoological" is ultimately derived from the Greek word for animal, "zoon" (that's pronounced "zoo-on," by the way, and not to rhyme with "soon"!).

What is the most popular zoo animal?

Yes, everyone wants to see the elephants, and the monkey cages are always good for a few laughs. But if a zoo wants to make its customers happy and keep them coming back for more, it'll pull some strings with the appropriate authorities and land itself a genuine, Chinese-born giant panda.

Today, only four zoos in the U.S. have Giant Pandas: the San Diego, Memphis, and Atlanta Zoos, as well as the National Zoo in Washington, D.C. Because these creatures are so rare—not to mention so cute and cuddly-looking—they attract many people who wouldn't ordinarily go to zoos. If a male and female panda happen to produce a baby panda, a zoo stands to reap enormous publicity—for instance, when the National Zoo's pandas had a bouncing baby boy, the news made a big splash all over the U.S.

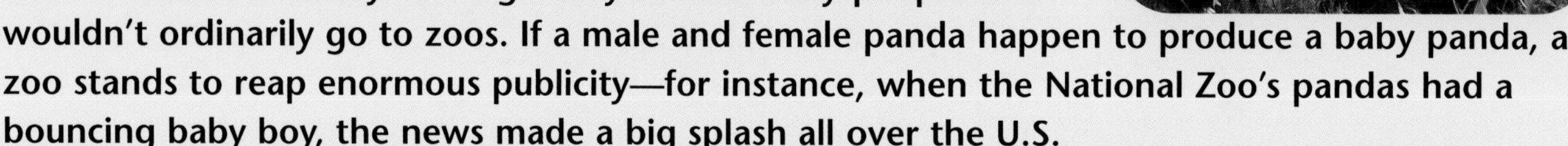

While pandas are good for a zoo's image, they're also extremely expensive. The Chinese government will only loan out pandas in exchange for multimillion-dollar fees, and these finicky creatures have to be fed a special diet and kept in climate-controlled environments. Amazingly, a panda is five times more expensive to keep in a zoo than an elephant!

What does a zoo do with its animal poop?

Zoos have lots and lots of animals, and all those animals produce lots and lots of poop, of all different sizes, shapes, and smells. Although a lot of this poop is simply discarded, much of it is resold as fertilizer—there's nothing like a few hundred pounds of elephant poop to get your azaleas blooming!

Why do some people disapprove of zoos?

As careful as zookeepers are to attend to their animals' needs, there's no getting around the fact that the inhabitants aren't there by choice—they've been taken out of their natural habitats and placed in a restricted (if not quite prison-like) environment. Although this makes some people uneasy, the fact is that if it weren't for zoos, many of these creatures might have disappeared long ago—and compared to extinction, a few iron bars don't seem too bad!

What was the first zoo?

That all depends on how you define "zoo." In medieval times, kings and emperors liked to collect strange beasts from foreign lands and put them in "menageries," small, zoo-like enclosures meant to be enjoyed by the ruler's family and higher nobles. However, since most commoners couldn't hope to visit the king's menagerie, it's not clear if these really qualified as "zoos." The Vienna Zoo—which has been operating continuously since 1752—was founded as an imperial menagerie, and some experts consider it the first modern zoo (that is, if you define "zoo" as "a place to go and look at animals").

But wait, we're not finished. A zoo, in the modern sense of the term, isn't simply a fun place for a family to visit on a lazy weekend—it's a scientific institution, run by professionals, that helps to nurture and conserve vanishing species. By this definition, the world's first zoo was the "Menagerie du Jardin des Plantes," founded in Paris in 1794. The concept of a menagerie with a scientific (and educational) mission soon caught on, and over the next few decades major zoos were founded in cities all over the world.

What do zoo animals do at night?

They put on their clothes, punch out on a time clock and return home to their families. Seriously, though, at night—when they're not sleeping—zoo animals do pretty much what they do during the day, only without hundreds of noisy people milling around looking at them!

Basketball

How tall is the average basketball player?

The stats are constantly changing, of course, but in the past few years the typical NBA player has towered about 6 feet, 6 inches. In fact, players are becoming so tall that some basketball fans have suggested raising the height of the hoop from 10 feet above the court to 11 or 12 feet. This would have the effect of making sheer height less important than talent, which most fans enjoy a lot more!

Why was the three-point shot added to basketball?

Before the NBA adopted the three-point shot in 1979, there was a tendency for the biggest, strongest basketball players to cluster under the hoop, which wasn't particularly fun for fans to watch. By making a shot from about 23 feet out worth three points rather than the usual two, the NBA "opened up" the game by encouraging players to take advantage of their "outside" (rather than their "inside") skills and of their aiming ability rather than their height.

How was basketball invented?

Basketball is the only team sport that, unlike baseball or football, can definitely be traced back to a single person. In 1891, Dr. James Naismith, a teacher at the YMCA Training School in Springfield, Massachusetts, invented a sport that students could play indoors during the long New England winters. The first game of his newfangled "basketball" was played with a soccer ball and two elevated peach baskets, and quickly spread throughout the country by way of local YMCAs.

As with football, the first organized games of basketball, in the late 1890s, were played by college students rather than by professional teams (which may explain why the NCAA Championships are so popular today!). It was only in the 1920s that various pro leagues came into existence, usually centered around a particular city (these early teams played their games in high-school gyms and dance halls rather than big arenas, and traded players the way you trade Pokémon cards with your friends). The National Basketball Association was finally founded in 1946, paving the way for the fast, high-powered game we enjoy today.

Why are basketballs orange?

Since basketball is such a fast-moving game, it's important for spectators to be able to see the action clearly. Before the late 1950s, most basketballs were a dark, dull brown, with a smattering of garish yellow balls. As a compromise, a coach named Tony Hinkle proposed the orange balls used today. (By the way, the American Basketball Association—a rival league that competed with the NBA from 1967 to 1976—used red, white, and blue balls!)

What is the "Final Four"?

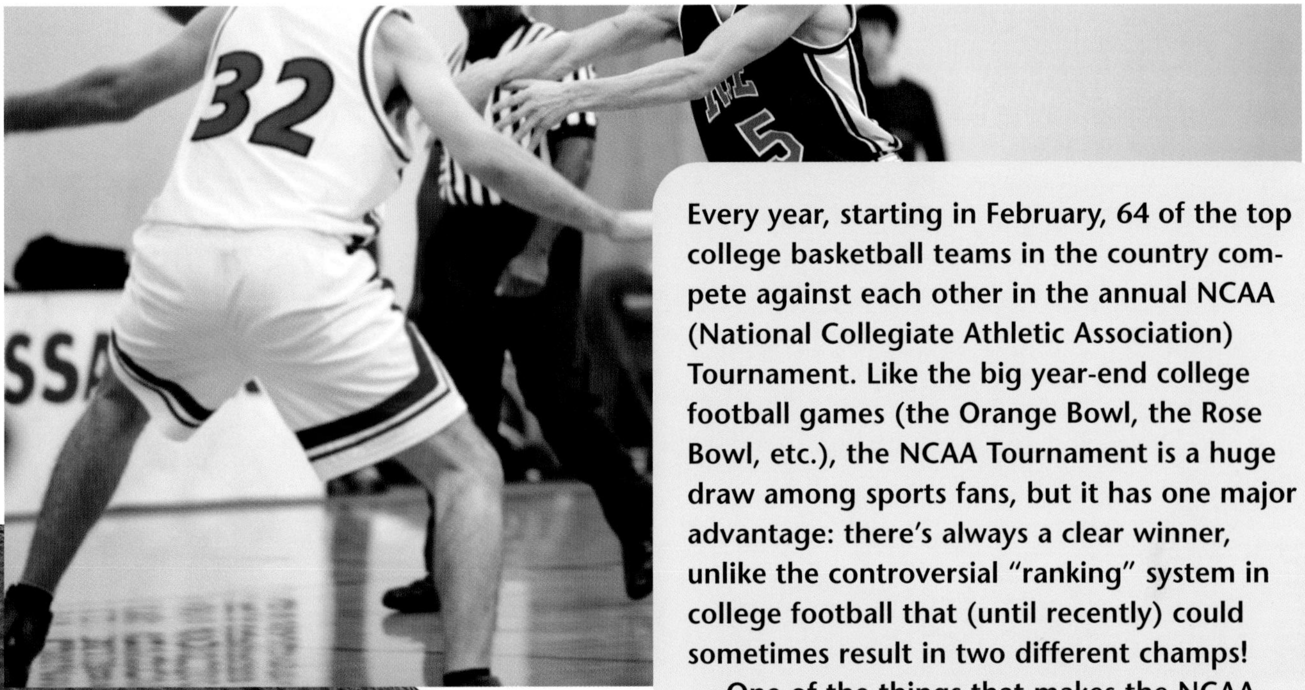

Every year, starting in February, 64 of the top college basketball teams in the country compete against each other in the annual NCAA (National Collegiate Athletic Association) Tournament. Like the big year-end college football games (the Orange Bowl, the Rose Bowl, etc.), the NCAA Tournament is a huge draw among sports fans, but it has one major advantage: there's always a clear winner, unlike the controversial "ranking" system in college football that (until recently) could sometimes result in two different champs!

One of the things that makes the NCAA Tournament so popular is that, every now and then, an obscure, low-ranked team makes an amazing run to the championship game. If one of these teams manages to reach the "Final Four" (that is, the final four teams in the tournament, who play against each other to determine the championship matchup), the result is instant fame and notoriety. Most of the time, though, the NCAA Tournament is dominated by familiar teams with historically strong basketball programs, such as the Duke University Blue Devils or the Kansas Jayhawks.

Why is it called "dribbling"?

You have to admit, "dribbling" is a pretty undignified name for bouncing a basketball. The most likely explanation is that soccer players "dribble" a ball by kicking it down the field in small distances, and since the first games of basketball were played with soccer balls, the name was attached to the practice of bouncing a ball on the court. (Interestingly, dribbling wasn't one of the original rules devised by basketball's inventor, Dr. James Naismith—it was improvised by one of his players!)

Boating

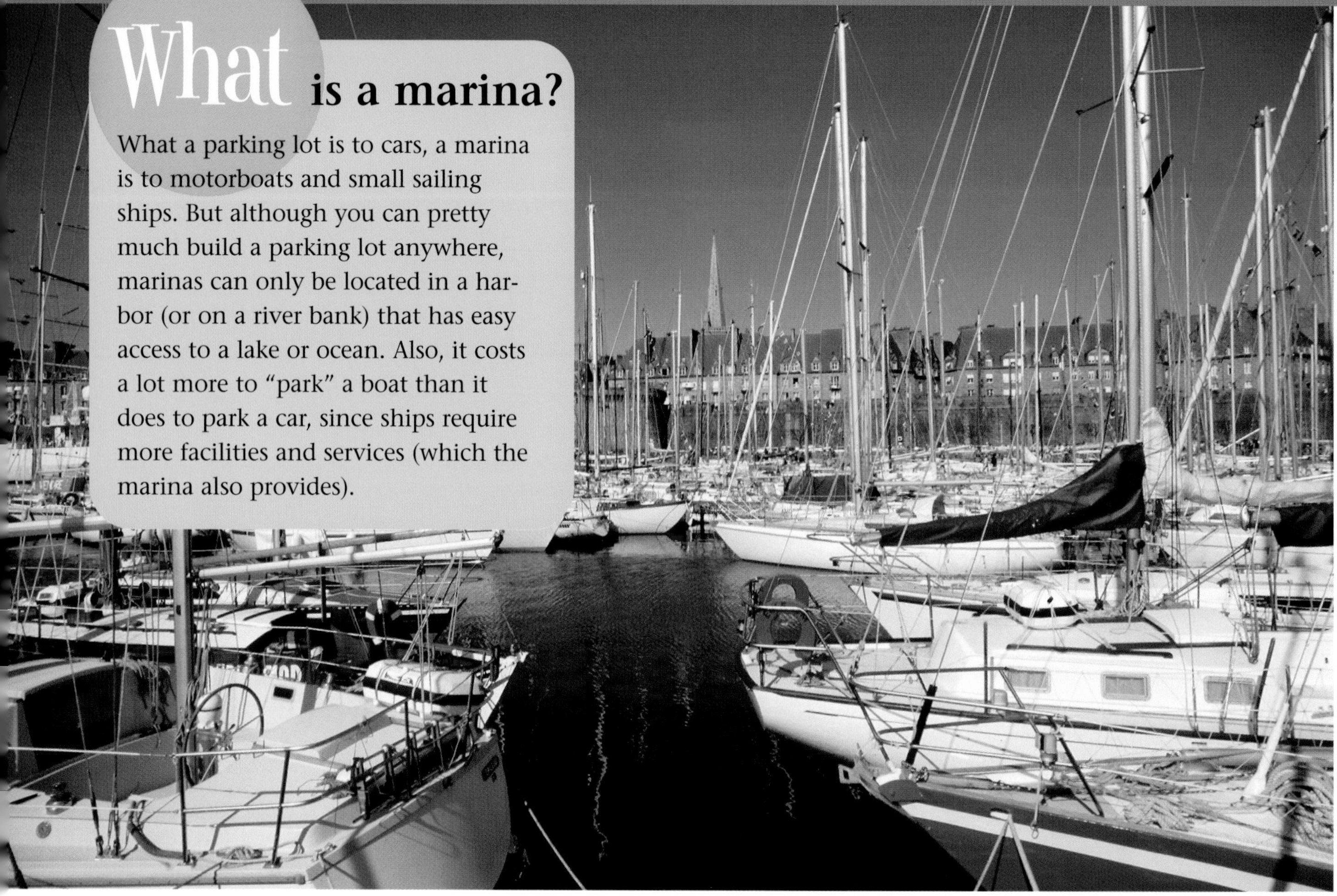

What is a marina?

What a parking lot is to cars, a marina is to motorboats and small sailing ships. But although you can pretty much build a parking lot anywhere, marinas can only be located in a harbor (or on a river bank) that has easy access to a lake or ocean. Also, it costs a lot more to "park" a boat than it does to park a car, since ships require more facilities and services (which the marina also provides).

How many rowers could a galley ship hold?

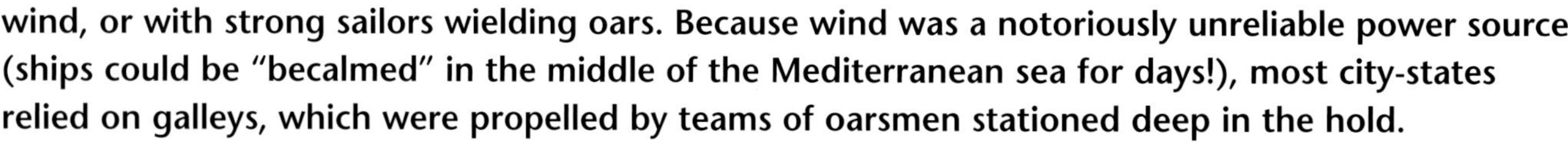

In ancient times—before the invention of steam propulsion—there were only two ways to power a ship: with sails that caught the wind, or with strong sailors wielding oars. Because wind was a notoriously unreliable power source (ships could be "becalmed" in the middle of the Mediterranean sea for days!), most city-states relied on galleys, which were propelled by teams of oarsmen stationed deep in the hold.

Just as there are all kinds of battleships today, there were all kinds of galleys 2,000 or 3,000 years ago. A "bireme" utilized two layers of oars (one on top of the other), while a faster "trireme" had three layers (there were also "quinqueremes" and "polyremes," with even more layers). The biggest galleys of all were built by the Romans and Egyptians, and required hundreds of oarsmen.

Because these huge ships needed more oarsmen than could reasonably be recruited and paid, they were usually manned by "galley slaves," whose sole function was to row, row, and row some more until they passed out or died!

Why do sailors say "port" and "starboard" instead of "left" and "right"?

In the early days of sailing, the "starboard" referred to a long rudder that hung from the side of a ship. Since most sailors (then as now) were right-handed, the starboard rudder came to signify the right side of the ship. As for "port," that doesn't refer to the kind of port where ships dock. Rather, this word is descended from the old Norse "bord," which simply means "side of a ship"—and since "starboard" meant right, "port" came to mean left.

Why are there fewer steamboats than there used to be?

The 19th century was the age of the steamboat—big, squat ships, fueled by coal, that used steam to power turbines. The reason steamboats have pretty much disappeared is that most ships today use clean-burning oil rather than soot-producing coal. Also, a steamboat's boiler needed to be constantly stoked with coal, a sweaty, dangerous job that very few sailors are willing to do nowadays!

Why is it called a "yacht"?

The word "yacht"—which is pronounced to rhyme with "swat"—derives from the old Dutch word "jacht," meaning "to hunt." The fast, sleek "jachtship" first came into prominence in the late 17th century, when the English king Charles II (who had been in exile in Holland) crossed the English Channel in a vessel borrowed from his Dutch hosts. Restored to the throne, Charles kept his "yacht," and the English nobility quickly followed suit, turning these big boats into very expensive status symbols.

Today, most yachts are used for recreational purposes, such as parties or pleasure cruises. But some folks like to rig up their yachts for races, the biggest of which is the America's Cup, an annual event conducted in various parts of the world (and which was first held back in 1851). Not just anybody can enter the America's Cup—outfitting a racing yacht and finding experienced sailors to man it can cost hundreds of thousands of dollars—but this is still one of the most competitive events in all of sports.

How fast can a motorboat go?

Despite what you see in movies, a motorboat can't go nearly as fast as a fast car on an open road. The most powerful motorboats (or "speedboats," as they're sometimes called) can attain a top speed of 40 or 50 miles per hour, compared to 90 or 100 mph for a car. (By the way, just as policemen patrol the highway, the Coast Guard patrols the shoreline—and they'll give you a ticket for driving your motorboat too fast!)

What are sails made of?

You can't just hang a bedsheet from a tall mast and go sailing: a sail has to be tough enough to withstand gale-force winds, yet light enough to be easily maneuverable. In olden times, sails were stitched together out of canvas or cloth, but most modern sails are made of space-age fabrics, which incorporate such exotic ingredients as high-strength carbon fibers.

Bowling

How was bowling invented?

Like golf, bowling is one of those games that seems to have been played by humans since the beginning of recorded history—with, of course, frequent changes in rules and equipment. There's some evidence that children in ancient Egypt enjoyed a primitive form of bowling—that is, if the word "bowling" applies to knocking over standing objects with a big, heavy ball. Historians agree that bowling was firmly established by the middle ages, when King Edward III of England prohibited this sport on Sundays so citizens could practice archery instead (oddly enough, he applied the same rule to golf). A few hundred years later, an early form of bowling using nine pins—which was called, appropriately enough, Ninepins—became popular in colonial New York (there's still a stop on the New York subway system called "Bowling Green"). By the late nineteenth century, most of the rules of modern bowling were established, including the length of the lanes and the number of pins used.

How hard is it to bowl a perfect game?

The way professional bowlers roll strikes, you'd think perfect games (12 strikes in a row, adding up to the highest possible score of 300) would be fairly common. But the fact is, even a champion bowler may bowl a perfect game only a handful of times over the course of his career, and the feat is rare enough at the amateur level that most bowling alleys will give you a prize for the accomplishment.

Why does bowling have such a strange scoring system?

Although it's easy to figure where the words "spare" and "strike" come from (a spare is when your first ball leaves pins to spare, and a "strike" is when you strike down all ten pins at once), the origins of bowling's complex frame-by-frame scoring system are shrouded in mystery. Decades ago, players had no choice but to score their games manually—a task that made college-level physics look easy!—but today, fortunately, computers do all the work.

Why do you need to wear bowling shoes?

There are two reasons bowling alleys make you trade in your street shoes for bowling shoes: first, the soles of bowling shoes allow you to slide your feet properly as you approach the lane, thus improving your score. Second (and most important, from the alley's point of view), street shoes can scuff up or gouge holes in the lanes, which have to be kept in good condition for professional tournaments.

How many bowlers are there?

Perhaps because it's more social and informal than other sports—there's nothing like bowling to catch up with friends, grab a slice of pizza, and get a little exercise—bowling is one of the most popular recreational sports in the world. Today, about 100 million people worldwide bowl regularly, including tens of millions of folks in the U.S. (a large percentage of which are kids aged 12 to 17).

What is the hardest spare?

One of the odd things about bowling is that, the more off-target your first ball, the easier it is to pick up the spare (if you throw a gutter ball to begin with, "striking" for a spare is relatively easy). What bowlers fear most is a "split"—a first ball that leaves two separate pins standing—and the most difficult of all splits is the "7-10," consisting of the two most widely separated pins in the back row. Even the best bowlers in the world may only pick up a 7-10 split once or twice in their lifetimes!

How heavy is a bowling ball?

As you know if you've ever been to a bowling party, a regulation-size, adult bowling ball is much more difficult to handle than a ball designed for little kids. The weight of an adult ball ranges between 8 and 16 pounds, and has a diameter of 8.5 inches. This means that heavier balls are much denser than lighter balls, since they pack more weight into the same amount of space. Since even eight pounds is a lot for a five-year-old kid to safely wield, most balls used for kids' parties are much lighter.

By the way, one thing that sets bowling apart from other sports is that a bowler can use any ball he pleases, as long as it conforms to these weight and width requirements. Balls can be made out of a variety of ingredients (though plastic and rubber are the most common), and can be any color—even transparent! Even the number of holes on a bowling ball is only loosely regulated; standard balls have three holes, for the ring finger, middle finger and thumb, but some balls have as many as five holes—and fit the bowler's hand like a (very heavy) glove.

What was the first animated movie?

Nowadays, kids can count on a half-dozen or so big-budget animated films being released every year. But back in the 1930s, when the cartoon pioneer Walt Disney started work on *Snow White and the Seven Dwarfs*, his decision was widely known as "Disney's Folly." Because hand-drawn animation is such an expensive process, *Snow White* wound up costing a whopping $1.5 million, more than most big-budget live-action films at the time. Even worse, no one knew if a full-length cartoon (no matter how expensive) would have any appeal for kids or their parents.

Well, Walt Disney was completely vindicated, because *Snow White* went on to become the biggest movie of 1938 (and the highest-grossing movie of all time, until *Gone with the Wind* a year later). Based on its success, over the next few years Disney embarked on a series of animated movies, including such classics as *Pinocchio*, *Fantasia*, and *Dumbo*. Because of the expertise of his animators (and the money he had to spend), Walt Disney pretty much had a monopoly on animated movies for the next 30 years!

How does computer animation work?

Basically, there are two kinds of animation: hand-drawn and computer. Hand-drawn animation relies on thousands (or hundreds of thousands) of separate drawings that are photographed in sequence, an expensive and time-consuming process. Computer animation, on the other hand, draws on the processing power of computers to generate realistic (or not-so-realistic) images on the screen, which can be stored on a hard drive and converted into film.

The history of computer animation closely mirrors the history of computers. The very first computer-animated cartoons, made a couple of dozen years ago, were only a few minutes long and hugely expensive, because of the limited capacity of computers at that time. Today, though, even a kid can use his home computer to create a short animated film, and professionals are doing amazing things with the form. It's even possible to create computerized characters that look almost human, what some people in Hollywood call "vactors" (short for "virtual actors").

Why are there so many cartoons on Saturday mornings?

That's an easy one: since kids don't have school, Saturday morning is the perfect time to plop down in front of the tube and watch 'toons. The reason there are fewer cartoons on Sunday mornings is that most networks use that time for "serious" programming, though that has changed somewhat with the advent of 24-hour cartoon and kids' channels.

What is anime?

Anime, a Japanese style of animation featuring lots of action, bug-eyed characters, and fantastic story lines, has had an enormous influence on American cartoons. Even when your parents were kids, early Japanese "anime" shows like *Gigantor* and *Speed Racer* were aired (dubbed into English, of course) on American TV.

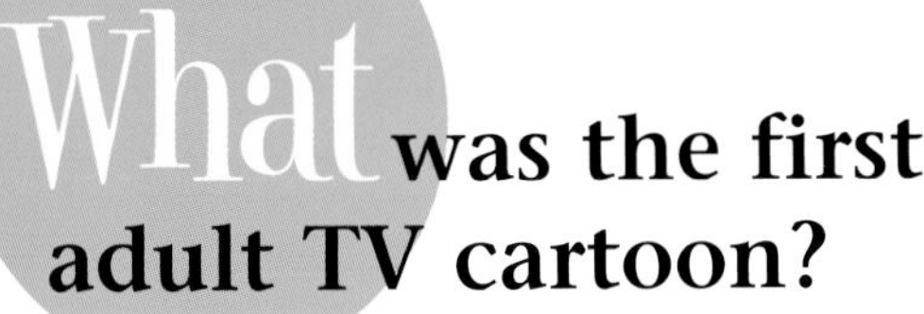

What was the first adult TV cartoon?

It may seem hard to believe, but when it debuted in 1960, *The Flintstones* was intended mostly for adults (or, at least, parents and their kids). The show ran for six years in prime time (the first animated show to air in the evenings), and has been recycled endlessly ever since. The closest equivalent to *The Flintstones* today is *The Simpsons*, which is also targeted at families and is one of the longest-running shows on TV, at more than 15 years and counting!

Why are cels worth so much money?

A "cel" (a piece of clear plastic that can be drawn on with colored ink) is the basic unit of hand-drawn animation: if you draw thousands of these in succession and put them on film, the result is an animated movie. Cels are expensive for two reasons: first, collectors are constantly seeking cels from classic films and cartoons (like *Bambi* and *Bugs Bunny*), and second, most animation today is done on computers, so hand-drawn cels are rapidly becoming a thing of the past.

What was the first TV cartoon?

In the early days of TV, it was common to fill airtime with old *Bugs Bunny* or *Popeye* cartoons. As incredible as it may seem, these cartoons weren't made for TV—they had first been shown in movie theaters, years before, as the "shorts" before the main attraction. The first cartoon made specifically for TV, *Crusader Rabbit*, debuted in 1950. Though the show (about an armor-wearing bunny and his tiger pal) has since been forgotten, it's famous for another reason: it was created by Jay Ward, the genius behind *The Rocky and Bullwinkle Show* ten years later.

How were fireworks invented?

As you can imagine, the history of fireworks started off with a bang—literally. About 2,000 years ago, in China, a military cook accidentally mixed together charcoal, sulphur, and a mineral called saltpeter, which promptly exploded when it was exposed to heat. Within a few centuries, Chinese monks had learned how to use this formula for peaceful purposes, stuffing it into tubes to propel colorful fireworks into the sky (usually as a way of celebrating birthdays or fending off evil spirits).

"Gunpowder" (as this explosive mixture was called) found its way into the West as long ago as the 13th century, but unlike the Chinese, the warring nations of Europe preferred to use this chemical for weapons rather than fireworks. It wasn't until the 16th century or so that the Italians "reinvented" the art of fireworks, creating colorful, technically advanced displays that soon made their way north and west. Fireworks became especially popular in England, where major events like royal births and coronations would be celebrated with enormous fireworks displays.

What is the Festival of Lights?

The U.S. isn't the only country that celebrates major holidays with fireworks. In India, the five-day holiday known as "Deepavali" (which celebrates the victory of good over evil, and usually falls in October or November) is marked by numerous fireworks displays, either by entire towns or by individual families. (In India, unlike in the U.S., pretty much anyone can buy and set off fireworks!)

How does a sparkler work?

They seem harmless enough, but sparklers—hand-held fireworks that burn slowly, emitting colorful sparks—can reach temperatures as high as 2,000 degrees Fahrenheit! Sparklers are made from metal rods that have been dipped in flammable material, then allowed to dry. The reason they emit sparks when they're lit is that the solid fuel contains flecks of aluminum or iron, which emit characteristic colors as they ignite.

How can fireworks spell words?

They can't, really. The technology doesn't yet exist that would allow fireworks to spell a simple word in the sky, much less a complete phrase like "I Love You, Mary." This is because the split-second timing that would be required is beyond the capacity of today's electronically detonated fuses, though progress is being made—the most advanced pyrotechnicians (as fireworks experts are called) have managed to spell out individual letters! If you see a word spelled out at a fireworks display, that's because a bunch of shells have been mounted on a big sign and detonated simultaneously (though the fireworks company would prefer you not to know that).

Complete words will have to wait for the future, but pyrotechnicians are getting better and better at "choreographing" displays in time to music—kind of like a real-time music video. This is a very complicated process, involving a computerized control system that launches a pattern of fireworks much more precisely than could ever be done by hand, as well as accurately placed speakers (the speed of sound is much slower than the speed of light, so synchronizing a fireworks display with music requires careful preparation).

What is a bottle rocket?

As its name implies, a bottle rocket is essentially a small rocket that's launched from a glass or plastic bottle, emitting a piercing sound before it explodes colorfully in the sky. If you've never launched a bottle rocket, there's a good reason: most states ban the sale of these fireworks, which can cause injury if they're launched incorrectly (especially if they're not aimed at the sky!).

What is the difference between a firecracker and an M-80?

Technically, an M-80 (a two-inch-long paper tube filled with gunpowder) is nothing more than a bigger, louder firecracker. Although they can be obtained illegally, M-80s have been banned in the U.S. for years, because kids (and some adults) have been known to light their M-80s and foolishly attempt to throw them like grenades. The result is that a lot of M-80s blow up in people's hands—and sometimes blow off their fingers!

What is a "fallout zone"?

During a fireworks display, the gathered crowd has to be kept safely beyond the reach of any potentially misfired shells. For the biggest shows—such as the annual Fourth of July fireworks display over New York's East River—this "fallout zone" can extend for a radius of 2,000 feet from the launching area. Safety precautions such as this make the average fireworks display far safer for spectators than, say, the average air show!

Gardening

What is a perennial?

A particular favorite of gardeners—because they require less work—perennials are flowers that bloom many times over the course of their lives, rather than blossoming once and then dropping dead. Because perennials are more durable than "annuals" or "biennials," their seeds tend to be a bit more expensive, but gardeners find they pay for themselves over the long haul.

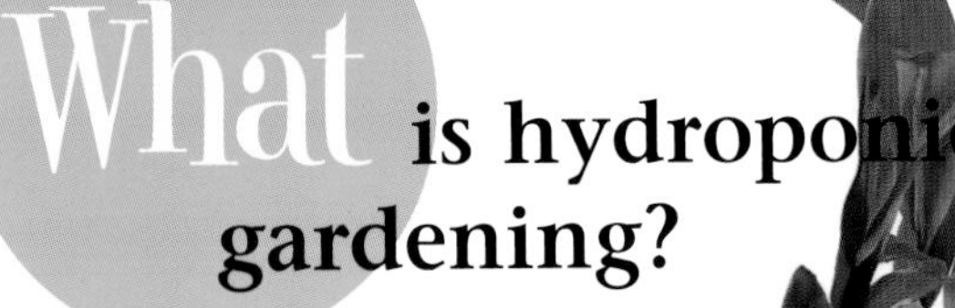

What is hydroponic gardening?

A longtime favorite of science-fiction writers, hydroponics is the art of gardening without soil—instead, plants are grown in a solution of nutrient-rich water. Not only does hydroponics allow food to be cultivated in areas without suitable soil, but it's also a way to protect growing plants from pesky weeds and insects. Today, hydroponic gardening is practiced around the world on a small scale, but (for economic reasons) it's a long way from supplanting traditional soil-based farming.

What is a topiary garden?

In ancient Rome, imperial gardeners learned the art of clipping shrubs and plants to resemble animals, symbols, and geometrical shapes. These "topiary gardens," as they were called, were the equivalent of modern-day museums, as visitors would come from near and far to marvel at the gardeners' art. ("Topiary," by the way, is derived from the Latin word for "shape.")

As you can guess, topiary isn't the easiest skill in the world to master. Although some types of plants and shrubs (such as rosemary, thyme, and yew) can be easily trimmed into simple geometrical shapes, turning a big bush into, say, a badger requires a lot more effort. This is accomplished with the use of metal frames that gradually force the young plant to grow into the desired shape—a process that can take as long as ten years!

If you're not willing to wait that long, though, there's at least one popular form of topiary that yields quick results. "Chia Pets," as they're called, are small clay sculptures that kids coat with the seeds of fast-growing grass. Within days of watering a Chia Pet, the result is a genuine (though not very long-lived) grass sculpture in the shape of an animal or cartoon character.

Why are ladybugs good for gardens?

You may think the last thing a gardener would want is a bunch of ladybugs prowling around in her backyard. However, unlike some other insects, ladybugs actually help gardens grow by eating aphids (tiny pests that feed on plants) and other slow-moving bugs, while leaving the flowers and vegetables alone. A single ladybug can consume as many as 5,000 aphids in its lifetime, a terrific return on a small investment!

What kind of manure is best for gardens?

You may think all manures (that is, number 2s made by animals) are pretty much the same when it comes to using them as fertilizer. However, most gardeners prefer the manure produced by vegetarian animals (such as cows and horses) over that produced by omnivores or carnivores (such as pigs or dogs). This is because the manure from meat-eating animals contains ingredients that can be injurious, rather than helpful, to growing plants.

Why are marigolds such popular flowers?

Gardeners don't only plant marigolds because they look good—these flowers have also been known to keep away nematodes, tiny, almost microscopic worms that eat away at the roots of plants. On a related note, planting Artemisia (also known as wormwood) can be a good way to keep away pesky rabbits!

Why are greenhouses hot?

By definition, tropical plants will grow only in tropical climates—meaning they require high humidity levels and temperatures well into the 80s and 90s. Since tropical plants are among the most colorful and interesting in the world, gardeners in, say, Canada need a way to cultivate them in their considerably cooler climate.

That's where greenhouses come in. These spacious gardens are surrounded by glass or plastic walls specially designed to allow in only certain frequencies of sunlight, and to block others from escaping. The result is that the greenhouse traps heat at the level where the plants grow, allowing the cultivation of hot-weather fruits and flowers. Of course, it's necessary to keep the plants moist (either with constant watering or mechanical humidifiers), and at night electric heaters are turned on to maintain the temperature.

The biggest greenhouses are complete ecosystems in their own right. Greenhouse gardeners are careful to introduce the "right" kinds of bugs and pests, such as bumblebees, to pollinate their flowers, and may even add a few colorful butterflies just for the heck of it!

Golf

How was golf invented?

The idea of hitting a tiny ball with a stick or club is almost as old as civilization itself: variants of this simple game were played by the people of ancient Rome, China, and Europe. It was up to Scotland, though, to come up with the innovation that led to the modern game of golf: aiming the ball at a little hole in the ground.

In the 14th century, Scottish sportsmen developed a taste for hitting pebbles (or primitive balls stuffed with feathers) into rabbit holes. The country's craggy landscape—dotted with hills, bunkers, and assorted trees and undergrowth—made this simple game so challenging that it quickly grew in popularity. Soon, players were digging their own holes and creating tees from which to hit their increasingly well-made balls.

By the middle of the 15th century, the game of "gowf" was so widespread that the king of Scotland issued a decree banning it on Sundays. On that day, he wanted his subjects to practice archery instead, to ready them for a possible war with England to the south.

Why is it called a "bogie"?

One of the things that makes golf so interesting (or baffling) is its terminology—words like "mashie," "niblick," "bogie" and "mulligan" can make you feel like you're in the middle of a Dr. Seuss book. As you might have guessed from reading the other questions on this page, most of these strange golf terms originated in the country that invented golf, Scotland—where even English speakers can have a hard time understanding the local dialect!

What is the most difficult golf course?

If you're an amateur, every golf course is difficult. But the toughest regulation golf course in the United States is Ko'olau in Hawaii, which is carved out of a tropical rain forest next to a 2,000-foot-high mountain. As for the rest of the world, some professional golfers might point to one or two courses in Scotland, where just making par (that is, an "average" score) can be enough to win major tournaments.

Why do golfers yell "fore"?

Golfers don't yell "fore!" on every swing—only if the ball has gone off in the wrong direction, and only if there are other players in the ball's path. Since "fore" is a British word for "ahead," it's much easier to yell "fore!" than something like "watch out for that ball I hit!"—which, by the time you finished saying it, might be way too late.

What is the Grand Slam?

Like its counterpart in tennis, the Grand Slam of golf refers to when a player wins all four major golf tournaments in the same calendar year: the Masters in April (held in Augusta, Georgia); the U.S. Open in June (held in a different location in the U.S. each year); the British Open in July (held in England, Ireland, or Scotland); and the PGA Championship (like the U.S. Open, held in a variety of U.S. golf courses) in September.

Since it's much harder for the same player to consistently win major golf tournaments than major tennis tournaments, the golf Grand Slam is one of the most difficult achievements in all of sports. A few years ago, there was some controversy when Tiger Woods claimed to have achieved a Grand Slam—true, he had won four consecutive major tournaments, but not in the same year. For this reason, some people refer to his feat as a "Tiger Slam," and reserve the term "Grand Slam" for scooping up all the majors in the same year.

How fast can a golf cart go?

The folks at the country club won't appreciate it, but a modern golf cart can rev up to about 20 miles per hour—meaning you can zip from hole to hole faster than any other player can run. By the way, most golfers are required to walk from hole to hole during professional tournaments, which can add up to a few miles in the course of a day.

Why do golf courses have 18 holes?

Up until the middle of the 18th century, golf courses didn't have a standard number of holes—the count varied from a dozen or so to as many as 22. That changed when the St. Andrews Golf Club in Scotland started an open tournament in which anyone could play, which boosted the sport's popularity. Since the St. Andrews course had 18 holes, it became the standard for all golf courses thereafter.

Horse Racing

Why are jockeys so small?

Think about it: if you wanted your horse to win a race, would you rather the person riding it was big and heavy or small and light? Most jockeys are small in stature because a horse will run faster with less weight (although a talented jockey can make up for his extra weight if has exceptionally good technique).

What is a trifecta?

In the United States, betting on horse races is legal. Most folks usually bet on a horse to win, place (come in second), or show (come in third), with a win earning the most money. A trifecta is when a bettor predicts which horses will win, place, and show in a single race, and it's so hard to pull off that the payoff can amount to hundreds of dollars for a two-dollar bet!

What is a thoroughbred?

Most people think of the word "thoroughbred" as a description referring to a horse that's been "thoroughly bred" to succeed at racing. But in fact, "thoroughbred" refers to a specific horse breed, created in 18th-century Britain by mating Arabian stallions with English mares.

Because a champion horse can earn millions of dollars, thoroughbred breeding is a big business. In the U.S., tens of thousands of thoroughbreds are born every year, mostly in big horseracing states like Florida, California, and Kentucky. Before a foal is sold to investors, it's carefully classified according to its bloodline (that is, whether its father or grandfather happened to win the Kentucky Derby), its physical condition, and how athletic it is. Needless to say, a foal that scores high in all three categories is worth more than one from an obscure background that has thin, gangly legs (though occasionally these "ugly ducklings" grow up to become champions themselves!).

By the way, although a thoroughbred can live for more than twenty years, only three-year-olds are allowed to compete in big racing events like the Kentucky Derby or the Preakness Stakes.

What happens when a racehorse breaks its leg?

Unfortunately, when a racehorse sustains a serious injury, it can be nearly impossible to nurse him back to top form. Since a horse can't lie down and "stay off" a broken leg, sometimes the only option is to administer a lethal injection and put him out of his misery. As veterinary medicine improves, though, many injured thoroughbreds that would have been "put down" years ago have gone on to live happy and productive lives.

Why are most racehorses male?

There are a couple of reasons for this. First, just as with humans, male horses (known as stallions) tend to be slightly faster and more muscular than female horses (known as mares). Second, even a fast mare may be more valuable to her owner as a mother than as a racer. Pregnant females can't race, but a stallion can impregnate a mare and race the very same day!

Why are racetracks oval rather than straight?

That's an easy one: even though horse races are extremely short compared to car races (one of the longest, the Belmont Stakes, is only a mile and a half long, compared to the 500-mile Indy 500), that length is better taken in by spectators on an oval track than a straight track. If a horse-racing track were laid out straight, the spectators near the starting line wouldn't be able to see who won!

What is the Triple Crown?

For most everyday fans, the horseracing season boils down to three events: the Kentucky Derby (held on the first Saturday in May in Louisville, Kentucky); the Preakness Stakes (run two weeks later in Baltimore, Maryland); and the Belmont Stakes (held two weeks after the Preakness in Belmont, New York). Winning any one of these races is an amazing accomplishment for a thoroughbred, but taking all three is extremely rare. In fact, as this book was written, the last horse to win the Triple Crown was Affirmed in 1978—since then, a handful of horses have won the first two races, but came up short in the finale.

Why is the Triple Crown so hard to win? First of all, each of the three races covers a different distance: the Kentucky Derby (one and one-quarter miles long) and the Preakness (one and three-sixteenths miles long) are similar in length, but the Belmont Stakes is an exhausting one and a half miles long—so a horse that wins the first two races may not have the endurance to win the third. Also, since these races take place rain or shine, they're often run on different track conditions—and a thoroughbred that's blazingly fast on a dry track may be only so-so in the mud!

Martial Arts

What is "Ultimate Fighting"?

Originally, the event known as The Ultimate Fighting Championship embraced a "no holds barred" philosophy: fighters were allowed to use any moves they liked, short of shooting or stabbing each other, and the last man left standing was declared the winner. Today, the rules are a bit stricter—no biting or hair pulling!—but true martial arts enthusiasts are still unimpressed with the UFC's "almost everything goes" style of combat.

Why are they called "martial arts"?

Since the word "martial" means "related to the military," it's easy to draw the conclusion that martial arts exist for one purpose: to aid a weaponless soldier in hand-to-hand combat. It's true that some martial arts were invented for fighting purposes, but today, the vast majority of people learn ju-jitsu or kung fu strictly for recreational purposes (and yes, occasionally to defend themselves in dangerous situations).

What does it mean to have a "black belt"?

In most martial arts, a "black belt" is awarded as a symbol of complete mastery. In other words, you can't just walk into a beginning karate class and walk out two hours later with a black belt; it usually takes years of study to attain this honor.

When this system was invented for Japanese Judo students in the late 19th century, the "black belt" was known as a "black obi," a kind of wide sash worn by Japanese men. At first, there were only two kinds of sash: white for beginners, and black for masters. (Some people believe that the white belt slowly turned black with dirt and grime as a student spent years perfecting his moves, but this probably isn't true—after all, people did laundry back then!) Since there's such a huge gap between white and black belts, kids in martial arts classes are usually given colored belts according to their achievement level.

By the way, in some martial arts, it's possible to attain a ranking higher than black belt. In Korea, for example, tae kwon do masters are awarded extra stripes on their black belts that correspond to their level of experience.

How was kickboxing invented?

In the 20th century, the popularity of traditional martial arts was threatened by plain, old-fashioned American boxing. In the 1950s, a Japanese boxing promoter combined elements of the Thai martial art known as "Muay Thai" with traditional boxing, allowing fighters to hit each other with their feet as well as their fists. This hybrid sport was a hit with the Japanese public, and spread shortly afterward to other countries.

How many martial arts are there?

Years ago, the only martial arts most Americans were familiar with were Japanese karate and Chinese kung fu. Today, though, an eager fighter can learn dozens of martial arts, ranging from the relatively familiar tae kwon do (which originated in Korea) to the arcane art of capoiera, a fighting form from Brazil that combines elements of dance with dangerous kicks and jabs.

Why were Shaolin warriors once so feared?

You see them all over movies and TV cartoons these days, but if a real Shaolin warrior felt he was being treated disrespectfully, he'd probably kill you five separate ways before you hit the ground!

In China, in the first millennium A.D., temples devoted to Shaolin Buddhism became a refuge for monks eager to escape the endless battles among Chinese warlords. In these temples, monks learned the Shaolin version of kung fu, and became so proficient that the very name "Shaolin" was enough to strike fear into opponents. Most monks used their kung-fu skills for peaceful purposes, though it's likely that at least a few renegades hired themselves out to the highest bidder.

Today, so many myths have been attached to the Shaolin tradition that it's hard to tell fact from fiction. We do know that Shaolin kung fu originally consisted of 18 different moves, or "techniques," and gradually expanded to almost 200, grouped into five animal families: tiger, crane, leopard, snake, and dragon. We also know that Shaolin warriors didn't have any supernatural abilities—they fought with their hands and feet, just like everyone else!

Why are there more martial arts in the East than in the West?

It's hard to figure out why specific styles of hand-to-hand fighting didn't evolve in Europe as they did in Asia—perhaps Europeans were more confident fighting with guns and swords than with their bare hands! In any event, Europe did develop some martial arts, after a fashion: jousting can be (roughly) put in this category, as can wrestling, bare-knuckle boxing, and even some kinds of gymnastics.

Photography

What were daguerrotypes?

Enormously popular in the 19th century, daguerrotypes (named after their inventor, Louis Daguerre) were an early kind of photograph involving the direct etching of images onto a sheet of specially prepared silver. Daguerrotypes were soon supplanted by modern photographs, for two reasons: first, the daguerreotype process didn't produce a "negative" from which multiple prints could be made, and second, the subject of a daguerreotype portrait had to stay perfectly still for more than a minute!

Why is it called a camera?

In a way, the concept of photography was invented long before cameras or film. As early as the 16th century, some European painters learned to fix images with a device called a "camera obscura," a large box with a hole in its side that projected a reduced image of a scene onto a nearby wall (which the artist could then use as a guide). Artists could also avail themselves of a "camera lucida," which used a different optical technique to project the scene being painted directly onto the canvas.

So what does the "camera" in these phrases signify? Well, "camera obscura" means "dark room" (since this device could be used only in the dark), while the less popular "camera lucida" means "lit room" (since this smaller gadget could be used in brighter conditions). As the art of photography developed, the projection and focusing of a reduced-size image onto film seemed naturally akin to these Renaissance inventions, so the name "camera" stuck to the earliest film-based contraptions when they were invented in the 18th century.

Why are darkrooms dark?

The film in old-fashioned cameras is coated with a substance that's sensitive to light, which is how it captures photographic images. Until it's treated with the proper chemicals, though, this film remains sensitive to light, which is why it needs to be unrolled in a darkened room (otherwise it might capture a "ghost" image that ruins the original snapshot). Darkrooms aren't completely dark, though; they're equipped with special reddish lights that don't affect film and allow the photo developer to see.

What is a digital camera?

Up until the last decade or so, the vast majority of cameras captured images chemically: that is, they were loaded with plain old film, the chemical composition of which changes according to how much light it absorbs (resulting, after the film is developed, in a detailed black-and-white or color photograph). Today, though, most cameras have dispensed with film entirely, and capture images digitally on sophisticated microchips (meaning the information is stored computer-fashion, as bazillions of 1s or 0s).

It's easy to see why digital cameras have become so popular. With most old-fashioned cameras, you have to wait until your film is developed to see the results, but digital cameras offer instant gratification: as soon as you take a picture, you can upload it onto your computer and e-mail it to friends. Also, as digital technology has advanced, these cameras have approached the quality of even the best film-based cameras, so more and more professional photographers are learning to use them. In fact, the way things have been going, you may soon only be able to find film cameras in museums!

What is the most expensive photograph?

Today, some early photographic prints are as rare (and as expensive) as paintings by masters like Degas or Picasso. The current record-holder is a 1904 print by Edward Steichen called *Pond-Moonlight*, which recently sold at auction for close to three million dollars! There are only three known copies of *Pond-Moonlight* (the negative has long since been destroyed); the other two reside at the Metropolitan Museum of Art and the Museum of Modern Art, both in New York.

What are megapixels?

Digital cameras are classified according to how many "megapixels" can be captured by their microchips (megapixel means, literally, a million pixels, a "pixel" being one of the microscopic dots that makes up a digital photograph). Today, most mass-market digital cameras are in the 4 to 6 megapixel range, which is more than enough visual detail for all but the most demanding photographers.

What does "SLR" stand for?

Until the early 20th century, the viewfinders of cameras were slightly off-center from the image being photographed, requiring a significant amount of guessing on the part of the photographer. Single-lens reflex (SLR) cameras solved this problem, transmitting the image directly through the view piece by means of mirrors and lenses. Today, most film-based cameras use SLR technology of one form or another.

Playground Games

How was hopscotch invented?

The next time your older brother makes fun of you for playing hopscotch, tell him that this playground game dates back to the Roman Empire, and was used as a training exercise for soldiers! During the Roman occupation of Britain, in the first few centuries A.D., Roman legions kept fit and nimble by jumping onto hopscotch squares in full body armor (try doing that on the playground!). This game caught on among onlookers, and soon "hopscotch" was being played all over Europe.

Why do schools have recess?

In a sense, it's unnatural for kids to be cooped up in school all day: children (especially boys) are naturally active and fidgety, and need a way to release their pent-up energy. That's the reason elementary schools schedule 15- or 30-minute recess periods: if students can bounce around in the playground at least once a day, usually at lunchtime, they're more likely to sit still in math class later on.

Now here's the part adults don't want you to know. First, recess isn't only a good way for jittery kids to blow off steam—teachers also look forward to it, because it gives them the chance to relax for a few minutes! And second, even though no books or blackboards are involved, recess has an educational function. During recess, kids learn valuable lessons about sharing (say, by taking turns on the swings) and cooperating (say, by playing a quick game of basketball), without requiring the intervention of adults. The fact is, the skills you learn on the playground can still pay off when you're an adult!

What happens if you swing over the bar?

Well, everyone knows the answer to this one: you turn inside-out! Seriously, though, it's nearly impossible to gather enough momentum, on your own, to swing all the way over a swing set's bar, and you probably couldn't accomplish this feat even if you had all your friends pushing you at the same time. (In case you're still tempted to try, the most likely result of swinging over the bar would be that you'd fall out of the swing, hit the ground head-first, and be seriously injured.)

How was kickball invented?

Like hopscotch (see the facing page), the game of kickball has a surprisingly militaristic origin. In 1942, a war correspondent reported this game being improvised by bored American soldiers posted in North Africa. Of course, games in which balls are kicked (such as soccer) have been around since recorded history; what made kickball innovative was that it loosely adapted the rules of baseball (which those servicemen probably would have been playing, if they'd remembered to bring their bats and gloves).

Because the balls used in kickball are big, red, and easy to, well, kick, this game has proved especially popular among little kids during recess. But that hasn't prevented some adults (again) from trying to get a piece of the action: in 1998, the World Adult Kickball Federation was founded in Washington, D.C. As you can guess, the main difference between kids' kickball and adult kickball is that grownups kick the ball much, much harder!

Why do playgrounds have gates?

On a city playground, kids as young as 5 or 6 can pretty much be counted on to stay in the immediate vicinity. The reason many of these playgrounds have gates is to prevent toddlers from wandering away when their parents or babysitters aren't watching. That's why the locks on these gates are located at adult level, rather than a couple of feet off the ground, which would make more sense from a kid's point of view.

Why don't some schools allow dodgeball?

Although you can make the case, just barely, that playing dodgeball is a good way to hone your reflexes, a lot of adults don't see it that way: to them, allowing kids to deliberately hurl rubber balls at each others' heads is just short of criminal. For this reason, many schools have prohibited dodgeball games, either organized in gym class or in pickup games out on the playground.

What is that spongy stuff under the monkey bars?

As you can guess, most playground injuries are caused by falls, usually because kids are horsing around and not paying attention. For this reason, modern playgrounds are covered with a soft, springy material, which is made out of recycled tires. This bouncy surface absorbs the force of small falls, but that doesn't mean you still can't get hurt if you take a big tumble (say, from the top of the swings).

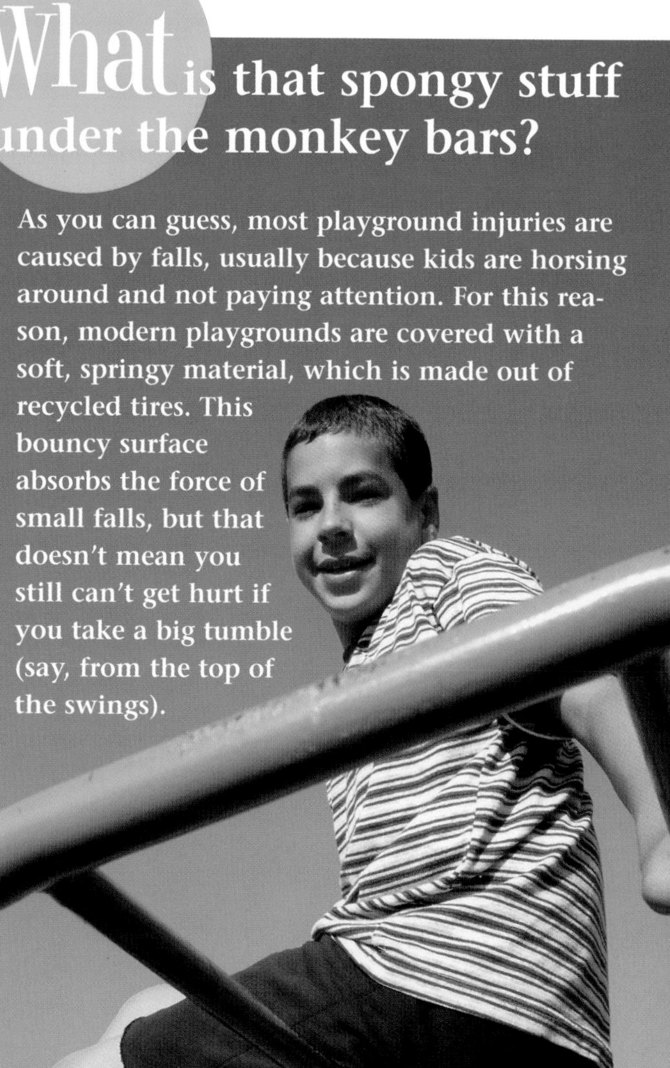

How were the Boy Scouts founded?

It may seem odd that an activity as wholesome as scouting could have been inspired by a bloody (and mostly pointless) war, but that's the way history often works! During the Boer War of 1899–1902, which was fought between English and Dutch settlers in South Africa, a British officer named Robert Baden-Powell was impressed by the boys of Mafeking, who banded together and helped out the British army while their town was under siege. A few years later, Baden-Powell wrote a book called *Scouting for Boys,* in which he outlined the principles of honor, discipline, and helpfulness that the boys of Mafeking so ably demonstrated.

Given Baden-Powell's background, it shouldn't be surprising that the earliest Boy Scout troops borrowed heavily from military routine, with uniforms, ranks, special flags, and even brass marching bands. As scouting evolved over the 20th century, it lost much of this militaristic character, though "merit badges" (based loosely on military medals) are still an important part of the scouting experience.

Why do Girl Scouts sell cookies?

Because Girl Scout cookies have become so deeply ingrained in American culture, it's easy to lose sight of the fact that Girl Scouts engage in many of the same character-building activities as Boy Scouts—camping, pioneering, etc. There are two main reasons Girl Scouts sell cookies: first, to help raise funds to pay for scouting activities, and second, to teach members responsibility and self-reliance.

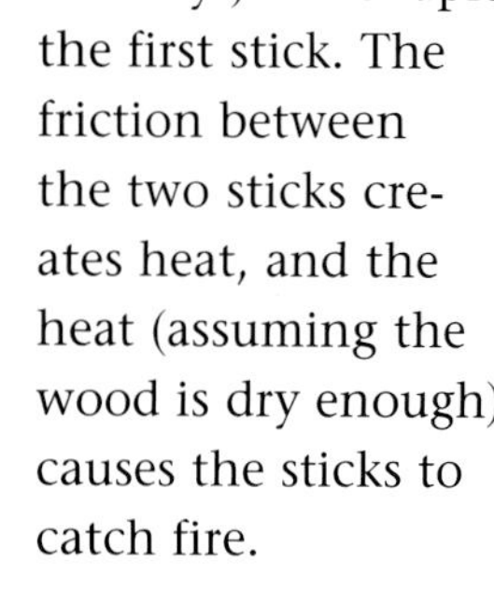

How does rubbing two sticks together start a fire?

In order to start a fire, you can't just listlessly rub two sticks together and wait for them to explode in flame. The trick is to place one stick on the ground, make a small indentation in its side with a second stick, and rub the second stick quickly between your palms (don't try this at home, by the way!) so its rapidly spinning end drills into the first stick. The friction between the two sticks creates heat, and the heat (assuming the wood is dry enough) causes the sticks to catch fire.

Why don't some national parks allow camping?

Boy and Girl Scouts (and ordinary folks on camping vacations) can't just pitch their tents wherever they please. Because campers can interfere with natural ecosystems—and because, unfortunately, some campers don't know enough not to leave their litter lying around or to extinguish their campfires—many national parks don't allow campers of any stripe to spend the night.

What country has the most Scouts?

You may be surprised by the answer to this one. Although the Boy and Girl Scouts were founded in Great Britain, and have always been popular in the U.S., the country with the largest amount of Scouts, hands-down, is Indonesia. Today, Indonesia has more than 8 million Boy and Girl Scouts, almost twice as many as can be found in the U.S.!

What are sleeping bags made of?

Only a generation ago, sleeping bags were so bulky that toting them around on a camping trip was like rolling up a full-sized blanket and strapping it onto your back. Today, most sleeping bags are covered with lightweight shells of nylon or polyester, and they roll up into a tight, compact bundle that's much easier to carry (not to mention much easier to take along on a 20-mile hike).

How many merit badges are there?

Scouting merit badges have come a long way from "campfire safety" and "knot tying." Today, there are almost as many merit badges as there are courses at a major university—though some, of course, are much harder to earn than others.

As you might expect, the Boy and Girl Scouts offer badges for such camping-related activities as canoeing, hiking, and first aid, and it may not surprise you to learn that you can also earn badges for such "artsy-craftsy" skills as painting, model design, and metalwork. For example, to earn a merit badge in music, you have to (among other options) play in your school band, make a traditional instrument from scratch and play it convincingly, or teach three songs to a small chorus.

If you really want to impress your friends, though, you might want to explore earning a merit badge in plumbing, salesmanship, or, best of all, nuclear science. (Though you don't have to build an actual nuclear bomb to receive this badge, you do need to know how a nuclear reactor works, as well as how to define such terms as "ionization" and "particle accelerator.")

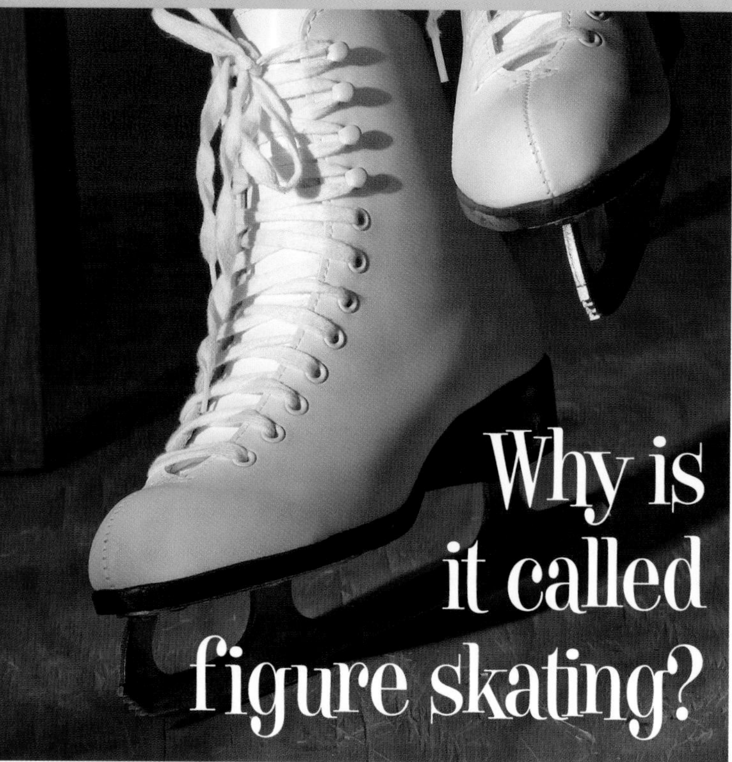

Why is it called figure skating?

In early skating competitions, "compulsory figures" counted for a large part of a contestant's score. The most familiar of these is the "figure eight," for which a skater had to trace out a perfect double loop using a specific part of her skates—but she would also have to master more obscure figures like the "serpentine," "double three," and "change loop." It was from these figures that "figure skating" derived its name.

Today, most international competitions (as well as the Olympics) have eliminated compulsory figures entirely, for two reasons. First, these events aren't as much fun to watch as the freestyle competition. And second, in the early days of the Olympics, compulsory figures caused confusion among spectators—people tuning in to the freestyle competition wouldn't realize that a large part of their favorite skater's score had already been determined by the (usually untelevised) compulsories.

How fast can a speed skater go?

Olympic speed skaters can attain speeds of more than 35 miles per hour, almost twice as fast as the fastest sprinters. The reason is twofold: first, a speed racer's skates are always in contact with the ice, while a runner has to waste at least some time lifting his feet; and second, the friction of ice is low, meaning a moving object can attain faster speeds with less of an initial push.

What is the difference between speed skates and regular skates?

At the Olympic level, most speed skaters use "clap" skates, which are hinged in front so the skater can lift his heel (while the blade of the shoe maintains contact with the ice). Another difference is that speed skates have a longer, narrower blade that's shaped for speed, while a hockey skate's shorter blade is shaped for maneuverability (that is, the ability to make sudden left or right turns or to stop completely).

Why is it called a triple Lutz?

In figure skating, popular moves are named after the skaters who created them. The Lutz—a fast, twirling jump—was invented by the skater Alois Lutz in 1913. Lutz contented himself with a single Lutz (that is, one complete rotation in the air), but skaters were soon performing double Lutzes, and triple Lutzes are now standard. It's not for lack of trying, but to date, no skater has been able to successfully complete a quadruple Lutz!

Why is hockey so popular in Canada?

Well, the short answer is that Canada has lots of frozen-over ponds and lakes during the winter and fall. Before the invention of refrigeration, you couldn't play a game of ice hockey in Florida if you wanted to, but our neighbor to the north was a natural incubator for the sport. (Ice hockey is also wildly popular in northern U.S. states like Minnesota.)

Although Canada claims to be the birthplace of hockey, there's some evidence that this sport was originally played on the frozen canals of Holland. Hockey is also closely related to the Scottish sport "shinty" (which is kind of like an early version of field hockey) and the Irish sport "hurling" (which is also played on a field rather than a patch of ice). Whatever the case, there's no question that hockey took root more deeply in Canada than in any other nation.

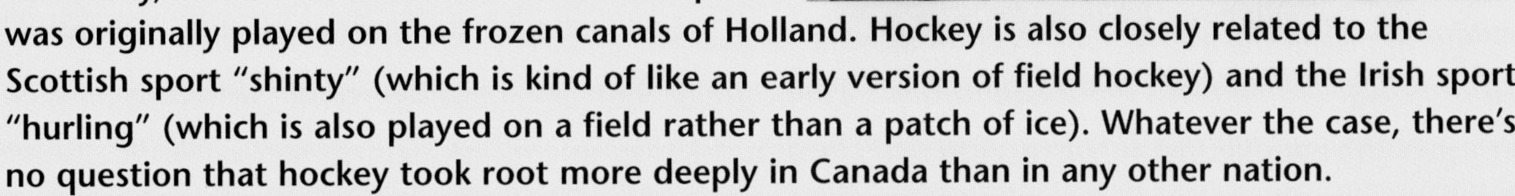

By the way, experts still aren't sure where the word "hockey" comes from. Some people point to Nova Scotia, in Canada, where a man named Hockey is said have originated the sport (there are still people named Hockey in the area). But it's more probable that "hockey" came either from the French word "hoquet" (meaning a shepherd's crook) or the Dutch word "hokkie" (meaning a small doghouse, referring to the goals on either end of the rink).

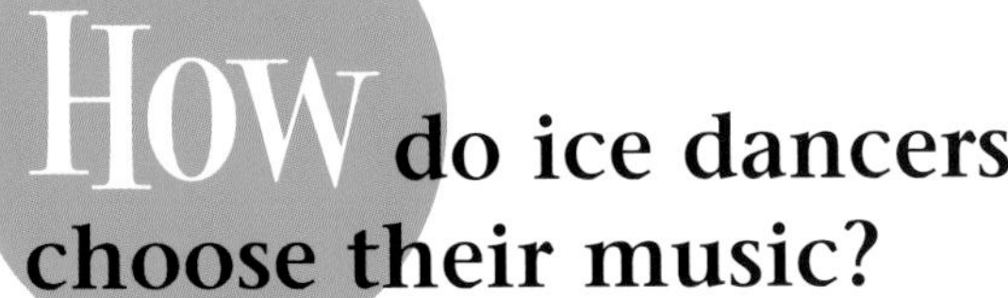

How do ice dancers choose their music?

First and foremost, ice dancers choose a piece of music that's easy to dance to! Beyond that, though, Olympic judges are always impressed by a bold choice of music, so the best ice dancers try to be original in their selections. One of the most famous ice dances of all time was at the 1984 Winter Olympics in Sarajevo, Yugoslavia, when Jane Torvill and Christopher Dean danced to a piece of classical music, Ravel's Bolero, earning perfect scores.

Why do skaters twirl faster when they pull their arms inward?

You probably weren't expecting a physics lesson, but here we go. A twirling ice skater has a certain amount of angular momentum, a physical quantity that relates the size of rotating objects to their speed of rotation. When she pulls her arms in, the skater decreases her effective "size," so she spins faster as her angular momentum transforms itself into speed to make up for the difference.

Swimming & Diving

What is the most difficult swimming stroke?

The butterfly is widely considered the most exhausting (and difficult to learn) swimming stroke. This stroke gets its name from the synchronized motion of the swimmer's arms as she pushes forward on her belly and flings them up from her sides, but it might just as well have been called the "dolphin"—because that's what swimmers look like when they're doing it!

Why is cliff diving dangerous?

You mean, besides the fact that you're jumping hundreds of feet into the water? The reason cliff diving is dangerous is that an extremely high dive requires extremely deep water on the other end—for example, if you dove 100 feet into a six-foot-deep swimming pool, you'd break your neck on the bottom. Professional divers can usually tell when conditions are safe for a cliff dive, but a slight miscalculation can mean extreme injury (such as paralysis) or even death.

What determines a dive's degree of difficulty?

One of the most confusing things about a dive meet is figuring out what a dive's "degree of difficulty" has to do with the judge's score. The difficulty of a dive is determined in advance by five elements: approach, entry, somersaults, twists, and "flight position." Divers have to submit a list of their intended dives before the competition starts, so the judges know what they're looking at.

So how does the degree of difficulty affect scoring? A high-difficulty dive, executed with a slight flaw, can sometimes earn a higher score than a lower-difficulty dive that's executed flawlessly. This encourages divers to challenge themselves with newer and more difficult dives, and also makes dive meets more fun for spectators.

By the way, even a seemingly perfect dive can unravel at the end, at the point where the diver enters the water. Judges look for a vertical entry with little or no splash—a big upsurge of water (not to mention a complete belly flop) can take the diver out of medal contention.

Why is it called "freestyle" swimming?

At swim meets, some events are designed for specific strokes (such as, say, the 200-meter breaststroke), but there are also freestyle events, meaning the swimmers can use whatever stroke they want. What's confusing is that virtually all freestyle swimmers use the front crawl (the stroke that most ordinary people use to swim), because this is the fastest stroke. In the Olympics, for example, you'll never see anyone swimming the backstroke or sidestroke during a freestyle event!

How big is an Olympic-size swimming pool?

There's a reason very few people have Olympic-size pools in their backyards. These swimming pools are 50 meters long (a meter is a little bit longer than a yard, so you can do the math) and 25 meters wide, and they're usually divided into 8 separate lanes. As for depth, that can vary, though all regulation Olympic pools have to be at least 6 feet deep (and a lot deeper than that for diving events!).

What is the difference between a platform and springboard?

Diving competitions usually feature separate events for springboard and platform dives. A springboard is the type of board you're familiar with from your local pool: you can bounce up and down on the end, giving you more height on your dive than you'd have if you simply jumped. A platform board, though, is just a big slab of non-springy wood or concrete, which produces less spectacular (but often more physically demanding) dives.

Why do swimmers shave their heads?

Competitive swimmers are constantly looking for ways to improve their speeds, even if it's by only one-hundredth of a second over 100 meters. One proven way to become more "hydrodynamic" (that is, to reduce your resistance to water as you push through it) is to shave your head and even your forearms. For a long time, people thought this effect was purely psychological— after all, showing up at a swim meet totally bald has a way of getting a guy's adrenaline going—but scientists have proven that shaving does in fact, well, shave seconds off a swimmer's time.

In the past few years, hardcore swimmers have started to use another competitive edge: scientifically designed, full-body swimsuits patterned after the most hydrodynamic creature on earth, the shark. The fact is, whenever you go for a swim, your skin is surrounded by a millimeter or so of "still" water, which drags against the water surrounding it and slows you down. A "fastsuit," as it's called, breaks down this layer of water, resulting in ever-so-slightly faster lap speeds.

What was the most famous TV commercial of all time?

In January 1984, during the third quarter of Super Bowl XVIII, a 60-second commercial from Apple introduced TV viewers to the Macintosh personal computer. This commercial, based on a famous novel by George Orwell called *1984*, showed a woman running through a futuristic convention hall and throwing a sledgehammer at the image of a talking man on a giant TV screen. The ad was so elaborate that it cost nearly $1 million to produce (and nearly $1 million more to air), and yet it was shown only once, adding to its legendary status.

In a way, Apple's Macintosh commercial had a bigger effect on TV advertising than it had on computer sales. In every Super Bowl since, companies have jockeyed to air ever-more-expensive, movie-quality TV commercials, to the extent that some people tune in to the big game just to see the ads! This trend peaked in the late 1990s, when some brand-new Internet companies (who could ill afford it) spent millions of dollars to shoot and air blockbuster commercials, then went out of business shortly afterward when their sales didn't increase.

What was the first TV commercial?

In July 1941, right before the broadcast of a Brooklyn Dodgers game, the Bulova Corp. aired a 10-second commercial that included a picture of a clock, a map of the U.S., and the spoken slogan, "America runs on Bulova time." This ad set Bulova back all of nine bucks, a far cry from the hundreds of thousands (or millions) of dollars that it costs to air major commercials today.

What is an infomercial?

A bit like the opposite of a 15-second TV ad, an infomercial is a 30- or 60-minute long scheduled program in which a host demonstrates a product's amazing qualities in front of an enthusiastic studio audience. When they first appeared, many people mistook infomercials for genuine TV shows, but nowadays most viewers understand that these shows are paid for by the products' manufacturers.

What is product placement?

In recent years, a closely guarded TV secret has leaked out to the public—some companies pay the producers of TV shows to have their products prominently featured (the hero of a detective show, for instance, might drive a particular model of car because the car's maker paid for the product placement). While this practice isn't illegal, some people think it's deceptive—but there's not much they can do about it except to not buy the offending product.

Why do kids' shows say "we'll return after these messages"?

You may have noticed that Saturday-morning cartoons inform viewers when it's time for a commercial break, and welcome them back ("now back to our show!") when the commercials are over. The government requires these announcements because many little kids don't understand the concept of commercials, and think that the ads telling them to buy products are part of the programs they're watching.

Why do some commercials have disclaimers?

You may have noticed that ads for cars and prescription medicines often have a fast-talking announcer at the end, who, if you listen closely, runs through all the "fine print" that the commercial neglected to mention (such as, "this sales price is for qualified people only" or "studies have shown that this medication may cause your head to explode"). Usually, these "disclaimers" are mandated by federal regulators, whose job it is to protect TV viewers from being fooled.

Why are TV commercials getting shorter and shorter?

In the early days of TV—the 1950s and 1960s—most commercials were slow, leisurely affairs that lasted for an entire minute, or sometimes longer. This was partly because the average viewer didn't engage in channel-surfing (back then, there were only a dozen or so channels anyway), and partly because people used to have much longer attention spans than they do today! In the 1970s and 1980s, TV commercials became much shorter, averaging about 30 seconds each, and today they're even shorter still, averaging a mere 15 seconds.

Oddly enough, this decrease in the length of TV commercials has gone hand-in-hand with an increase in the amount of time devoted to commercials. In the golden age of TV, an hour-long drama was about 51 minutes long, with 9 minutes devoted to commercials—but today, that same show would be 42 minutes long, with 18 minutes of ads! Not surprisingly, this explosion in the amount of advertising has led many people to subscribe to premium cable TV channels, which (in exchange for a monthly fee) don't show any distracting commercials at all.

Word Games

What is the hardest tongue twister?

There's no definitive answer to this question—after all, you may find "rubber baby buggy bumpers" impossible to say, while the next person trips over "she sells seashells by the sea shore." However, one tongue twister that's especially notorious for giving people fits is "the sixth sick sheik's sixth sheep's sick." This phrase is difficult to say clearly even once, let alone five times in a row!

Why do so many figures of speech have Greek names?

The ancient Greeks were masters of rhetoric—that is, the use of various verbal "tricks" to drive points home and win debates. Some of these techniques are familiar to grade-school kids; for example, a "simile" is when you compare one thing to another, and "hyperbole" is when you deliberately exaggerate. But some are much more obscure: you've probably never heard of "paraprosdokian," which means ending a sentence with a surprising word or phrase (as in, "today's forecast calls for rain . . . and more rain").

Why are some Scrabble tiles worth more than others?

When Alfred Butts, the inventor of Scrabble, was devising the rules for his board game in the 1930s, he studied the front page of the *New York Times* to determine how often various letters appear in everyday English. It didn't take him long to figure out that while English employs tons of "e"s and "t"s, letters like "z" and "q" appear much less frequently. Based on his analysis, he assigned common letters like "a" a point value of 1, while "p" merited a 3 and "z" a 10. (By the way, "s" is the only letter that's less common in Scrabble than in everyday English, because Butts wanted to limit the ability of players to make new words by adding an "s" at the end of existing ones.)

As things turned out, Butts didn't invent just a game, but a national craze. Today, practically every family in America owns a Scrabble set, and there are international tournaments where players try to outdo each other with strange two-letter words like "ut" or "ne." At the professional level, Scrabble success pretty much boils down to memorizing every word in the dictionary—an ordinary player would be hard-pressed to make a word out of the letters L, N, I, T, P, and H, but a pro Scrabbler would instantly spell out "plinth."

How was the crossword puzzle invented?

The very first crossword puzzle, by a man named Arthur Wynne, appeared under the title "Word-Cross" in a New York newspaper in 1913. Unlike modern crosswords, Wynne's puzzle was diamond-shaped rather than rectangular, and it had no black squares (meaning every square had to be filled in with a letter). However, if you're willing to stretch the definition of the term, crosswords date back a century or so earlier to "word squares"—puzzles in which letters are arranged so that the same words can be read in rows or columns.

Whatever the case, it wasn't long before Wynne's invention caught on, though under the more pleasing name "crossword" rather than "word-cross." Crosswords really took off when the first book of crossword puzzles (published in 1924) became a bestseller, and since then, practically every newspaper in the U.S. has a daily or Sunday crossword. Probably the most famous weekly crossword puzzle appears in the *New York Times Sunday Magazine*; it's likely that as many people buy the Sunday *Times* just to do the crossword as to read the day's news!

What is the best way to solve a word search puzzle?

Some kids, when they're faced with a solid square of printed letters and a list of hidden words underneath, immediately want to run screaming out of the room. But there's an easy way to start a word search: don't try to look for the entire word at once, but zero in on the first one or two letters. Once you find this starting portion, it's easy to tell if the hidden word continues from there, or if you need to look somewhere else.

What is a cryptic crossword?

In terms of difficulty, a cryptic crossword is to a regular crossword as a game of chess is to a game of checkers. The clues of a cryptic crossword can involve anything from subtle word games to obscure references to outrageous puns and anagrams. For instance: what's a nine-letter word for "unable to be decimalized"? The clue makes no sense in a regular crossword, but in a cryptic puzzle the answer would be "untenable" (un-TEN-able, get it? No? Don't worry—most adults are every bit as baffled by cryptic crosswords as you are!).

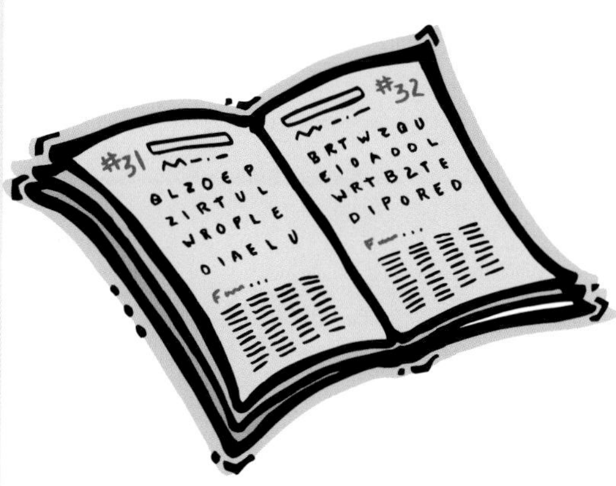

Index

A

B

C

D

E

S

T

U

V

W

Y

Z

Photo Credits

p.2: all photos.com

p. 3: shutterstock.com

p. 5: (top) photos.com, (middle) photos.com, (bottom) shutterstock.com

p. 6: (top) photos.com, (middle) shutterstock.com, (bottom) photos.com

p. 7: all photos.com

p. 8: (top) photos.com, (bottom) shutterstock.com

p. 10: (top) photos.com, (bottom) shutterstock.com

p. 11: (top) shutterstock.com, (bottom left) photos.com, (bottom right) photos.com

p. 12: (top) shutterstock.com, (bottom) clipart.com

p. 13: (top) shutterstock.com, (bottom) photos.com

p. 14: (top) shutterstock.com, (bottom) shutterstock.com

p. 15: (left) shutterstock.com, (top right) shutterstock.com, (bottom right) clipart.com

p. 16: (top left) shutterstock.com, (bottom left) photos.com, (top right) shutterstock.com

p. 17: (top) shutterstock.com, (bottom) clipart.com

p. 18: shutterstock.com

p. 19: (top) clipart.com, (bottom left) shutterstock.com, (bottom right) shutterstock.com

p. 20: (top) photos.com, (bottom) istockphotos.com

p. 21: (top) photos.com, (bottom) clipart.com

p. 22: (top) photos.com, (bottom) photos.com

p. 23: (top) photos.com, (bottom left) clipart.com, (bottom right) photos.com

p. 24: (top) photos.com, (bottom) photos.com

p. 25: (middle left) photos.com, (top right) clipart.com, (bottom right) clipart.com

p. 26: (top) shutterstock.com, (bottom) photos.com

p. 27: (top) clipart.com, (bottom) istockphotos.com

p. 28: (top left) clipart.com, (top right) shutterstock.com, (bottom) photos.com

p. 29: (top) shutterstock.com, (middle) shutterstock.com

p. 30: (top) photos.com, (middle) photos.com

p. 31: (top left) photos.com, (top right) shutterstock.com, (bottom) istockphotos.com

p. 32: (spread) shutterstock.com, (inset) clipart.com

p. 34: photos.com

p. 35: (top) photos.com, (bottom) istockphotos.com

p. 36: (top) photos.com, (bottom left) photos.com, (bottom right) clipart.com

p. 37: (top) photos.com, (bottom) clipart.com

p. 38: photos.com

p. 39: (top right) photos.com, (top left) clipart.com, (bottom) photos.com

p. 40: (top left) photos.com, (top right) photos.com, (bottom) photos.com

p. 41: (top left) photos.com, (bottom right) photos.com

p. 42: photos.com

p. 43: (top left) photos.com, (right) photos.com, (bottom left) clipart.com

p. 44: (top left) photos.com, (bottom) photos.com

p. 45: (top right) shutterstock.com, (bottom right) photos.com

p. 46: (top) photos.com, (bottom) shutterstock.com

p. 47: (top) istockphotos.com, (bottom left) shutterstock.com, (bottom right) shutterstock.com

p. 48: (top left) photos.com, (bottom right) clipart.com

p. 49: (top) photos.com, (bottom) photos.com

p. 50: (top left) istockphotos.com, (top right) photos.com, (bottom right) istockphotos.com

p. 51: photos.com

p. 52: (top left) photos.com, (bottom) photos.com

p. 53: (middle left) shutterstock.com, (bottom right) shutterstock.com

p. 54: (top) photos.com, (bottom left) shutterstock.com, (bottom right) shutterstock.com

p. 55: (top) clipart.com, (bottom) shutterstock.com

p. 56: (top) shutterstock.com, (bottom) clipart.com

p. 57: (top) clipart.com, (bottom) istockphotos.com

p. 58: clipart.com

p. 59: (top) shutterstock.com, (bottom) shutterstock.com

p. 60: (top) clipart.com, (bottom) photos.com

p. 61: (left) photos.com, (right) shutterstock.com

p. 62: (top) shutterstock.com, (bottom) shutterstock.com

p. 63: (left) clipart.com, (right) shutterstock.com

p. 64: (left) photos.com, (right) clipart.com

p. 65: (top) photos.com, (bottom) photos.com

p. 66: (top) photos.com, (bottom) clipart.com

p. 67: (top left) shutterstock.com, (top right) photos.com, (bottom left) istockphotos.com

p. 68: (top left) photos.com, (top right) photos.com, (bottom right) shutterstock.com

p. 69: (top right) photos.com, (bottom right) photos.com

p. 70: (top left) shutterstock.com, (top right) photos.com, (bottom right) photos.com

p. 71: (top) shutterstock.com, (bottom) photos.com

p. 72: (top) photos.com, (bottom) photos.com

p. 73: (top) photos.com, (bottom) photos.com

p. 74: (top left) istockphotos.com, (top right) photos.com, (bottom right) photos.com

p. 75: (top left) photos.com, (right) shutterstock.com

p. 76: (left) shutterstock.com, (right) clipart.com

p. 77: (top left) shutterstock.com, (top right) clipart.com, (bottom right) shutterstock.com

p. 78: (left) shutterstock.com, (right) shutterstock.com

p. 79: (top) photos.com, (bottom) photos.com

p. 80: (top left) istockphotos.com, (top right) photos.com, (bottom right) clipart.com

p. 81: (left) photos.com, (right) photos.com

p. 82: (top left) photos.com, (top right) shutterstock.com, (bottom) photos.com

p. 84: (top) clipart.com, (bottom left) clipart.com

p. 85: (top) photos.com, (bottom) photos.com

p. 86: (top left) photos.com, (top right) clipart.com, (bottom) shutterstock.com

p. 87: (left) clipart.com, (right) photos.com

p. 88: (top left) photos.com, (bottom right) clipart.com

p. 89: (top) photos.com

p. 90: (top left) photos.com, (top right) shutterstock.com, (bottom right) clipart.com

p. 91: (top) clipart.com, (bottom) clipart.com

p. 92: (top) photos.com, (bottom) clipart.com

p. 93: (top right) photos.com, (bottom left) shutterstock.com, (bottom right) clipart.com

p. 94: (top) shutterstock.com, (bottom) shutterstock.com

p. 95: (top) clipart.com, (bottom) clipart.com

p. 96: clipart.com

p. 97: (top) photos.com, (bottom left) shutterstock.com, (bottom right) photos.com

p. 98: (left) photos.com, (right) clipart.com

p. 99: (top) shutterstock.com, (bottom) shutterstock.com

p. 100: (top) clipart.com, (bottom) clipart.com

p. 101: (left) shutterstock.com, (right) clipart.com

p. 102: (top) shutterstock.com, (bottom) photos.com

p. 103: (top) clipart.com, (bottom) photos.com

p. 104: (left) photos.com, (right) shutterstock.com

p. 105: (top) shutterstock.com, (bottom left) clipart.com, (bottom right) shutterstock.com

p. 106: (spread) shutterstock.com

p. 107: (left) clipart.com, (right) clipart.com

p. 108: (top) clipart.com, (middle) shutterstock.com

p. 109: (top left) clipart.com, (middle right) clipart.com, (bottom left) shutterstock.com

p. 110: (top) photos.com, (bottom) photos.com

p. 111: shutterstock.com

p. 112: photos.com

p. 113: (top) shutterstock.com, (bottom) shutterstock.com

p. 114: (top) shutterstock.com, (bottom) photostock.com

p. 115: (top) shutterstock.com, (bottom) photos.com

p. 116: (left) shutterstock.com, (right) clipart.com

p. 117: (top) shutterstock.com, (bottom) photos.com

p. 118: clipart.com

p. 119: (top right) photos.com, (middle left) clipart.com, (bottom right) istockphotos.com

p. 120: (top) shutterstock.com, (bottom) shutterstock.com

p. 121: (top left) shutterstock.com, (top right) photos.com

p. 122: (top) photos.com, (bottom) istockphotos.com

p. 123: (top) clipart.com, (bottom) photos.com

p. 124: (top) shutterstock.com, (bottom) shutterstock.com

p. 125: (top) clipart.com, (bottom) clipart.com

p. 126: istockphotos.com

p. 127: (top) istockphotos.com, (bottom) istockphotos.com

p. 128: (top) shutterstock.com, (middle) shutterstock.com

p. 129: (top) clipart.com, (bottom) shutterstock.com

p. 130: (top) photos.com, (bottom) photos.com

p. 131: (left) photos.com, (right) shutterstock.com

p. 132: (top) shutterstock.com, (bottom) photo.com [sic]

p. 133: (left) photos.com, (right) clipart.com

p. 134: (top left) shutterstock.com, (middle right) photos.com, (bottom left) shutterstock.com

p. 135: shutterstock.com

p. 136: (top left) shutterstock.com,

(top right) photos.com, (bottom left) clipart.com

p. 137: (top) clipart.com, (bottom) photos.com

p. 138: (top left) shutterstock.com, (top right) photos.com, (middle left) shutterstock.com

p. 139: photos.com

p. 140: (top) clipart.com, (bottom) shutterstock.com

p. 141: (top) clipart.com, (bottom) istockphotos.com

p. 142: (left) istockphotos.com, (top right) clipart.com, (bottom right) photos.com

p. 143: (top) clipart.com, (bottom) photos.com

p. 144: (top) photos.com, (bottom) photos.com

p. 145: (top) istockphotos.com, (bottom) shutterstock.com

p. 146: (top) photos.com, (middle) photos.com

p. 147: (left) photos.com, (right) photos.com

p. 148: (top) photos.com, (bottom) photos.com

p. 149: (top left) clipart.com, (top right) photos.com, (bottom left) photos.com

p. 150: (top) shutterstock.com, (bottom) clipart.com

p. 151: (top) photos.com, (bottom) clipart.com

p. 152: (top) photos.com

p. 153: (top right) photos.com, (bottom left) photos.com, (bottom right) photos.com

p. 154: (top) photos.com, (bottom) photos.com

p. 155: (top left) clipart.com, (bottom left) photos.com

p. 156: photos.com

p. 157: shutterstock.com

p. 158: istockphotos.com

p. 159: (top) photos.com, (bottom) clipart.com

p. 160: (top) photos.com, (bottom left) clipart.com, (bottom right) istockphotos.com

p. 161: (left) shutterstock.com, (right) clipart.com

p. 162: (top left) photos.com, (top right) clipart.com, (bottom right) shutterstock.com

p. 163: (left) photos.com, (right) photos.com

p. 164: shutterstock.com

p. 165: (left) photos.com, (right) photos.com

p. 166–167: (spread) shutterstock.com

p. 168: (top left) photos.com, (top right) shutterstock.com, (bottom right) clipart.com

p. 169: (top) photos.com, (bottom) istockphotos.com

p. 170: (left) photos.com, (right) photos.com

p. 171: (top right) photos.com, (middle left) clipart.com, (bottom right) photos.com

p. 172: (top) photos.com, (bottom) photos.com

p. 173: (top left) clipart.com, (top right) photos.com, (bottom left) photos.com

p. 174: shutterstock.com

p. 176: photos.com

p. 177: (top right) clipart.com, (bottom left) photos.com

p. 178: (left) photos.com, (right) photos.com

p. 179: (top right) clipart.com, (bottom right) istockphotos.com

p. 180: (top) istockphotos.com, (bottom) photos.com

p. 181: (left) shutterstock.com, (right) shutterstock.com

p. 182: (top left) photos.com, (bottom) photos.com

p. 183: (top right) photos.com, (bottom left) clipart.com

p. 184: (top left) photos.com, (bottom right) photos.com

p. 185: (left) clipart.com, (right) photos.com

p. 186: shutterstock.com

p. 188: (top left) photos.com, (top right) photos.com

p. 189: (left) clipart.com, (top right) photos.com, (bottom right) photos.com

p. 190: (top) photos.com, (bottom) istockphotos.com

p. 191: (top) shutterstock.com, (bottom) shutterstock.com

p. 192: (top) shutterstock.com, (bottom) clipart.com

p. 193: (top right) clipart.com, (bottom) photos.com

p. 194: (top) photos.com, (bottom) istockphotos.com

p. 195: (top left) photos.com, (top right) istockphotos.com, (middle) shutterstock.com

p. 196: istockphotos.com

p. 198: istockphotos.com

p. 200: (top) photos.com, (bottom) shutterstock.com

p. 201: (top) photos.com, (bottom) photos.com

p. 202: istockphotos.com

p. 204: (top) shutterstock.com, (bottom left) photos.com, (bottom right) photos.com

p. 205: (left) photos.com, (right) photos.com

p. 206: (bottom left) shutterstock.com, (middle right) photos.com

p. 207: (middle left) photos.com, (top right) photos.com, (bottom right) shutterstock.com

p. 208: (top left) photos.com, (bottom right) shutterstock.com

p. 209: (top left) clipart.com, (top right) shutterstock.com, (bottom right) photos.com

p. 210: (top) clipart.com, (bottom) clipart.com

p. 211: (top) clipart.com, (bottom) photos.com

p. 212: (left) photos.com, (right) clipart.com

p. 213: (top) clipart.com, (bottom) shutterstock.com

p. 214: photos.com

p. 215: (top) clipart.com, (bottom) photos.com

p. 216: istockphotos.com

p. 217: photos.com

p. 218: (top) clipart.com, (bottom) shutterstock.com

p. 219: (top left) clipart.com, (top right) shutterstock.com, (bottom right) clipart.com

p. 220: (top) photos.com, (bottom) clipart.com

p. 221: (top) shutterstock.com, (bottom) photos.com

p. 222: (top) clipart.com, (middle) photos.com

p. 223: (left) photos.com (right) clipart.com

p. 224: (left) istockphotos.com, (right) clipart.com

p. 225: (left) photos.com, (bottom right) clipart.com

p. 226: (top left) istockphotos.com, (bottom right) clipart.com

p. 227: (top left) clipart.com, (top right) clipart.com, (bottom left) photos.com

p. 228: (top left) clipart.com, (top right) shutterstock.com, (bottom left) shutterstock.com

p. 229: (top right) clipart.com, (bottom left) clipart.com

p. 230: (top) photos.com, (bottom left) clipart.com, (bottom right) clipart.com

p. 231: (top left) shutterstock.com, (middle left) clipart.com

p. 232: (top left) photos.com, (middle left) clipart.com, (bottom right) clipart.com

p. 233: (top) photos.com, (bottom) clipart.com

p. 234: (left) photos.com, (right) istockphotos.com

p. 235: (top) istockphotos.com, (middle) photos.com

p. 236: (top) photos.com, (bottom) photos.com

p. 237: (top right) clipart.com, (top left) photos.com, (bottom) photos.com

p. 238: (top) clipart.com, (bottom) shutterstock.com

p. 239: (left) shutterstock.com, (right) shutterstock.com

p. 240: (top left) photos.com, (bottom right) photos.com

p. 241: (top left) shutterstock.com, (top right) shutterstock.com, (bottom right) photos.com

p. 242: (top left) photos.com, (bottom right) photos.com

p. 243: (top) istockphotos.com, (bottom) photos.com

p. 244: (top) photos.com, (middle right) clipart.com

p. 245: shutterstock.com

p. 246: shutterstock.com

p. 247: photos.com

p. 248: (top) photos.com, (bottom left) photos.com, (bottom right) clipart.com

p. 249: (top) photos.com, (bottom) photos.com

p. 250: (top) istockphotos.com, (bottom) clipart.com

p. 251: (top right) shutterstock.com, (bottom right) clipart.com, (middle left) clipart.com

p. 252: (top left) photos.com, (bottom left) clipart.com, (bottom right) shutterstock.com

p. 253: shutterstock.com

p. 254: (top left) photos.com, (top right) photos.com, (bottom left) photos.com

p. 255: (top) photos.com, (bottom) photos.com

p. 256: (top left) photos.com, (bottom left) clipart.com, (bottom right) photos.com

p. 257: (top right) photos.com, (bottom right) clipart.com

p. 258: (top) photos.com, (bottom) istockphotos.com

p. 259: photos.com

p. 260: shutterstock.com

p. 261: photos.com

p. 262: (top) istockphotos.com, (bottom) photos.com

p. 263: (top left) photos.com, (top right) photos.com, (middle) shutterstock.com

p. 264: (top left) photos.com, (top right) photos.com, (bottom left) photos.com

p. 265: photos.com

p. 266: (top) photos.com, (bottom) photos.com

p. 267: (top) photos.com, (bottom) photos.com

p. 268: (top) clipart.com, (bottom left) photos.com, (bottom right) clipart.com

p. 269: (top) clipart.com, (bottom) photos.com

p. 270: (left) photos.com, (right) photos.com

p. 271: (top) photos.com, (bottom left) clipart.com, (bottom right) clipart.com

p. 272: (top) photos.com, (bottom) photos.com

p. 273: istockphotos.com

p. 274: shutterstock.com

p. 275: photos.com

p. 276: (top) clipart.com, (bottom) istockphotos.com

p. 277: clipart.com

p. 278: (top) clipart.com

p. 279: (top) shutterstock.com, (bottom) clipart.com